sappi
tree spot

LOWVELD

INCLUDING KRUGER NATIONAL PARK

TREE IDENTIFICATION MADE EASY

Silver Cluster-leaf
Terminalia sericea

Rina Grant and Val Thomas
Illustrations by Joan van Gogh

Jacana

Acknowledgements

Sappi Tree Spotting Lowveld originally took two years of intensive research and testing to reach publication date. Jacana is grateful to all the people from many different fields who gave their time and commitment to produce this superb publication. We would like specifically to thank the following individuals and organisations sincerely for their dedication, their time and expertise during the project.

The research and development of **Sappi Tree Spotting** was carried out by Jacana and Twisisa. This would not have been possible without the assistance of the following scientists: Nick Zambatis and Dr Freek Venter (National Parks Board), Mike Peel (Agricultural Research Council) and Dr Rina Grant (Twisisa).

Our special thanks and warmest congratulations to Joan van Gogh for the beautifully illustrated artwork which will assist tree spotters to discover and identify trees of the Lowveld. We would also like to acknowledge and thank Sally MacLarty for her contributions to the line-artwork.

Jacana was responsible for the text production of the book. We thank the following editors for their contributions: Rachel Adatia, Jessie Albert, Tony Davidson, Jill Dunstone, John Rushworth and Matthew Seal.

The book itself was designed by Jacana, and the cover by David Selfe Designs. We sincerely thank Resolution for some of the DTP origination.

We thank the various companies and individuals who helped in the production of the Maps: CartoGraphics for layout and DTP; the National Botanical Institute (Cape Town), Clive Webber, Barry Low and Twisisa for their expert help on the geology. The tree distribution maps of South Africa were supplied by Trevor Arnold and Mrs Hannelie Snyman (National Botanical Institute, Pretoria).

Many people gave generously of their time in order to test and check the book, and we thank them for their invaluable assistance:

Sidney Miller, Nick Zambatis, Guin Zambatis, Dr Harry Biggs, Christo van der Linde and Robbie Clarke (National Parks Board); Honorary Rangers Corps; Penny and Gordon Brodie; John and Tish Payne; Shirley Clarke; BB Bengis; Duan Biggs; Sharon Pollard (Wits Rural Facility); Mike Peel (Agricultural Research Council), Johan Kluge (Lowveld Botanical Gardens, Nelspruit); Brandon Kemp and Debbie White.

The polished surfaces of the wood samples were photographed by André Pretorius (StringLite), by courtesy of Stephanie Dyer, Division of Water Environment and Forestry Technology (Environmentek), CSIR, Timber Utilisation Programme, Forestek. The wood ornaments were donated to Pretoria University by the late WEC van Wyk, and photographed by courtesy of Magda Nel and Professor AE Van Wyk (Department of Botany).

We sincerely thank Professor Kader Asmal, Minister of Education, for his support, and for writing the Foreword.

We are proud to acknowledge the work of the whole Jacana Team who have contributed in their specialised fields to produce **Sappi Tree Spotting:** Janet Bartlet, Carol Broomhall, Hayley Butler, Paula Correia, Ntkozo Dubazana, Tracey Fisher, Ruth Friedland, Dr Rina Grant, Ingrid Glashoff, Ashwell Glasson, Mpho Hlabela, Ruth Longridge, Zandi Luvuno, Joanne Mallet, Obed Molobe, Fortune Ncube, Davidson Ndebele, Jannett Ndebele, David Ngwenya, Bambi Nunes, Jenny Prangley, Mariette Strydom, Amanda Thoane, Peter Thomas, Val Thomas.

Finally, we would like to thank Sappi Limited for their vision and commitment in helping to fund the research and development of a book that we believe will add significantly towards helping South Africans and their visitors to be aware of, to care for, to protect and to enjoy our magnificent Lowveld trees.

Foreword

The **Sappi Tree Spotting** series are, without a doubt, educational and inspirational. Should you have any interest in trees, their place in our landscapes or their management and care, then this is what this series most definitely provides.

As our immediate environment and natural areas come under increased pressure, there is a growing need to enhance environmental learning, and for taking up action to restore the fragile balance. Raised public awareness highlights the need for greater insight and understanding. This is because ecological relationships and processes, the role of plants in general, and trees in particular are indeed complex. Because of increased ecological awareness worldwide, more and more people are becoming interested in the role trees play in the environment. This emphasises the need for books which make it easy, accessible and enjoyable, to identify trees in their natural environment.

This unique resource can provide us with the wisdom on the intricacies of the "web of life". We are all integral parts of our environment, and an aspect of the fascination of being in Nature is to understand why things are the way they are.

Trees provide food, shade, oxygen, fuel for wood, materials for crafts and furniture; they filter pollution and noise, they are an indispensable part of the habitats of our animal life. In these days of global warming, they are also vital "sinks" for carbon sequestration; and they are, in their own right, magnificent living wonders. We must treat them with reverence, for they are fundamental to our own survival.

I wrote the forewords to the previous books in my former capacity as Minister of Water Affairs and Forestry. Now, I am delighted to write this introduction as Minister of Education for two reasons. Firstly, these books are exceptional environmental resource materials, and deserve recognition as such. Secondly, this accords with my drive to make environmental education a central focus of my tenure as Minister of Education.

The **Sappi Tree Spotting** series reminds us of our responsibilities to conserve the ecological integrity of our natural systems, and to take care in clearing invading alien plants, which are seen as a great threat to our biological diversity and ecological health.

Many people have often perceived tree identification as being so complicated as to rather remain the domain of the expert Dendrologist; but the **Sappi Tree Spotting** series goes a long way to demystify the subject. The novice and advanced amateur are provided with a wealth of practical details and skills, which lead not only to correct tree identification, but also to greater ecological insight.

The latest in the series is the revised edition of the first title, the **Lowveld**. This new edition covers name-changes made since the first edition in 1997, to keep abreast with taxonomic developments. It also features additional species text, as well as photographs for each tree. Another exciting innovation has been added – "*Tree Trails*" that will provide the reader with tree adventures that can be followed in the Kruger National Park.

The knowledge, enthusiasm and commitment that Jacana has lavished on producing these books bode well for the botanical, ecological and spiritual benefits of the user. I have no hesitation in recommending the individual books, and the series as a whole, and in commending Sappi for their foresight and support. Sappi for their foresight and support.

Kader Asmal

Professor Kader Asmal, MP
Minister of Education
(previously Minister of
Water Affairs
and Forestry)

Jacket-plum
page 274

sappi

The lure of the Lowveld

Travelling through the Lowveld is an unforgettable experience, whether you choose to travel by foot or by vehicle – for this lush and varied territory is home to a marvellous number of species of indigenous trees.

In contrast to Europe, which has fewer than 100 tree species, the southern part of Africa can claim over 1 300 listed species – and in the Lowveld alone, some 800 trees confirm this particular region's intricate and diverse wealth.

The challenge

Sappi is a major landowner in the Lowveld, but only 70% of its land is afforested. The balance is dedicated to the conservation of water, fauna and flora. Annual environmental audits (since 1989) have greatly enhanced our efforts in protecting resources and conserving indigenous forests, grasslands and wetlands, as well as nurturing threatened and endangered species.

Sappi Forests began the implementation of ISO 14001 throughout its forests in South Africa in 1995, and was accredited in April 1999 – the first multi-site operation in Africa, and one of only a few in the world, to receive this sought-after certification in international environmental standards.

Sappi is also voluntarily pledged to the South African Natural Heritage Programme. To date, Sappi has 18 Natural Heritage sites on 6 500 hectares, and 48 sites of Conservation Significance covering 4 000 hectares.

In addition, as part of the Lowveld's rich arboreal heritage, Sappi is dedicated to conserving prime areas of unique flora and fauna. On Sappi's tree farms of Elandshoogte, Mashonamien, Kalkoenskrans and Shonalanga, visitors to the Lowveld are offered the rare opportunity to explore some of South Africa's treasured indigenous forests.

The experience

Fortunately, the pleasure of observing South Africa's rich diversity of tree species is not restricted to particular areas. It is possible to observe beautiful indigenous trees throughout South Africa, in both town and country. It is gratifying to contemplate the beauty of indigenous trees, and to wonder at the possibilities trees hold to future discoveries in medicine, wellness and universal quality of life.

Our country's traditional and natural healers treasure a healing lore concerning the trees and plants indigenous to South Africa. For them especially, the Lowveld is a well-stocked apothecary.

Whether an amateur enthusiast or scientist, the trees of the Lowveld – both abundant and rare, whose ancient habitat is the Lowveld – beckon the beholder to witness their life, appreciate their glory, and soak in their beauty. This is why Sappi has been enthusiastic in its support of the revised edition of this publication.

The book

Sappi Tree Spotting Lowveld is an essential guide to each tree's role in the natural order in which it is found. The book explains their relationship with other life forms and gives clues as to where to locate both the more common trees as well as those more difficult to identify in each area.

In an easy-to-use, uncomplicated way, this book takes the mystery out of identifying trees, and introduces you to a silent friend.

Happy tree spotting in the Lowveld!

The Mac Mac River on Sappi's Venus Tree Farm is an essential part of the unique ecosystem in this Lowveld region.

The National Botanical Institute (NBI)

NATIONAL
$\mathscr{B}$OTANICAL
INSTITUTE

The mission of the National Botanical Institute is to promote the sustainable use, conservation, appreciation and enjoyment of the exceptionally rich plant life of South Africa, for the benefit of all its people.

The NBI is an autonomous, state-supported, statutory organisation, which has its head office in the Kirstenbosch National Botanical Garden. It has physical resources such as the eight National Botanical Gardens, three Herbaria and two Research Units. In addition, it boasts the human resources of many highly qualified scientists, horticulturists, academics and support staff.

National Botanical Gardens

The eight National Botanical Gardens propagate and display the unique wealth and diversity of South African flora. Our National Botanical Gardens are situated throughout the country and specialise in local flora.

Herbaria

The combined collections of dried plant material of the three NBI herbaria, in Pretoria, Cape Town and Durban, contain over 1,8 million specimens of mainly Southern African plant material. They are invaluable resources to researchers throughout the African continent, as well as internationally.

Education

Environmental Education, both within the National Botanical Gardens and working with communities on outreach greening projects country-wide, is a major priority of the National Botanical Institute.

Research

The Ecology Research Programme focuses on conservation of plant diversity and plant resources in Southern Africa.

Many plants could prove invaluable to humans in terms of new food crops or medicinally as cures for diseases for which, at present, there are no cures. However, many are being eradicated before their potential has been investigated.

The Ecology Research Programme focuses on responses of vegetation to environmental stress and global climate change. These are crucial questions facing mankind to which answers must be found before it is too late.

Botanical Society membership

Members of the public who are interested in the work of the NBI can join their nearest branch of the Botanical Society, or can visit their local National Botanical Garden.

NBI and Sappi Tree Spotting

As a sheer coincidence of positive energy the early phase of planning the Tree Spotting series overlapped with the NBI publication of the Low and Rebelo *Vegetation Map of South Africa* (see page 4).

Defining the boundaries of each Tree Spotting book, and the zones within each boundary, was automatically facilitated by this essential piece of scientific work. It is services and relationships such as these that make the NBI an unique and invaluable asset to South Africa. As part of the information about each tree, there are mini maps of their South African distribution. The information for each of these maps was supplied by the NBI from data collected throughout the country.

Botanical Society of South Africa

The Botanical Society of South Africa is a non-governmental organization whose mission is to win the hearts, minds and material support of individuals and organizations, wherever they may be, for the conservation, cultivation, study and wise use of the indigenous flora and vegetation of southern Africa.

Botanical Society Branches' Membership

Information and application forms are obtainable from the various National Botanical Gardens, Botanical Society head office or branches.

Head Office: Kirstenbosch

Tel: (021) 797-2090 Fax: (021) 797-2376
e-mail: info@botanicalsociety.org.za
Private Bag X10, Claremont, 7735
New members are welcome.
Members enjoy the following benefits:

- The privilege of visiting any of South Africa's National Botanical Gardens free of charge.
- The opportunity to create an indigenous garden from your annual allocation of free seed.

- First hand experience can be gained of our magnificent indigenous plants on organised hikes and outings.
- The opportunity to increase your knowledge by attending demonstrations and lectures.
- The pleasure of receiving *Veld & Flora*, our quarterly magazine full of interesting articles, free of charge.
- A discount of 10% on purchases from botanical society shops and participating outlets.
- The opportunity to support and participate in plant conservation and environmental education projects and to assist with development projects for the National Botanical Institute.

Botanical Society Branches and Botanical Gardens

Botanical Society Branches

Albany Branch	(046) 636-1370
Bankenveld Branch	(011) 964-2890
Bredasdorp / Napier Branch	(028) 424-2587
Cederberg Branch	(027) 482-2763
Durban Branch	(031) 261-2197
Free State Branch	(051) 31-3530
Garden Route Branch	(044) 877-1360
Johannesburg Branch	(011) 489-2419
Kirstenbosch Branch	(021) 671-5468
Kogelberg Branch	(021) 782-2669
Lowveld Branch	(013) 744-0241
Pietermaritzburg Branch	(033) 343-1386
Pretoria Branch	(012) 333-4629
Villiersdorp Branch	(0225) 32224

Botanical Gardens

Free State National Botanical Garden	(051) 436-3530
Harold Porter National Botanical Garden	(028) 272-9311
Karoo National Botanical Garden	(023) 347-0785
Kirstenbosch National Botanical Garden	(021) 799-8800
Lowveld National Botanical Garden	(013) 752-5531
Natal National Botanical Garden	(033) 344-3585
Pretoria National Botanical Garden	(012) 804-3166
Witwatersrand National Botanical Garden	(011) 958-1750/1

Tree Society

The Tree Society of Southern Africa has been actively involved in promoting an interest in our natural eritage since 1946.

Outings, education and publications

Members are enthusiasts from all walks of life, including professional botanists, who will gladly assist in extending your knowledge of the environment.

- Enjoy visits to undisturbed areas not generally accessible to the public. Discussions on walks extend beyond trees to cover geology, general flora, fauna and history. Day outings, within reasonable driving distance of Johannesburg and Pretoria, as well as weekend and long-weekend visits, are organised to areas in neighbouring provinces.

- The Society collaborates with the C.E. Moss Herbarium offering courses on identifying trees.

- A prime objective is compiling vegetation checklists for landowners, and noting rare species and noxious invaders.

- The Society has been instrumental in establishing three prizes for excellence in the field of Plant Systematics at Wits University.

- Funds being available, the Society assists deserving students furthering studies in Botany.

- The Society journal, *"Trees in South Africa"* has been published since 1949, and back numbers of many issues are still available. Articles are of general and botanical interest.

- *"Peltophorum"* – The Society Newsletter is issued twice a year.

Membership

Details may be obtained from:

The Tree Society of Southern Africa
P.O. Box 70720, Bryanston, 2021

Walter Barker: Tel / Fax (011) 465-6045
e-mail: walterb@icon.co.za

Cheryl Dehning: Tel (011) 316-1426;
Fax (011) 316-1095
e-mail: dehning@mweb.co.za

Wits courses

For information contact:
Reneé Reddy: Tel (011) 717-6467
e-mail: kevinb@gecko.biol.wits.ac.za

Dendrological Society

Arborum silvarumque conservatio salus mundi est. – The conservation of trees and forests is the salvation of the world.

Aims, activities and publications

The Dendrological Foundation, formed in 1979 by Dr F. von Breitenbach, was created as an independent, non-profit, non-racial association aimed at the promotion of the knowledge of trees. In 1980 the Dendrological Society was formed, with similar aims, focusing on conservation and education.

- *Dendron* is the Society magazine, and the *Journal of Dendrology* contains more scientific essays on all aspects of dendrology.

- The Society runs correspondence Tree Knowledge Courses aiming to spread the joy of trees through information.

- It provides a Tree Identification Service for members who submit specimens for ID.

- Tree Name and Number Plates are available.

Branches

Branches around the country are named after a tree species, or a significant geographical feature.
- "Magalies" – Head office, Pretoria, (012) 567-4009 Jutta von Breitenbach
- "Atalaya" – Port Elizabeth
- "Boekenhout" – Witbank
- "Celtis" – P'termaritzburg
- "Erythrina"– Pietersburg
- "Kameeldoring" - Potgietersrus
- "Kwambonambi" – Zululand
- "Langeberg" – Swellendam
- "Manketti" – Ellisras
- "Olienhout" – Groot Marico
- "Outeniqua" – Knysna
- "Soutpansberg" – Louis Trichardt
- "Tafelberg" – Cape Town
- "Umdoni" – Durban
- "Vaal" – Meyerton
- "Witwatersrand" – Johannesburg
- "Wolkberg" – Tzaneen

Food & Trees for Africa

Food and Trees for Africa (FTFA)'s mission is to contribute to a healthy and sustainable quality of life for all through environmental awareness and greening programmes.

Objectives

FTFA, established in 1990, is the only national, non-governmental, non-profit organisation in South Africa addressing sustainable national resources management and food security through permaculture and urban greening. Its objectives are to create an awareness of the benefits of environmental upliftment activities amongst all communities of Southern Africa. It is currently involved in diverse projects ranging from urban greening, permaculture, environmental awareness and education to township nurseries.

- Over 1,7 million trees have been distributed to thousands of disadvantaged communities throughout the country.
- Three newsletters are produced and distributed annually, to over 4 500 organisations and individuals, locally and internationally. Five environmental education booklets have been published and are available for FTFA.
- Plant a tree to celebrate or honour someone you know and FTFA will send a personalised certificate to register this.

- FTFA encourages South Africans to celebrate trees, and anyone wishing to contribute to the greening of Southern Africa can assist by becoming a member of FTFA.

Membership

- R50 Individual membership per year - receive FTFA's newsletter, *Newsleaf*, quarterly.
- R150 Family membership per year - receive a certificate in the family name, three newsletters quarterly, and trees will be planted where they are really needed.
- All businesses that support FTFA receive a personalised certificate, coverage in FTFA's newsletters and Annual Review, and subscription to all three newsletters. FTFA links companies with meaningful community upliftment programmes.

For more information contact:
FTFA on (011) 803-9750, visit our website at www.trees.co.za
email: trees@cis.co.za

Names of South African trees

All trees that have been identified and "listed" internationally have a botanic, bi-nomial name. This is invaluable in recognising families and their linkages all over the Earth.

In South Africa there are over 1,200 woody species tall enough to offer shade to sit under – a daunting number of Latin names to learn – especially for beginners. In addition our rainbow nation has eleven official languages; many of our trees have at least that many "common" names, if not more. In early South African human history, names were given by Koi-San peoples, and later by black tribes moving southwards from central Africa. The arrival of settlers from Europe led to many trees being named by farmers, timber merchants, carpenters and builders, the majority of whom were of Dutch descent. English speakers were, in the main, not people of the land, and the vast majority of trees did not have English names until the mid 1950s, except as translations.

Since then various groups have attempted to "co-ordinate' or "improve" the early translations, and this has led to a series of changes in the literature. Currently there is a world-wide move towards international standardisation, accuracy and the "marketing" of trees to make them accessible, interesting and exciting for members of the general public who want to tree spot for recreation. The final lists have not been written, and in the interim changes are inevitable!

The Sappi Tree Spotting series is committed to ease of identification, and our names too have changed over the series. For example, we have attached the surnames Acacia, Bushwillow and Bauhinia to the appropriate tree names. This is to help beginner tree spotters, even though we are aware of the rather ridiculous anomaly: Scented-pod Thorn Acacia! All tree names that have changed are marked with an asterisk in the Contents (see the following 2 pages). Their original names are also given in the main section of this book where each tree is described in detail.

Contents

Pride-of-De
Kaap Bauhinia,
page 106

TREES GREET YOU

FIND TREES BY ECOZONE

Large-fruit Bushwillow,
page 288

The tree groups in the contents have been graded from easy-to-spot to the most difficult-to-spot. The colours of the tabs on the side of each page cross-correlate with the colours in each section of the contents. These colours have nothing to do with the Ecozones.

*These tree names have changed since the last edition. See "Names of South African trees" on page ix.

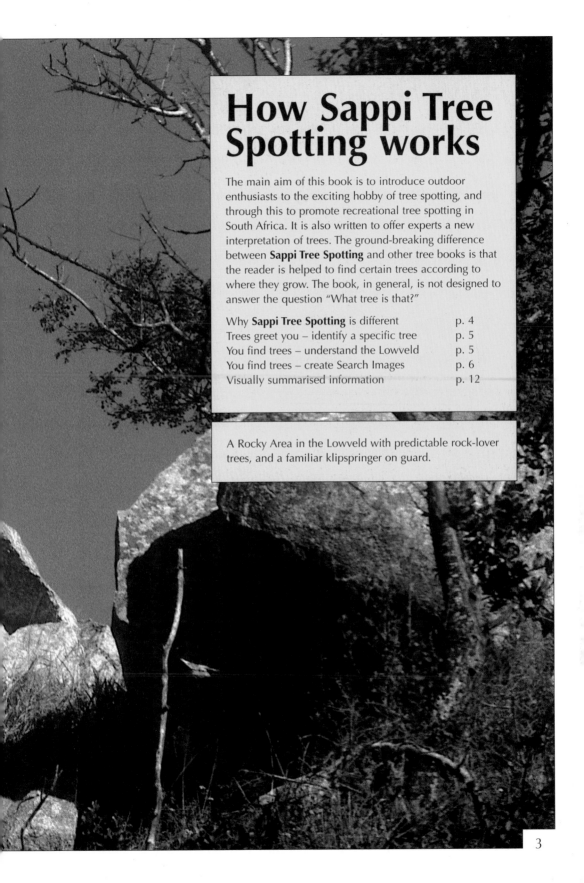

How Sappi Tree Spotting works

The main aim of this book is to introduce outdoor enthusiasts to the exciting hobby of tree spotting, and through this to promote recreational tree spotting in South Africa. It is also written to offer experts a new interpretation of trees. The ground-breaking difference between **Sappi Tree Spotting** and other tree books is that the reader is helped to find certain trees according to where they grow. The book, in general, is not designed to answer the question "What tree is that?"

A Rocky Area in the Lowveld with predictable rock-lover trees, and a familiar klipspringer on guard.

How Sappi Tree Spotting works
WHY SAPPI TREE SPOTTING IS DIFFERENT

Sappi Tree Spotting is a creative new way to make the most of the outdoors. It is designed to do for trees what Roberts and Newman have done for birds. Eight years of intensive, scientific field and market research have gone into fine-tuning a simple and innovative method of getting to know trees in their natural environments. Until recently trees have remained inaccessible to all but the most devoted, botanically minded, tree-key followers.

Sappi Tree Spotting changes this with innovative methods of linking real trees to book theory. In most other field guides, for either animals or plants, the systems is based on:

• seeing a species in the wild
• looking it up in the guidebook to identify it, and to gain further information

In Sappi Tree Spotting that system changes in 4 ways:

1 Trees greet you – Identify a specific tree because it is spectacular (see opposite)

This is similar to the traditional method described above, because these trees are spectacular enough to be recognised easily. Some feature of the tree is so Distinctively Striking, or Unique, or Seasonally Striking that you cannot fail to identify it (see opposite page).

2 You find trees – Understand the Lowveld, and look for the right trees in the right places (see opposite)

This is a Sappi Tree Spotting innovation, and is based on you setting out to look for specific trees in specific places. In natural environments most trees flourish and reach maturity in areas that suit them best. That is the right place for you to learn them first. Thinking the other way around – when you are in the area it makes sense to first learn those trees that thrive there best. Much of the layout and philosophy of this book series is to make this identification of the right trees as easy as possible.

3 You find trees – Create Search Images by using simple language (see page 6)

This series highlights aspects of the chosen trees which are easiest to visualise. Whichever area you are in, you can work out which trees you are likely to find, and build up a mental picture of their most Striking Features. All the text is easy-to-follow in simple English. The average recreational tree spotter will never use 'pubescent' when 'hairy' will do! Learning to know and love trees need not only be for the botanically trained.

4 Visually summarised information (see page 12)

This series helps the tree spotter by means of accessible, easy-to-use information like: height and shade density icons; grids indicating seasonal changes; maps and information blocks that direct you to the most convenient park, lodge or game reserve. It also gives information on modern and traditional uses for trees, and their gardening possibilities.

1 TREES GREET YOU – IDENTIFY A SPECIFIC TREE BECAUSE IT IS SO SPECTACULAR

There are a number of Lowveld trees that you can identify easily. None of these trees need a complex system of 'keying', because they are instantly recognisable, in many instances even from a distance. There are three ways, using this book, to find the names of these distinctive trees.

Distinctive Striking Features

On pages 50 - 65 you will find a series of visual summaries of striking leaves, flowers, fruit and bark, as well as comparisons of a number of families. Using these pages you could well come across a **Distinctive Striking Feature** on a tree in the wild, and look it up here, and be able to identify it immediately.

Long-tail Cassia flowers, page 102

Unique Trees

On pages 68 - 87 are the **Unique Trees** that are so unusual in their growth form that, after you have browsed through the book once or twice, you will not fail to recognise them if you see them in the wild.

Lala-palm leaves, page 76

Seasonally Striking Trees

On pages 90 - 125 are the trees that have very striking flowers or fruit, in certain seasons, **and** they are difficult to identify without these features. The recommendation is that if you want instant recognition, you first look for these trees in the specified season. This is made easier by the Seasonal Grid on the last page of each tree's description.

Purple-pod Cluster-leaf pods, page 110

2 YOU FIND TREES – UNDERSTAND THE LOWVELD AND LOOK FOR THE RIGHT TREES IN THE RIGHT PLACES

From pages 20 - 40, there are descriptions of the various Habitats and Ecozones of the Lowveld. There is always a strong correlation between an area and the trees you can look for. It is worthwhile familiarising yourself with at least the area where you intend to go tree spotting. Use the maps on pages 332 - 345, the cross-section diagram and the Ecozone blocks shown below. A seven step guide is summarised on page 47.

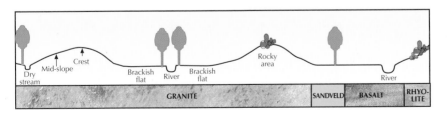

3 YOU FIND TREES — CREATE SEARCH IMAGES BY USING SIMPLE LANGUAGE

Finding a tree that you do not know, is like looking for a stranger in a crowded room. You need to have a clear Search Image of certain Striking Features that you can visualise easily. For example, when looking for a specific person, you may think of a tall, red-haired woman with glasses. In the same way most trees covered in this book have a specific form and look about them, that will help you find them.

Look at a number of different trees carefully and you will see many patterns. The fascinating part is that most species do have their own pattern so strongly encoded that it is repeated to a greater or lesser degree in each individual tree. As you learn these patterns of growth you will learn to recognise many trees at a glance.

Sappi Tree Spotting descibes these patterns in this order:

- **Main branches** splitting off the **trunk/stem**.
- **Branchlets** splitting off the **branches**, then splitting into **twigs**.
- **Leaf-stalks** attaching the leaves to the twigs, or in a few trees, the leaves to the branchlets.

Main branches always leave the main trunk (or stem) in a generally upward or horizontal direction.
However, branchlets and twigs can tend to be in an upward, horizontal or even downward pattern, or they can be a mixture.

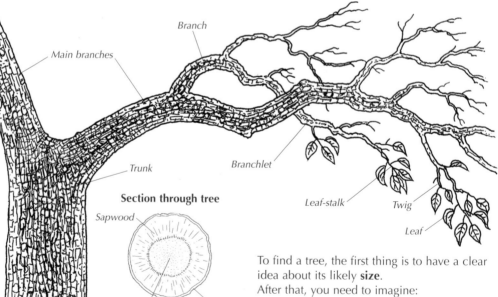

Branch
Main branches
Trunk
Branchlet
Leaf-stalk
Twig
Leaf

Section through tree
Sapwood
Heartwood
Bark

Thorns and spines
They are both sharp.
Thorns are protuberances not covered in bark. **Spines** are bark-covered twigs that may carry leaves.

To find a tree, the first thing is to have a clear idea about its likely **size**.
After that, you need to imagine:
- the trunk form
- how this trunk splits up into branches, branchlets and twigs
- the form and density of the canopy

Finally the shape, size and colour of the leaves, flowers, fruit or pods will help you with a positive identification.
On the following pages you will find the terms used in **Sappi Tree Spotting**. These will help you to create your Search Images.

TRUNKS AND STEMS

"Trunk" is used for larger trees and "stems" for smaller and/or multi-stemmed trees.

Multi-stemmed
eg. Many-stemmed Albizia
- p. 174

**Single-trunked,
low-branching**
eg. Sycamore Fig
- p. 218

**Single-trunked,
high-branching**
eg. Leadwood
Bushwillow
- p. 136

Straight trunk
eg. Marula
- p. 140

Crooked trunk
eg. Apple-leaf
- p. 128

Fluted trunk
eg. Green-thorn
- p. 162

Buttressed trunk
eg. Sycamore Fig
- p. 218

CANOPIES

The canopy is the upper area of a tree, formed by the branches and the leaves.

Round
eg. Natal-mahogany
- p. 232

Semi-circular
eg. Marula
- p. 140

Umbrella
eg. Umbrella Thorn Acacia
- p. 80

Wide spreading
eg. Pod-mahogany
- p. 200

V-shaped
eg. Many-stemmed Albizia
- p. 174

Narrow
eg. Tree Wisteria
- p. 118

Irregular
eg. Apple-leaf
- p. 128

LEAVES

A leaf grows on a leaf-stalk that attaches the leaf to the twig or branchlet. It snaps off the twig or branchlet relatively easily at the leaf-bud (axillary bud). You can often see this bud as a swelling at the base of the leaf-stalk.

All leaves are described as simple or compound.

Sometimes it is not easy to tell the difference between a simple and a compound leaf. Some of the ways are:

- Look for the position of the leaf-bud.
- Compound leaves look organised on their leaf-stalk. Most simple leaves that are grouped close together look irregular on the twig.
- The leaflet of a compound leaf tends to tear off the leaf-stalk – it does not snap off neatly, the way the leaf itself usually snaps off the twig at the leaf-bud. Please note this is not true for all species, nor at all times of the year.

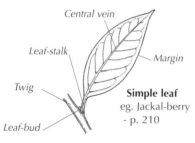

Central vein
Leaf-stalk
Margin
Twig
Simple leaf
eg. Jackal-berry
- p. 210
Leaf-bud

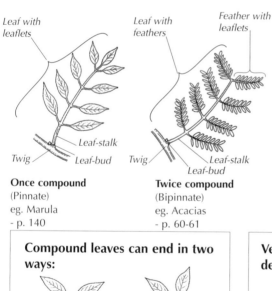

Leaf with leaflets
Leaf with feathers
Feather with leaflets
Leaf-stalk
Twig
Leaf-bud

Once compound
(Pinnate)
eg. Marula
- p. 140

Twig
Leaf-stalk
Leaf-bud

Twice compound
(Bipinnate)
eg. Acacias
- p. 60-61

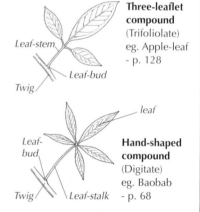

Leaf-stem
Leaf-bud
Twig

Three-leaflet compound
(Trifoliolate)
eg. Apple-leaf
- p. 128

leaf
Leaf-bud
Twig
Leaf-stalk

Hand-shaped compound
(Digitate)
eg. Baobab
- p. 68

Compound leaves can end in two ways:

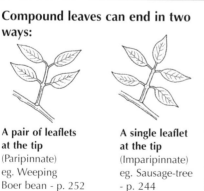

A pair of leaflets at the tip
(Paripinnate)
eg. Weeping Boer bean - p. 252

A single leaflet at the tip
(Imparipinnate)
eg. Sausage-tree
- p. 244

Vein patterns on leaves vary a great deal. Two distinctive patterns are:

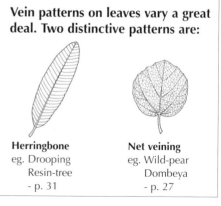

Herringbone
eg. Drooping Resin-tree
- p. 31

Net veining
eg. Wild-pear Dombeya
- p. 27

LEAF ATTACHMENTS TO TWIGS OR BRANCHLETS

Leaf-stalks can attach to the twigs in a number of ways and these tend to be predictable, species by species. Sometimes, however, you will find a variety of attachments on a single tree – this is done simply to confuse you and to make traditional keying methods difficult to follow! Attachments of the leaves to the twig or branchlet can be:

Opposite
eg. Water
Nuxia
- p. 248

Alternate
eg. Buffalo-thorn
- p. 258

Spiral
eg. Purple-pod
Cluster-leaf
- p. 110

Clustered
eg. Bushveld
Gardenia
- p. 262

Winged
None in this
book

LEAF OR LEAFLET SHAPE

There are many varieties of leaf shape. As a basis for all descriptions this book refers to them as:

Round
eg. Round-
leaved
Bloodwood
- p. 296

Heart-shaped
eg. Large-leaved
Rock Fig
- p. 196

Narrow elliptic
eg. Water Nuxia
- p. 248

Broad elliptic
eg. Jackal-berry
- p. 210

Butterfly
eg.
Mopane
- p. 144

Needle
None in
this book

Triangular
eg. Feverberry
Croton
- p. 37

LEAF MARGINS

The edge of the leaf can be:

Smooth
eg. Sycamore
Fig - p. 218

Wavy
eg. Magic Guarri
- p. 278

Toothed
eg. Tamboti
- p. 222

FLOWER PARTS

All flowers are made up of these parts:

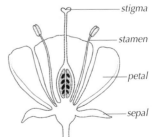

- stigma
- stamen
- petal
- sepal

9

BARK

The bark texture, and/or colour, is often characteristic of a tree. However, it often differs between trunk and branches, older and younger trunks, and older and younger branches. Thinner and younger branches mostly have smoother and paler bark.

Smooth
eg. Fever Tree Acacia
- p. 72

Coarse
eg. Jackal-berry
- p. 210

Fissured or grooved
eg. Knob Thorn Acacia
- p. 132

Blocky
eg. Tamboti
- p. 222

Flaking, peeling
eg. Flaky Thorn Acacia
- p. 284

FLOWERS

Plants, including trees, are scientifically classified and named according to their flower shape. Looking carefully at flower-shapes can help with family identification, but this is often very technical and not easy to see.

Most species within a family, however, share general flower-shapes (pages 398 - 401). Some flowers have a unique shape, eg. Baobab, page 86, or are inconspicuous, eg. Tall Firethorn Corkwood, page 300. These are described in detail in the specific texts.

Ball
eg. Fever Tree Acacia
- p. 72

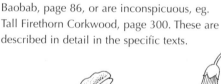

Spike
eg. Knob Thorn Acacia
- p. 132

Pea-like
eg. Apple-leaf
- p. 128

Trumpet
eg. Bushveld Gardenia
- p. 262

Star
eg. Raisins
- p. 308

Protea
None in this book

Pincushion
Albizias
- p. 59

FRUIT

Fruit has a fleshy pulp covering the seed/s. The pulp may be oily, watery or dry, and must be removed before the seeds can germinate.

Birds and animals are attracted to the fruit and help distribute the seeds.

Berry – small, single
eg. Jackal-berry
- p. 210

Grape – small, in bunches
eg. Wild Date-palm
- p. 84

Plum – larger, single
eg. Jacket-plum
- p. 274

PODS

Pods are hard envelopes covering a seed, or more often, several seeds.

Flat bean
eg. Knob Thorn
Acacia
- p. 132

Broad bean
eg. African-wattle
- p. 90

Bumpy bean
eg. Scented-pod
Thorn Acacia
- p. 270

Coiled
eg. Umbrella
Thorn Acacia
- p. 80

Sickle/kidney
eg. Mopane
- p. 144

Capsule
eg. White Kirkia
- p. 204

Two-winged
eg. Cluster-leafs
- p. 63

Four-winged
eg. Bushwillows
- p. 62-63

4 VISUALLY SUMMARISED INFORMATION

English name/Scientific species name/Scientific family name English family name/Other South African names

These identify the specific tree. The majority of the names in different South African languages were compiled by the Dendrological Society in 9 of our 11 languages.

Previous English names

These are the **original names** published in the 1st Edition. See page ix for more information about names of South African Trees.

Where you'll find this tree easily

As with the cross-section diagram below, the **red tree icon** shows the easiest place to find the tree. The **green tree icon** shows the other Habitats where the tree is likely to be found.

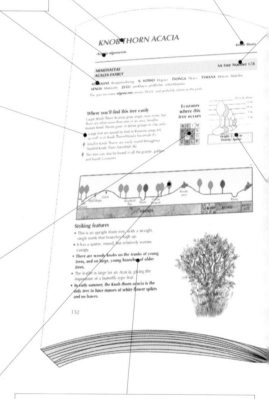

Ecozone blocks

The blocks that are coloured show the Ecozones in which you can find this tree easily.

The colours and their letters are the same ones you will find on the Maps – pages 332 - 345.

Cross-section diagram of the Lowveld

The **red tree icons** show the Habitat where it is easiest to find the tree. The **green tree icons** show the Habitat to look in as second choice. Note that the icons of trees are proportionally too large for the scale of the landscape.

Striking Features of mature trees

These are features of mature trees which will help you find an example of the tree with the greatest ease.

The bold items are those Striking Features which are the most important in helping you with positive identification.

South African tree number

The numbers are according to the National List of Indigenous Trees, compiled by the National Botanical Institute.

Line drawing

This drawing will indicate the most important Striking Feature that will help you to differentiate the tree from any others.

Artwork of the tree

Trees vary greatly and no single photograph or illustration can represent every tree you will find. However this artwork gives an overall impression of the size and the common form of mature trees, which are easiest to find. It emphasises the Striking Features listed on the opposite page.

Identification tab

For easy reference the colour-coded tabs indicate **Sappi Tree Spotting** groups, as well as the specific tree. These same groups are colour-coded in the Contents. The green colour-codes are purely to separate sections of the book, and have no correlation to Ecozones.

Dendrological Society record tree

This information is from the society's register indicating the largest tree of this species currently registered. The location of the tree is also given.

Density and height icon

This will help you form a more accurate Search Image.
The tree which is coloured gives an idea of the average height of mature trees you will find easiest to identify in the Lowveld, in comparison with other common trees. The height is given in metres.
The density of the colour indicates the average summer density of the leaves and branches, as well as the resultant density of the shade.

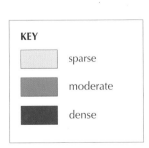

KEY

	sparse
	moderate
	dense

4 VISUALLY SUMMARISED INFORMATION – CONTINUED

Wood samples and ornaments

Many South African trees have beautiful wood that is workable for carving, turning or furniture. Where possible a picture of the polished wood, as well as a finished product, are included to show the texture and the colour. Not all the workable timbers are included in the book.

These pictures should help with the appreciation of the value, beauty and diversity of South Africa's indigenous woods, and should encourage sustainable usage. Wasteful chopping and burning of our rarer trees is leading to a number of them becoming "endangered" in the wild, although none of these trees are covered here.

The photographs of these wood samples were taken courtesy of the CSIR, Pretoria.

Sets of wood samples and technical details of different woods can be obtained from CSIR (Environmentek). The photographs of the ornaments were taken courtesy of Prof A E van Wyk, University of Pretoria.

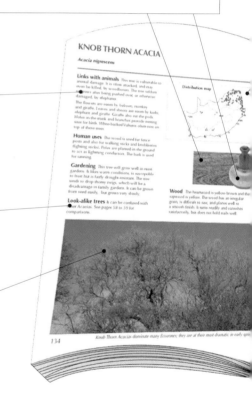

General information and usages

Details of interest about the tree, in relation to people and to animals, as well as gardening, are given here.

Look-alike trees

Noted here are trees that can be confused with the featured tree. They are not necessarily in the same family or genus.

Photographs/Look-alikes

These are **photographs** of the tree, or its features, chosen to increase either your information or your pleasure!

In some trees there is a **diagram** and/or text which covers look-alike trees.

Map of South Africa

This is an adaptation from maps supplied by the National Botanical Institute in Pretoria, and the Dendrological Society.

Abbreviations:

BLM:	Bloemfontein	GR:	Graaff Reinet	PE:	Port Elizabeth
BW:	Beaufort West	JHB:	Johannesburg	PS:	Port Shepstone
CT:	Cape Town	K:	Kimberley	RB:	Richard's Bay
DBN:	Durban	MB:	Mossel Bay	SC:	Sun City
EL:	East London	N:	Nelspruit	SPR:	Springbok
		P:	Pietersburg	UP:	Upington

Growth details

These details will help you to check your identification. They build up a wider Search Image so you can find the same tree elsewhere. For each specific tree the size of the leaves, flowers, fruit and/or pods are shown in relation to one another. However this size relationship does not carry through proportionately from one species to another.

Seasonal changes

This grid is to help you find trees at different times of the year. However, Lowveld Habitats offer varying protection, therefore it is an average guide only.

- The information will vary from year to year depending on temperature and rainfall.
- The information also varies from Ecozone to Ecozone and within Habitats.
- The colours represent the months during which the leaves, flowers, fruit / pods are most likely to be seen.
- The colours themselves are a very rough guide only. You should refer to the artwork for more accurate colours.
- Pale grey is used for inconspicuous flowers or pods.
- Whether a fruit/pod is ripe or not, it is shown on the grid, while it is still visible on the tree, even after losing its seeds.

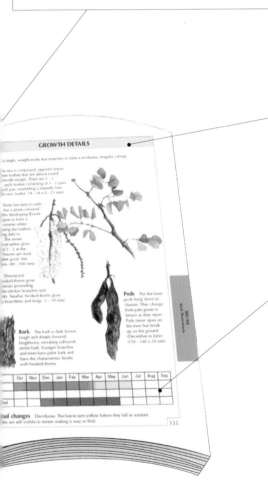

15

The Lowveld

Understanding different areas of the Lowveld will help with tree identification. Trees have evolved and are adapted to specific soil, temperature and moisture conditions, as well as to specific patterns of animal utilisation and fire. In addition, a tree will only thrive and become part of the plant community when it is well enough adapted to also compete with the other trees and plants that grow in that area. Trees that are common in the Lowveld can withstand long seasonal droughts, many are susceptible to frost, and all are in some way protected against overutilisation by browsing animals.

The following pages have information that describes the different areas of the Lowveld, and some of the trees you can expect to look for.

Here the meandering Olifants River runs from west to east through the rugged hills of Ecozone J.

The Lowveld

The Lowveld as defined for this book, is a lowlying area between two mountain ranges – the Drakensberg in the west and Lebombos in the east. A narrow tongue extends through Swaziland to northern Natal. Northwards the Lowveld and its vegetation patterns are evident well into Zimbabwe. The altitude ranges from 150 to 600 metres above sea level.

The Lowveld is a summer rainfall area receiving between 200 and 600 mm per annum. This decreases from west to east, and from south to north. The summers are hot and humid with temperatures up to 44°C, while winters are mild, with frost occurring only rarely in most of the area.

About 130 million years ago the Lowveld was formed by massive movements of the continental plates. Due to tilting and subsequent erosion, different layers of underlying geology were exposed.

The diverse geology of the Lowveld is very important because it forms the basis of the Habitats and Ecozones which influence the distribution of different species of trees. In addition to the ranges in altitude, rainfall and geology the large geographic area ensures you can look for a wide variety of trees.

Some of these trees are the common-place South African favourites, like Marula (page 140) and Tamboti (page 222). Others are truly unique, and even breathtaking, and are found only in very limited ranges. They obviously include the well-loved Baobab (page 68), as well as the lesser known but equally magnificent Pod-mahogany (page 200). You are going to have fun tree spotting in the Lowveld!

The Lowveld in Southern Africa

WHAT IS A HABITAT?

For the purpose of **Sappi Tree Spotting**, "Habitats" is used to mean something very specific. To find trees easily, you will need to notice whether you are on a hill, a midslope or in a valley bottom; you will naturally be more aware if you are alongside a river or near a Rocky Area. These are all different Habitats, and they occur with varying reliability in the different Ecozones. Habitats are discussed on pages 20 - 25.

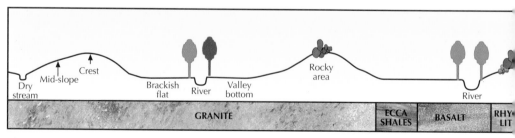

These cross-section diagrams are next to every tree discription. The red and green trees here indicate in which habitat you are most likely to find each tree easily.

WHAT IS AN ECOZONE?

An Ecozone is an area where there is uniform landform, rainfall and geology, leading to relatively uniform soils. As a result you can expect to find specific trees in each Ecozone, but still subject to changes in Habitat.

Lowveld Ecozones

The Lowveld can be longitudinally divided into two main geological zones with older more resistant granites and gabbro in the west, and younger Ecca shales, basalts and rhyolites in the east. As different rocks erode, soils form with different characteristics.

The Ecozones are on the Maps, pages 332 - 345, each one in a different colour, with a letter A to P linked to their names. They are also discussed in detail on pages 26 - 40.

You will find blocks like this next to every tree. The coloured blocks indicate the Ecozones where you will find this tree easily.

A	E	I	M
B	F	J	N
C	G	K	O
D	H	L	P

Granite Ecozones – Rolling Hills

A	Mixed Bushwillow Woodlands
B	Pretoriuskop Sourveld
C	Malelane Mountain Bushveld
D	Sabie / Crocodile Thorn Thickets
P	Mopane / Bushwillow Woodlands

Gabbro Ecozone – Flat Plains

| E | Thorn Veld |

Ecca shale Ecozones – Flat Plains

| G | Delagoa Thorn Thickets |
| O | Tree Mopane Savannah |

Basalt Ecozones

F	Knob Thorn / Marula Savannah
J	Olifants Rugged Veld
K	Stunted Knob Thorn Savannah
L	Mopane Shrubveld

Rhyolite Ecozone

| I | Lebombo Mountain Bushveld |

Specialist Ecozone

| M | Alluvial Plains |
| N | Sandveld |

| H 〜〜〜 Riverine (This Ecozone is described as a Habitat) |

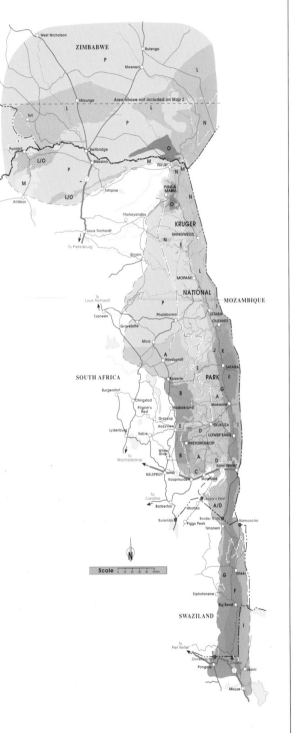

Habitats

CRESTS, VALLEYS, SEEPLINES AND PLAINS

Crests of granite Ecozones A, B, C, D and P

The oldest, exposed layers of the Lowveld are the ancient granites in the west. These granites have eroded to form an undulating landscape, criss-crossed by many drainage lines, where rain-water flows, above or below ground level. The soils derived from the granites are coarse and sandy. They are low in nutrients and water drains easily into these soils. Water caught between the sandy grains can be readily absorbed by plant roots. These sandy soils are typically found on the crests of the granite hills, and between the rocks of granite Rocky Outcrops.

Trees that grow on sandy soils normally have large leaves, like Bushwillows (*Combretum* species). This is because the trees have to absorb large amounts of water to obtain enough nutrients for growth. They need to get rid of excess water, and larger leaves facilitate evaporation.

These large leaves are very prone to insect attacks, and form chemicals to protect themselves. These same chemicals make the leaves unpalatable to browsers, and they only tend to eat the leaves when there is little else available. The most common tree on the crests in the granites in the south is the Red Bushwillow (*Combretum apiculatum,* page 292).

Seeplines in granite

In the granite undulations, water flows down hill from the Crests. Where the sand meets the hard rock on the midslope, water seepage into the soil is stopped. The water runs along the rock, onto the soil surface, to form a seepline. These seeplines are clearly visible in years of high rainfall. During these periods, soils here are very damp and water can often be seen on the surface. These areas often have a dense grass cover, interspersed with the tall Silver Cluster-leaf (*Terminalia sericea,* page 148).Lower down the slopes the Crest evens out, with some clay being deposited. These areas generally have shallower soils, with more clay, than the Crests, and both broad-leaved and fine-leaved trees are found here. (See explanation of fine-leaved trees, growing on clay, on opposite page).

Giraffe on the crest add excitement to your tree spotting!

Valleys of granite Ecozones A, B, C, D, and P. Plains of gabbro E; basalt F, J, K and L; Ecca shale G and O.

In clay, particles lie close together, and water is held between them, like water in milled flour. Here water does not seep into the soils easily, but once held, gives rise to areas that become very muddy, and water-logged in the rainy season. Clay soils are rich in nutrients, but water molecules are held tight, and plants have more difficulty extracting water from them.

Trees growing on clay soils can only absorb small amounts of water, and they therefore have to conserve water, and **not** lose too much through large-leaved evaporation. They tend to have smaller, finer leaves. These small leaves are less accessible to insects, and the trees only have to defend themselves against animals that find the small leaves very palatable. Most of these trees therefore have thorns, such as the Acacia family. The Knob Thorn Acacia (*Acacia nigrescens*, page 132) is one of the most common trees, both in granite valley bottoms and on the southern basalt plains, while the Scented-pod Thorn Acacia (*Acacia nilotica*, page 270) is common in Brack areas and on gabbro plains.

Because of the slopes in the granite Ecozones, smaller sand particles, and animal and plant material are carried downhill, resulting in fine-grained clay soils in the valleys.

In the soils of the other Ecozones, listed in the heading above, the soils are all naturally clay-like. The clay soils of the basalts and Ecca shales support less varied vegetation than the granites, and are often dominated by a few tree species. It could be easier for beginners to start identifying trees in these Ecozones – F, G, J, K and L.

Valleys in the granites tend to be dominated by various Acacia Thorn trees.

RIVERINE HABITAT; ALSO ECOZONE H

There is Riverine vegetation along all of the large perennial rivers, as well as many smaller rivers and stream banks, throughout the Lowveld. The most magnificent, huge trees can be found here. This is because their root systems are able to access enough moisture all year round, often from underground water flow. In addition, the mean temperature in the Lowveld does not often drop to frost or freezing levels, giving year round warmth for some growth.

Water-loving trees such as the Water Nuxia (*Nuxia oppositifolia*, page 248), and River Bushwillow (*Combretum erythrophyllum*, page, 236), occur on the banks of large

perennial rivers near the water, while the Matumi (*Breonadia salicina*, page 228), often grows in the rocky reaches of the same rivers.

Large evergreen trees such as the Sausage-tree (*Kigelia africana*, page 244), and the Natal-mahogany (*Trichilia emetica*, page 232), are found on the banks of almost all the larger rivers. The Nyala-tree (*Xanthocercis zambesiaca*, page 214), however, is more common along the rivers from the Olifants northwards. During spring the red flowers of the Flame Climbing Bushwillow (*Combretum microphyllum*, page 98), form a striking picture in the riverbeds.

The majestic Olifants River running through the Lebombo mountains has typical riverine trees.

Umdoni/Waterberry
***Syzygium cordatum** SA Tree no 555*
This tree occurs along the banks of permanent rivers and on the hills of the Pretoriuskop Sourveld Ecozone B. It is a single-trunked, low-branching, evergreen tree, and has a dense, semi-circular canopy. The stemless leaves are round, simple, blue-green, leathery, with a distinct, yellow central vein. Leaves grow at branchlet ends, forming rosettes. Flowers are sweet-smelling, creamy-white to pinkish, pincushion-like and grow in bunches in leaf rosettes (October to June). Fruit is fleshy, berry-like, deep purple when ripe, and grows in bunches in leaf rosettes (November to June).

BRACKISH FLATS

These areas tend to occur on the inner bends of rivers as they flow through the granites. These areas have a different salt composition. This is the result of the movement of salts down the crests and along the drainage lines, although there is no hard data as to why these areas occur on the bends.

The vegetation growing here is very palatable and often high in sodium. There are often large, open patches of short, very palatable grasses that are usually heavily grazed, leaving bare, exposed soil. Some trees can tolerate these salty soils well,

and they are often quite distinctive and easy to find. The most common is the Magic Guarri (*Euclea divinorum*, page 278), which is one of the indicator trees of the sodic (salty) or brack patches. Because these areas are so open, animals like to rest here where they can see approaching predators. These are therefore always good areas to look for game.

Jacket-plum (*Pappea capensis,* page 274), Bushveld Gardenia (*Gardenia volkensii,* page 262), and Bushveld Saffron (*Elaeodendron transvaalense,* page 266) are also common here.

An open area with short grass surrounded by Magic Guarri.

Young Tamboti
Spirostachys africana *SA Tree no. 341*
Large stands of young, light-barked, spiny Tamboti trees can most easily be identified on clay soils that form near drainage lines in the granite Ecozones. They can also be found in Ecozone G (Ecca shale), further from water. The grass cover in these areas is mostly sparse and animals tend to congregate here to rest in the shade. During the dry months the fallen Tamboti leaves are eaten by smaller browsers such as impala. These patches differ from the sodic patches where the Magic Guarri grows, as they are not open, like the Brack areas above. Tambotis are described in detail on page 222.

ROCKY OUTCROPS

Rocky Outcrops are most commonly formed by granite boulders in the granite Ecozones, A, B, C, D and P. Rocky outcrops are also found in the Sandveld (Ecozone N) where the boulders are formed by sandstone. This is softer than granite and is often covered in a wide variety of lichen species. The dark coloured boulders of the gabbro in Thornveld (Ecozone E) also form some of the well-known landmarks of the Lowveld.

These Rocky Outcrops are well drained, and many of the drought-resistant species such as

Euphorbias and Corkwoods (*Commiphora* species) can be found growing here. White Kirkia (*Kirkia accuminata*, page 204), which are a favourite of elephants, can escape from them in this less accessible Habitat.

The long roots of Rock Figs are a common sight on most Rocky Outcrops, and the new red leaves of the Red-leaved Fig (*Ficus ingens*, see below), are conspicuous on these outcrops in early spring.

Granites erode to leave magnificent outcrops, forming a unique protective habitat.

Red-leaved Fig
Ficus ingens SA Tree Number 55
This Fig can be found on Rocky Outcrops and mountains throughout the Lowveld. It branches low down and spreads widely, to form a semi-circular canopy, often with obvious white roots,

or a fluted trunk if larger. Large, simple leaves are long and narrowly elliptic, with distinct, yellowish, indented central and side veins. In spring there is a spectacular flush of wine-red to coppery young leaves. Small berry-like figs are smooth, or slightly hairy, and dull-red to copper when ripe from June to December. All parts of the tree have some milky latex.

PANS

Pans are most common in Ecozones which are relatively flat, i.e. basalts (Ecozones F and K), and Ecca shales, as well as Ecozones G and O, where they form an important part of the drainage system. They are obviously also vital in the life of the animal populations living or moving nearby.

These Pans are mostly in very flat areas, away from any drainage lines and are often very similar to Brack Areas (see page 23). They are relatively open areas which have palatable grasses, and animals often visit these pans. Many pans are actually maintained, and/or enlarged, by animals such as rhino and warthog.

The most common trees are Fever Tree Acacias (*Acacia xanthophloea* page 72) and Lala-palms. The Northern Lala-palm (*Hyphaene petersiana*) is the one illustrated on page 76. It grows into a tall tree, has more-or-less round fruit, and is more common in the north. The Southern Lala-palm (*Hyphaene coriacea*) is usually a shrub with pear-shaped fruit, and is more common in the south. The Red Spike-thorn (*Gymnosporia senegalensis*, page 114), often form large stands near pans, while the Common Spike-thorn (*Gymnosporia buxifolia*, see below), may be found growing on the edges of the pan itself.

Pans tend to be in the flat clay-dominated basalts in the east.

Common Spikethorn
Gymnosporia buxifolia SA Tree no 399
This evergreen, single-stemmed, low-branching tree has an untidy angular outline formed by haphazardly upward-growing branchlets. Variable-lengthed, straight spines grow beneath the leaf-bud. The bark is pale to dark brown, maturing to

be deeply furrowed in regular, protruding blocks. The simple leaves are variable, mostly elliptic with a very short leaf-stem, broad tip and sharp base. They are clustered on ends of short, stubby twigs, forming a sleeve around the branchlets. Conspicuous clusters of white star-shaped flowers smell offensive. The berry-like fruit is three-celled (May to January).

Ecozones

ECOZONE A – MIXED BUSHWILLOW WOODLANDS (ON GRANITE)

This Ecozone is typical of the all the granite Ecozones (A, C, D and P), and occurs in the southern part of the Lowveld. The rainfall varies between 550 and 700 mm, and the altitude between 350 and 500 m. This landscape is large and occupies about 11% of the Kruger National Park.

These granitic areas consist of granite domes, intersected by drainage lines, creating undulating crests and valleys. These are discussed in detail on pages 20 - 21.

On the crests of the domes, boulders are often exposed by erosion to form Rocky Outcrops. The granite rocks weather to form sandy soils that vary in depth from deep to very shallow. The most

common tree on these crests is the Red Bushwillow (*Combretum apiculatum*, page 292). In the valleys where the soil is a heavier clay the most common trees are the Acacias, particularly the Knob Thorn Acacia (*Acacia nigrescens*, page 132).

Both towards the west and the south of this Ecozone the rainfall is slightly higher, and the Large-fruit Bushwillow (*Combretum zeyheri*, page 288) and the Weeping Bushwillow (*Combretum collinum*, see below) are more common.

Although this Ecozone does not have any large perennial rivers, there are a number of larger streams, where typical riverine vegetation can be found. It is a good Ecozone to find kudu.

Bushwillows tend to be formless, but their sheer numbers make them easy to find.

Weeping Bushwillow
Combretum collinum *SA Tree Number 541.2*
This Bushwillow is more common in areas of higher rainfall including the Pretoriuskop Sourveld Ecozone B. In the past this tree has been called Variable Bushwillow for good reason! Large, broad elliptic to oval leaves can be opposite or alternate, dark green above and paler green to silvery below. Flowers can be cream to yellow, sweetly scented in spikes (August to October). Pods are characteristically four-winged, as in all Bushwillows, but are rosy-red, not rusty-red when young, and dry to dark brown.

ECOZONE B – PRETORIUSKOP SOURVELD (ON GRANITE)

This Ecozone is located in the south-western corner of the Lowveld and is very similar to the Sour Bushveld discussed in **Sappi Tree Spotting – Bushveld**.

Ecozone B, like A, D and P, is a granite Ecozone with the typical undulating landscape of crests and valleys. This is more fully described on pages 20 - 21. The rainfall is higher than in most of the other granitic Ecozones, varying from 600 to 1 000 mm. The altitude varies from 550 to 600 m above sea level.

This Ecozone only covers about 3% of the Kruger National Park, however many of the private game reserves along the Sabie and Sand rivers are also located in this Ecozone. Many areas of this Ecozone are characterised by long grass typical of Sour Bushveld, as well as extensive stands of

Silver Cluster-leaf (*Terminalia sericea,* page 148). Some trees, that prefer higher rainfall, are only found in the Lowveld in this Ecozone. These include the Kiaat Bloodwood (*Pterocarpus angolensis*, page 166). The Black Monkey-orange (*Strychnos madagascariensis,* page 154) is also more common here. Many trees such as the Sycamore Fig (*Ficus sycomorus,* page 218) and Jackal-berry (*Diospyros mespiliformis,* page 210) that normally only occur along rivers in the rest of the Lowveld, are found here on the crests. Look for White Rhino and sable in the open, grassy areas.

Extensive stands of Silver Cluster-leaf are common.

Wild-pear Dombeya
Dombeya rotundifolia SA Tree Number 471
This deciduous, single-stemmed tree has an irregular, moderate canopy. Leaves are simple, hairy, rough and parchment-like, and are conspicuously round. It is spectacular in early spring when covered in star-like, cream to light brown flowers which appear before the leaves (July to October). Seeds grow in small capsules, surrounded by brownish, dry flower-petals (October to December).

ECOZONE C – MALELANE MOUNTAIN BUSHVELD (ON GRANITE)

This is the most mountainous of the Ecozones, with an altitude of 350 to 800 m. The undulating Malelane Mountains are formed by ancient granites, and the area has a high rainfall of 600 to 700 mm. Both because of its mountainous nature, and the higher rainfall, this area is, in fact, not truly part of the "Lowveld", but has been included here because it constitutes about 2.5% of the Kruger National Park.

Not unexpectedly many trees found here are different from the rest of the Lowveld. These include the Mountain Kirkia (*Kirkia wilmsii,* see below), that can be seen on some of the higher Rocky Outcrops. This tree also forms a splendid autumn landscape along the main tar road between Nelspruit and Komatipoort where it runs along the Crocodile River. This is the only Ecozone where Mountain Reedbuck can be found.

Malelane Mountains – near Mpondo Dam

Mountain Kirkia
Kirkia wilmsii *SA Tree no 269*
This deciduous tree boasts spectacular autumn colours (April to May) on the northern slopes of the mountainous areas of Ecozones B and C. It is a multi-stemmed tree with a spreading, irregular canopy. Branchlets and twigs end
bluntly with tightly clustered, slender, compound leaves at the tips of the branchlets. Leaves have 10 to 20 opposite pairs of tiny leaflets and a leaflet at the tip. Flowers grow in yellow-green, small, inconspicuous sprays (September to December). Fruit is brown and woody, and when mature splits into four sections joined at the apex (February to March).

ECOZONE D – SABIE / CROCODILE THORN THICKETS (ON GRANITE)

This is the least undulating of the granite Ecozones. It is a low-lying landscape between the Crocodile and Sabie rivers, and is characterised by dense stands of Acacia species. The rainfall varies between 500 and 550 mm per year, and the altitude between 200 and 350 m above sea level. The soils of this landscape have more clay than any of the other granite landscapes, which is why this landscape has such dense Acacia stands – a good Ecozone to get to know the common Acacias.

Many riverine trees (see page 22) and Brack areas (page 23) can be found along the banks of the two large rivers, as well as along the numerous other large streams. This Ecozone comprises

about 6% of the Kruger National Park, and for reasons which are not fully understood seems to be an Ecozone of the Kruger National Park only.

There are two tree species that are easier to find in this Ecozone than in any other in the Lowveld. The False Marula *(Lannea schweinfurthii, see below)* is common between Skukuza and Hazyview. The Green-thorn *(Balanites maughamii*, page 162) is also common here. It is easy to identify in all phases of its growth as they often grow in colonies of various ages, fairly close together. Because of the permanent water and riverine vegetation, bushbuck are fairly common along the major riverbanks.

Scented-pod Thorn Acacia are common in this Ecozone.

False Marula
Lannea schweinfurthii *SA Tree no. 363*
This deciduous tree has a single, bare, relatively straight stem and a spreading canopy. It is found throughout the Lowveld, but is not as common as its look-alike the Marula (Sclerrocarya birrea, page 140). The bark peels in large, irregular patches without the round, whitish, golf-ball patches unique to Marula. The compound leaves are smooth, shiny, fresh green with 1 – 3 pairs plus a terminal leaflet, tips broadly tapering. The flowers are unisexual and are found on separate trees. Male flowers are yellow-green, while female flowers are pale yellow and slightly smaller, both appearing November to December. The small, berry-like fruit grows in long bunches, is pale red while swelling, but turns dark wine-red when ripe (January to February).

29

ECOZONE E – THORN VELD (ON GABBRO)

This Ecozone occurs wherever volcanic gabbro has intruded into the granite of Ecozones A, B, D and P. Gabbro is a volcanic rock that was formed millions of years ago, when volcanic lava flowed out between the granite sheets. Because the parent rock is different, the resultant soils and landscape are noticeably different, even to the amateur eye. As a consequence, the Ecozone not only looks different, but has very different trees from those in the surrounding granites. Ecozone E is generally very flat with dark boulders strewn over the landscape. The rainfall average is 500 to 600 mm.

Knob Thorn Acacia *(Acacia nigrescens,* page 132*)* and Marula *(Sclerocarya birrea,* page 140) are very common, and it is also a good Ecozone to find the Long-tail Cassia (*Cassia abbreviata,* page 102). The long finger-like branchlets and twigs of the Rubber-hedge Euphorbia (*Euphorbia tirucalli,* see below) can be seen on some of the Rocky Outcrops.

The soils are rich and the vegetation very palatable, and it is therefore a good Ecozone to find large numbers of browsers such as kudu and giraffe, and grazers such as zebra and wildebeest.

This Ecozone is dotted throughout the south of Kruger National Park, covering about 3.5%, and also occurs west of Kruger in the private Game Reserves.

Open Woodland with tall trees and short grass attracts grazers.

Rubber-hedge Euphorbia
Euphorbia tirucalli
SA Tree no 355
This tree is so unusual in growth form that it is unique, and very easy to identify. It is most easily found on Rocky Outcrops, but also grows in most other Habitats. All parts have a milky toxic latex. Cylindrical, smooth, leafless, green branchlets and twigs are succulent, forming a rounded canopy usually on a single trunk. Inconspicuous yellowish-green flowers cluster at the tips of twigs (October to December). Fruit is a rounded, 3-lobed capsule (November to January).

ECOZONE F – KNOB THORN / MARULA SAVANNAH (ON BASALT)

This Ecozone is found in the southern part of the Lowveld in areas that have volcanic basalts as their parent rock. Basalts erode to form flat, rich clay soils that support open, grassy plains – the home to large numbers of zebra and wildebeest. The rainfall varies from 550 to 600 mm, and the area is about 250 m above sea level.

This very flat Ecozone does not develop distinct streamlets, streams and rivers. Rainwater drains into shallow drainage lines, depressions and pans where it collects. The water, however, does not run off easily, as it does in the undulating granites. Larger drainage lines form alluvial-like plains, where Fever Tree Acacias *(Acacias xanthophloea,* page 72) flourish.

The main vegetation of the plains of Ecozone F consists of large Marulas *(Sclerocarya birrea,* page 140) and Knob Thorn Acacias *(Acacia nigrescens,* page 132), with large stands of the smaller Round-leaved Bloodwood *(Pterocarpus rotundifolius,* page 296), and Sickle-bush *(Dichrostachys cinerea,* page 304). Red Spike-thorn *(Gymnosporia senegalensis,* page 114), grows near the drainage lines. The Drooping Resin-tree *(Ozoroa engleri,* see below), although not very common, is found south of the Olifants River, and is conspicuous in Ecozone F.

Southern Plains – westward from Nkumbe

Bushveld and Drooping Resin-trees
Ozoroa paniculosa SA Tree no 375
Ozoroa engleri SA Tree no 371
These trees are conspicuous in specific areas in the Lowveld. The Bushveld Resin-tree is more common in the basalt Ecozones and the Lebombos north of the Olifants River. The Drooping Resin-tree can be found south of the Olifants River. Resin-trees can be identfied by their long, narrow, peach-like leaves, clustered in whorls of three, *with distinct herringbone veins. Bushveld Resin-trees have a silvery tint in the canopy, while Drooping Resin-trees are bluish. Both have milky, resinous sap, and dark brown to grey rough bark, flaking in small square segments. White to creamy small flowers occur in sprays (October to February), and kidney-shaped fruit grows in loose clusters.*

31

ECOZONE G – DELAGOA THORN THICKETS (ON ECCA SHALE)

This flat Ecozone occurs on Ecca shales, which are a strip of Karoo sediment with some cave sandstone ridges. They run north-south between the undulating granites on the west, and the flat basalts in the east. It covers about 3% of the Kruger National Park. Rainfall is between 500 and 600 mm per year, and the altitude is between 260 and 320 m above sea level. A number of drainage lines run from north to south, because the soft shales weather so easily, and there are many small pans that are rich in bird-life. The soils are nutrient-rich, and the grasses very palatable.

The fact that Delagoa Thorn Acacia (*Acacia welwitschii*, page 158) and Many-stemmed Albizia (*Albizia petersiana*, page 174) dominate this Ecozone, makes it one of the most unique, vegetation-wise, in the Lowveld. It is very easy to find both these species once you are in the Ecozone, although some other Acacia species are also found here that can be confused with the Delagoa Thorn Acacia, particularly Black Monkey Thorn Acacia (*Acacia burkei*, see below). Giraffe like the flowers and pods of the Delagoa Thorn Acacia, and are often found here from November through to July.

This flat Ecozone is dominated by Delagoa Thorn Acacia, the large tree on the right.

Black Monkey Thorn Acacia
Acacia burkei *SA Tree no 161*
This Acacia is more common on the granites south of the Olifants River. It is tall, single-trunked and deciduous, and is often high-branching, with a dense, dark green, semi-circular to thick-umbrella canopy. The bark is dark, rough and deeply fissured lengthways, exposing yellowish underbark. Alternate, twice compound leaves are short and stiff and stand
upright, hardly moving in the wind. The leaflets are relatively large (4-20 x 2-12 mm). Thorns are short, dark, and sharply hooked, in pairs far apart below leaf-buds. White flower-spikes bloom after new leaves appear (October to January). Flat bean pods are dark brown when ripe with a pointed tip. This tree is favoured by elephants, and is less common where elephant densities are high.

Ecozone 1 – Lebombo Mountain Bushveld (on rhyolite)

The Lebombo Mountains form the eastern boundary of Kruger National Park, from as far north as Shingwedzi, and continue southwards through Swaziland, well into northern KwaZulu-Natal. The rainfall increases southwards from 400 mm in the north, to 700 mm near Crocodile Bridge. The average altitude varies between 300 and 400 m. This Ecozone covers about 8% of the Kruger National Park.

Volcanic rhyolite rocks form these mountains, and many of the large west-east rivers cut through them forming deep gorges. A wide variety of Euphorbias contrast with the red rhyolite rocks, and the Lebombo Euphorbia (*Euphorbia confinalis*, see below) is one of the more unique species found here. Suprisingly, waterbuck are often found on the rocky slopes. It is also a good place to look for klipspringer.

In the Lebombo Mountain Bushveld you often see reddish rhyolite rocks.

Lebombo Euphorbia
***Euphorbia confinalis** SA Tree No 345*
This leafless tree grows only in Ecozone 1, on the Lebombo Mountains, where it prefers rocky terrain. It is a single-trunked Euphorbia with a candelabra-like canopy of upward-growing branches. Individual branches form many side branchlets originating at the same level, unlike the Bushveld Candelabra Euphorbia (Euphorbia cooperi, page 192), with branches that do not split. The branches are square and form long rectangular segments. Flowers are small and pale yellow (June to August). Capsule-like fruit has three parts which ripen red (July to October).

ECOZONE J – OLIFANTS RUGGED VELD (ON RHYOLITE / BASALT)

This rugged Ecozone occurs on a mixture of volcanics. The rhyolite of the Lebombos means many rhyolite boulders are strewn across the landscape, while the basalt forms dark clays with dark basalt boulders. The altitude varies between 180 and 300 m above sea level, and the rainfall ranges between 450 and 500 mm per annum.

The Timbavati and Olifants rivers cross this Ecozone, and the dense, green Riverine belts contrast with the sparser vegetation of the Ecozone generally. The Purple-pod Cluster-leaf (*Terminalia prunioides*, page 110) is very common in Rocky Areas while the Shepherds-tree (*Boscia albitrunca*, see below) can be found in the hills around the Olifants River.

This Ecozone occurs only within the Kruger National Park, and covers about 1.5% of the Park. Steenbuck are often seen in open areas.

Euphorbias and White Kirkia are both striking trees in Ecozone J.

Shepherds-tree
Boscia albitrunca *SA Tree no 122*
This evergreen tree is associated with hot, dry areas, and prefers well-drained soils, such as the sandy or rocky areas around the Olifants River in Ecozone J. It is single-trunked, branching into a few large branches that divide profusely to form a rounded, dense canopy. Bark is noticeably pale grey with white, yellowish or black patches.

Young, dull green twigs stand out amongst the spirally-arranged, simple, elliptic, tough, leathery leaves. Yellow star-shaped flowers, with no individual petals, are inconspicuous, in bunches of 4 to 5 (July to November, depending on rain). Fruit is yellow and berry-like when ripe (December to March).

ECOZONE K – STUNTED KNOB THORN SAVANNAH (ON BASALT)

Small Knob Thorn Acacias dominate this slightly undulating Ecozone with underlying basalt rocks. The rainfall varies between 500 and 550 mm, and the altitude between 250 and 500 m above sea level. These soils are high in clay content, and are shallow and dark, and erode easily. The rainfall here is too low for the clay soils to provide the trees with enough water to grow tall. This fact, combined with the dense grass layer, and resulting hot veld fires, keep the trees small.

This area has one of the highest kudu populations in the Kruger National Park. Giraffe are also very fond of Knob-thorns, and because these trees are small, their leaves are easier to reach than in the other Ecozones. Due to the heavy utilisation by giraffe the small Knob Thorns have a regular Christmas-tree-like cone shape, with only the highest branches escaping to form a more irregular canopy (see below).

This Ecozone occurs only within the Kruger National Park and covers about 2% of the Park.

Stunted Knob Thorn Acacias, green in early spring, dominate this relatively flat Ecozone.

Small Knob Thorn Acacia
***Acacia nigrescens** SA Tree no 178*
The Knob-thorn in this Ecozone looks very different from the same tree in the other Ecozones. Here the trees are kept small by the low available soil moisture, hot fires and particularly by the heavy browsing of giraffe and kudu. Even in this Ecozone, when a tree grows

tall enough to be beyond the effect of the browsers, there is enough soil moisture to allow it to reach the full mature height of Knob Thorns in other Ecozones. See page 132 for a full description of the Knob Thorn Acacia. Everything that applies to the trees that are larger when they are mature, also applies to this stunted form, except the height, and overall browsed shape.

35

ECOZONE L – MOPANE SHRUBVELD (ON BASALT)

This Ecozone is based on flat, volcanic basalt which leads to very uniform vegetation, consisting mostly of dense Mopane shrubs (*Colophospermum mopane*, page 144). Mopane stay small here, because the dense clay soils dry out, and as they do so, they tend to break the roots of the trees. Regular fires also keep the trees low, as they have to resprout from the bottom after every fire.

The altitude varies between 300 and 400 m above sea level, and the rainfall ranges between 450 and 500 mm per annum.

This Ecozone covers about 15% of Kruger National Park, and is also found north of the Limpopo in the Lowveld of Zimbabwe.

Ecozone L is traversed by many broad, grass-covered drainage lines with Lala-palms (*Hyphaene coriacea*, page 76), along the banks. This is also where the small Acacia-like Bushveld Albizia (*Albizia harveyi*, see below) is common. Open vleis along the drainage line have very few trees making this Ecozone suitable for rare game such as roan and tsessebe. However, generally on the uplands, spotting game is not easy in the dense Mopane vegetation.

Shrub Mopane – looking eastward towards the Lebombo mountains

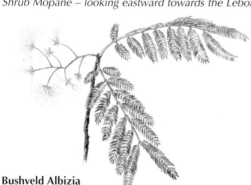

Bushveld Albizia
Albizia harveyi *SA Tree no 155*
This slender tree is deciduous. It is widely distributed in the Lowveld, and is also common on Brackish flats. Large trees are found along the Alluvial plains. The bark of large trees sub-divides into prominent vertical ridges. The feathery leaves *are twice compound with up to 16 feathers, with a large number of tiny, sickle-shaped leaflets per feather. White, powder-puff flowers are grouped at the end of twigs; stamens up to 20 mm (October to November). The large pods (180 x 20 - 30 mm) are pale brown, thin and flat, split open readily, and ripen in late summer (March to August).*

ECOZONE M – ALLUVIAL PLAINS

Ecozone M, Alluvial Plains, is found in the north. It occurs along the large rivers as they cross the basaltic plains flowing west to east towards the Lebombos and Mozambique. The Ecozone is best developed along the Shingwedzi, Luvuvhu and Limpopo rivers. These rivers regularly flood during periods of high rainfall, depositing rich clays along their banks, which alters the type of vegetation that grows there.

Rainfall ranges between 400 and 550 mm per annum, and altitude between 200 and 300 m above sea level. The area covers a little more that

1% of the Kruger National Park. Nyalas are common along the Luvuvhu River.

The floodplains of the Luvuvhu are the best example of these plains. Many interesting and unique trees can be found, including the very common Narrow-leaved Mustard-tree (*Salvadora australis*, page 178). Also of interest are Fever Tree Acacia forests (*Acacia xanthophloea*, page 72) and large stands of Sycamore Figs (*Ficus sycomorus*, page 218). The heart-shaped leaves of the Feverberry Croton (*Croton megalobotrys*, see below) are also very striking and easy to recognise.

Narrow-leaved Mustard-trees are very common around Shingwedzi, in Ecozone M.

Feverberry Croton
Croton megalobotrys *SA Tree no 329 Common along large rivers such as the Limpopo, Olifants and Sand, it has a slender, smooth, pale grey stems, and dense, drooping canopy. Large simple, alternate leaves are spirally arranged and triangular, with a toothed leaf-edge. The under-surface of young leaves has silvery-white hairs. Characteristic three-lobed, yellowish-brown fruit capsules look like small apples, and are covered by grey-white, woolly hairs when young (December to March).*

37

ECOZONE N – SANDVELD

The Sandveld Ecozone has unique geology. There are rugged sandstone hills in the north-west, and it is flat with deep sands in the north-east. The sandstone mountains form the lowest foothills of the Soutpansberg in the west. The deep Sandveld continues both across the Mocambique boundary, and northwards, over the Limpopo into Zimbabwe. This Ecozone covers about 2% of the Kruger National Park.

The rainfall varies from 450 mm per annum in the east, to 600 mm near Punda Maria in the west. These sandy soils are well drained and support drought-resistant trees such as the Corkwoods, (*Commiphora* species) of which a wide variety are found in this Ecozone (Zebra-bark Corkwood, *Commiphora viminea*, see below). Pod-mahogany (*Afzelia quanzensis*, page 200) and White Kirkia (*Kirkia acuminata*, page 204), are also fairly common.

Dramatic autumn leaves of White Kirkia and Baobab decorate the Sandstone Hills near Punda Maria.

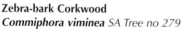

Zebra-bark Corkwood
Commiphora viminea *SA Tree no 279*
This exceptionally twiggy, deciduous tree is characterised by its yellow-white bark that peels in horizontal, dark bands to form the characteristic zebra-striped bark. It grows in low altitudes in hot, dry areas. It prefers well-drained sandy soils, but can also be found on the basalts of Ecozone L, east of Punda Maria. The simple leaves are bluish-green with a distinct, greyish bloom and are clustered in rosettes on dwarf, spine-tipped side shoots. They are oval, often narrowly so. Pale yellow flowers grow in inconspicuous clusters from November to December. The fruit has no stalk, is oblong and is red when ripe, in late summer.

Ecozone O – Tree Mopane Savannah (on Ecca shale)

Ecca shales, with deep soil that can support large trees, form this flat Ecozone. This is the same underlying geological shale as in Ecozone G down south. The altitude varies between 360 and 420 m above sea-level, and the rainfall between 500 and 550 mm per annum.

The Mopane trees here, (*Colophospermum mopane*, page 144) are unlike those found in Ecozones P and L, growing to a substantial height, between 10 and 15 m tall. The rare Arnot's Chat, that only occurs in tall woodland, is sought after here by serious birders, adding to their life list. Although not very common, the Bushveld Bead-bean (*Maerua angolensis*, see below), is very conspicuous, both when it flowers, and when it bears its bean-like pods, in early spring and summer.

The impressive, tall Mopanes create a woodland, very different from the shrub-form in other Ecozones.

Bushveld Bead-bean
Maerua angolensis SA Tree no 132
This tree can be found on Rocky Outcrops and termite mounds, and is usually evergreen. It has a single, pale grey trunk that branches high up to form a moderate, semi-circular canopy. Simple, broad, elliptic, dark green leaves spiral in clusters, and have a small, but distinct, hard, hair-like tip. Masses of sweet-scented, creamy-white, pin-cushion flowers

with very long stamens cover the tree from July to October. Characteristic, long, slender, yellow-green, bumpy-bean pods resemble a chain of unequal-sized beads from September to April.

39

ECOZONE P – MOPANE / BUSHWILLOW WOODLANDS (ON GRANITE)

This granite Ecozone covers 15% of the Kruger National Park. It is also the basic Ecozone of many farms and reserves still in the Lowveld (to the west and north-west of the Park) and is the base of a great deal of the land in Zimbabwe, across the Limpopo where Lowveld altitudes dominate the landscape. The altitude throughout varies between 250 and 400 m above sea level. The rainfall is variable between 450 and 500 mm per year.

As with the other granite Ecozones, this is an undulating landscape with many dissecting streams and rivers. This vegetation is more variable than on the basalts, and the crests of the granite are dominated by the Red Bushwillow (*Combretum apiculatum*, page 292). Although

Mopane (*Colophospermum mopane*, page 144) are also found on the crests, they are more common in the midslopes and valleys, where some *Acacia* species will also be found.

The Small False Mopane (*Guibourtia conjugata*, see below) is fairly common in the northern part of this Ecozone, and it can be confused with Mopane because of its similar butterfly-leaf. It is, however, easy to distinguish by its bark and closer inspection of its leaves. This is an important habitat for Sable Antelope, as are Ecozones A, B and C, because they prefer more undulating granites to flatter basalts. The reason for this is that mammal, and therefore predator densities, are generally lower in undulations. Large breeding herds of elephants are also common.

The undulating granite hills of this Ecozone are dominated by Shrub Mopane and Bushwillows.

Small False Mopane
Guibourtia conjugata SA Tree no 200
This deciduous, upright tree has heavy wood and grows slowly. It grows in deep, sandy soils in low altitude, open woodland and bush, often along rivers. It is most likely to be found in the far north

of this Ecozone, and in Ecozone N. The butterfly leaves are alternate, compound with 1 pair of leaflets, oval, but with a curved leaf-edge. They look very similar to Mopane. The star-shaped sprays of flowers have long stamens, are creamy-yellow (Mopane are greenish) and appear from November to January. The fruit is a thin, flat, circular pod (Mopane is kidney-shaped) which ripens in winter.

Ecozone Tree Lists

Sappi Tree Spotting is based on two fundamental concepts – Look for the right trees in the right place, and create Search Images of the trees you are looking for. On the following pages are the trees you are most likely to find in each Ecozone, and in each Habitat.

The trees you should look for first are shown at the top of the list in the darker colour. The trees in the paler colour are the next "easiest" to look for. The rest of the list is other trees that you could find, less easily, in each Habitat. Each list includes look-alike trees, and trees described in the introductory pages 22 - 40.

Ecozone A – Mixed Bushwillow Woodlands

CREST

Black Monkey-orange	**154**
Flaky Thorn Acacia	**284**
Marula	**140**
Red Bushwillow	**292**
Silver Cluster-leaf	148
Weeping Bushwillow	26
Zebrawood	122
Black Monkey Thorn Acacia	255
Buffalo-thorn	258
False Marula	29
Large-fruit Bushwillow	288
Naboom Euphorbia	192
Sickle-bush	304
Tall Firethorn Corkwood	186
Wild-pear Dombeya	27

ROCKY HILL

Large-leaved Rock Fig	**196**
Pod-mahogany	200
Red Bushwillow	292
Bushveld Candelabra Euphorbia	192
Purple-pod Cluster-leaf	110
Red-leaved Fig	24
Russet Bushwillow	300

SEEPLINE

Silver Cluster-leaf	**318**
African-wattle	90
Large-fruit Bushwillow	288
Marula	140
Red Thorn Acacia	182
Tree Wisteria	118
Bushveld Albizia	36
Red Bushwillow	292
Red Spike-thorn	114

BRACK

Horned Thorn Acacia	**270**
Jacket-plum	**274**
Magic Guarri	**278**
Scented-pod Thorn Acacia	**270**
Buffalo-thorn	258
Tamboti	222
Umbrella Thorn Acacia	80
Bushveld Gardenia	262
Bushveld Saffron	266
Russet Bushwillow	300

MIDSLOPE

African-wattle	**90**
Black Monkey-orange	**154**
Black Monkey Thorn Acacia	32
Marula	140
Red Thorn Acacia	182
Russet Bushwillow	300
Bushveld Albizia	36
Flaky Thorn Acacia	284
Sickle-bush	304
Umbrella Thorn Acacia	80
White-leaved Raisin	308

VALLEY BOTTOM

Apple-leaf	**128**
Green-thorn	**162**
Knob Thorn Acacia	**132**
Leadwood Bushwillow	**136**
African-wattle	90
Flaky Thorn Acacia	284
Red Thorn Acacia	182
Round-leaved Bloodwood	296
Scented-pod Thorn Acacia	270
Zebrawood	122
Black Monkey Thorn Acacia	32
False Marula	29
Horned Thorn Acacia	270
Long-tail Cassia	102
Tall Firethorn Corkwood	186
Umbrella Thorn Acacia	80
Weeping Boer-bean	252

DRAINAGE LINE

Matumi	**228**
Sycamore Fig	**218**
Apple-leaf	128
Jackal-berry	210
Knob Thorn Acacia	132
Leadwood Bushwillow	136
Marula	140
River Thorn Acacia	240
Tamboti	222
Umdoni/Waterberry	22
Broad-pod Albizia	94
Common Spike-thorn	25
Flame Climbing Bushwillow	98
Natal-mahogany	232
Red Bushwillow	292
River Bushwillow	236
Russet Bushwillow	300
Umbrella Thorn Acacia	80
Water Nuxia	248
Weeping Boer-bean	252
Wild Date-palm	84

Red Bushwillow, page 292

41

Ecozone B – Pretoriuskop Sourveld

CREST		SEEPLINE		VALLEY BOTTOM		DRAINAGE LINE	
Large-fruit Bushwillow	**288**	**Silver Cluster-leaf**	**148**	**Apple-leaf**	**128**	**Knob Thorn Acacia**	**1**
Marula	**140**	African-wattle	90	**Knob Thorn Acacia**	**132**	**Pride-of-De Kaap Bauhinia**	**1**
Red Bushwillow	**292**	Black Monkey-orange	154	**Umbrella Thorn Acacia**	**80**	**River Thorn Acacia**	**2**
African-wattle	90	Marula	140	African-wattle	90		
Black Monkey-orange	154	Tree Wisteria	118	Leadwood Bushwillow	136	Jackal-berry	2
Kiaat Bloodwood	166			Marula	140	Marula	1
Naboom Euphorbia	192	Buffalo-thorn	258	Red Thorn Acacia	182	Sycamore Fig	2
Sycamore Fig	218	False Marula	29	Scented-pod Thorn Acacia	270	Tamboti	2
		Red Spike-thorn	114			Weeping Boer-bean	2
Bushveld Candelabra Euphorbia	192	Umdoni/Waterberry	22	Buffalo-thorn	258	Buffalo-thorn	2
Jackal-berry	210			False Marula	29	Red Spike-thorn	1
Large-leaved Rock Fig	196	**ROCKY HILL**		Jackal-berry	210	Sausage-tree	2
Red-leaved Fig	24	**Bushveld Candelabra Euphorbia**	**192**	Long-tail Cassia	102	Umbrella Thorn Acacia	
Sickle-bush	304	**Large-leaved Rock Fig**	**196**	Red Bushwillow	292	Umdoni/Waterberry	
Spiny Monkey-orange	154			Russet Bushwillow	300	Wild Date-palm	
Weeping Boer-bean	252	Mountain Kirkia	28	Sickle-bush	304		
Weeping Bushwillow	26	Red-leaved Fig	24	Weeping Boer-bean	252	**BRACK**	
Wild-pear Dombeya	27	Wild-pear Dombeya	27	White-leaved Raisin	308	**Magic Guarri**	**2**
				Wild-pear Dombeya	27	**Tamboti**	**2**
						Buffalo-thorn	2
						Jacket-plum	2
						Bushveld Saffron	2
						Umbrella Thorn Acacia	8

Magic Guarri, page 278

Ecozone C – Malelane Mountain Bushveld

CREST		SEEPLINE		VALLEY BOTTOM		DRAINAGE LINE	
Large-fruit Bushwillow	**288**	**African-wattle**	**90**	**Knob Thorn Acacia**	**132**	**Knob Thorn Acacia**	**13**
Red Bushwillow	**292**	**Silver Cluster-leaf**	**148**	**Russet Bushwillow**	**300**	**Weeping Boer-bean**	**25**
African-wattle	90	Red Bushwillow	292	Bushveld Albizia	36	**Wild Date-palm**	**8**
Black Monkey-orange	154	Weeping Bushwillow	26	Jacket-plum	274	Apple-leaf	12
Weeping Bushwillow	26			Leadwood Bushwillow	136	Jackal-berry	21
		ROCKY HILL		Umbrella Thorn Acacia	80	River Thorn Acacia	24
Flaky Thorn Acacia	284	**Large-leaved Rock Fig**	**196**	White-leaved Raisin	308	Tamboti	22
Marula	140	**Red-leaved Fig**	**24**	Flaky Thorn Acacia	284		
Red Spike-thorn	114			Magic Guarri	278	Flaky Thorn Acacia	28
Round-leaved Bloodwood	296	Bushveld Candelabra Euphorbia	192	Red Thorn Acacia	182	Magic Guarri	27
Sickle-bush	304	Mountain Kirkia	28	Wild-pear Dombeya	27		
Zebrawood	122	Naboom Euphorbia	192				
		Purple-pod Cluster-leaf	110	**BRACK**			
				Buffalo-thorn	**258**		
		Red Bushwillow	292	**Tamboti**	**222**		
				Jacket-plum	274		

Buffalo-thorn, page 258

Ecozone D – Sabie/Crocodile Thorn Thickets

CREST		SEEPLINE		BRACK		MIDSLOPE	
False Marula	**29**	**Silver Cluster-leaf**	**148**	**Bushveld Gardenia**	**262**	**African-wattle**	**90**
Red Bushwillow	**292**			**Bushveld Saffron**	**266**	**Red Bushwillow**	**292**
Sickle-bush	**304**	**VALLEY BOTTOM**		**Magic Guarri**	**278**		
Knob Thorn Acacia	132	**Flaky Thorn Acacia**	**284**	Buffalo-thorn	258	**DRAINAGE LINE**	
Marula	140	**Green-thorn**	**162**	False Marula	29	**Broad-pod Albizia**	**94**
Purple-pod		**Knob Thorn Acacia**	**132**	Horned Thorn Acacia	270	**Matumi**	**228**
Cluster-leaf	110			Jacket-plum	274	**River Bushwillow**	**236**
Umbrella Thorn		Apple-leaf	128	Knob Thorn Acacia	132		
Acacia	80	Long-tail Cassia	102	Marula	140	Apple-leaf	128
		Marula	140	Round-leaved		Buffalo-thorn	258
Flaky Thorn Acacia	284	Red Spike-thorn	114	Bloodwood	296	Flame Climbing	
Sandpaper Raisin	308	Scented-pod		Scented-pod		Bushwillow	98
Weeping Boer-bean	252	Thorn Acacia	270	Thorn Acacia	270	Jackal-berry	210
		Tamboti	222	Tamboti	222	Knob Thorn Acacia	132
ROCKY HILL		Umbrella Thorn				Marula	140
Large-leaved Rock Fig	**196**	Acacia	80	Bushveld Resin-tree	31	Natal-mahogany	232
Purple-pod				Flaky Thorn Acacia	284	Nyala-tree	214
Cluster-leaf	**110**	Leadwood Bushwillow	136	Green-thorn	162	Red Spike-thorn	114
Red-leaved Fig	**24**	Russet Bushwillow	300	Jackal-berry	210	River Thorn Acacia	240
		Sickle-bush	304	Nyala-tree	214	Sausage-tree	244
Bushveld Candelabra				Russet Bushwillow	300	Sycamore Fig	218
Euphorbia	192			Sandpaper Raisin	308	Tamboti	222
				Weeping Boer-bean	252	Water Nuxia	248
Naboom Euphorbia	192					Weeping Boer-bean	252
Red Bushwillow	292						
Rubber-hedge						Pride-of-De Kaap	
Euphorbia	30					Bauhinia	106
						Umdoni Waterberry	22
						White-leaved Raisin	308
						Wild Date-palm	84

Ecozone E – Thorn Veld

PLAINS		ROCKY HILL	
Round-leaved Bloodwood	**296**	**Large-leaved Rock Fig**	**196**
Zebrawood	**122**		
		Bushveld Saffron	266
African-wattle	90	Green-thorn	162
Jacket-plum	274	Knob Thorn Acacia	132
Knob Thorn Acacia	132	Rubber-hedge Euphorbia	30
Marula	140		
Tamboti	222		
Tree Wisteria	118		
Umbrella Thorn Acacia	80		
Apple-leaf	128		
Buffalo-thorn	258		
Bushveld Albizia	36		
False Marula	29		
Leadwood Bushwillow	136		
Red Bushwillow	292		
Russet Bushwillow	300		
Sickle-bush	304		
Weeping Boer-bean	252		

Round-leaved Bloodwood,
page 296

Ecozone F – Knob Thorn / Marula Savannah

SOUTH		NORTH		DRAINAGE LINE	
Knob Thorn Acacia	132	Knob Thorn Acacia	132	Knob Thorn Acacia	132
Marula	140	Leadwood Bushwillow	136	Natal-mahogany	232
Red Spike-thorn	114	Marula	140		
Red Thorn Acacia	182			Apple-leaf	128
		African-wattle	90	Broad-pod Albizia	94
Apple-leaf	128	Buffalo-thorn	258	Fever Tree Acacia	72
Leadwood		Long-tail Cassia	102	Jackal-berry	210
Bushwillow	136	Red Thorn Acacia	182	Leadwood	
Long-tail Cassia	102	Tall Firethorn		Bushwillow	136
Round-leaved		Corkwood	186	Magic Guarri	278
Bloodwood	296	Umbrella Thorn Acacia	80	Red Spike-thorn	114
Tree Wisteria	118	White-leaved Raisin	308	Sausage-tree	244
Zebrawood	122	Zebrawood	122	Sycamore Fig	218
				Umbrella	
Bushveld Albizia	36	Bushveld Albizia	36	Thorn Acacia	80
Common Spike-thorn	25	Bushveld Bead-bean	39		
Drooping Resin-tree	31	Bushveld Resin-tree	31	Feverberry Croton	37
False Marula	29	False Marula	29	Lala-palm	76
Scented-pod		Russet Bushwillow	300	River Thorn Acacia	240
Thorn Acacia	270	Sickle-bush	304	Russet Bushwillow	300
Sickle-bush	304	Weeping Boer-bean	252	Wild Date-palm	84

Ecozone G – Delagoa Thorn Thicke[t]

PLAINS	
Delagoa Thorn	
Acacia	15
Many-stemmed	
Albizia	17
Apple-leaf	12
Black Monkey	
Thorn Acacia	3
Knob Thorn Acacia	13
Magic Guarri	27
Red Thorn Acacia	18
Tamboti	22
Umbrella Thorn	
Acacia	8
Bushveld Bead-bean	3
Sickle-bush	30
Tree Wisteria	11
Weeping Boer-bean	25
White-leaved Raisin	30

Ecozone H – Riverine Habitat

IN RIVERS		RIVER BANKS	
Matumi	228	Apple-leaf	128
Wild Date-palm	84	Jackal-berry	210
		Sausage-tree	244
Flame Climbing		Sycamore Fig	218
Bushwillow	98		
Pride-of-De Kaap		Broad-pod Albizia	94
Bauhinia	106	Feverberry Croton	37
Water Nuxia	248	Knob Thorn Acacia	132
		Leadwood Bushwillow	136
River Bushwillow	236	Marula	140
Umdoni/Waterberry	22	Natal-mahogany	232
		Nyala-tree	214
		Red Spike-thorn	114
		River Thorn Acacia	240
		Tamboti	222
		Umdoni/Waterberry	22
		Weeping Boer-bean	252
		Black Monkey	
		Thorn Acacia	32
		Common Spike-thorn	25
		False Marula	29
		Fever Tree Acacia	72
		Magic Guarri	278
		Mopane	44
		Narrow-leaved	
		Mustard-tree	178
		White-leaved Raisin	278

Wild Date-palm,
page 84

Ecozone I – Lebombo Mountain Bushveld

SOUTH		NORTH	
Bushveld Candelabra		Baobab	6
Euphorbia	192	Lebombo Euphorbia	3
Lebombo Euphorbia	33	Lebombo-ironwood	17
Red Bushwillow	292		
		Bushveld Candelabra	
African-wattle	90	Euphorbia	19
Jacket-plum	274	Marula	14
Large-leaved Rock Fig	196	Mopane	14
Long-tail Cassia	102	Pod-mahogany	20
Naboom Euphorbia	192	Shepherds-tree	3
Pod-mahogany	200	Tall Firethorn	
Shepherds-tree	34	Corkwood	18
Tall Firethorn Corkwood	186	White Kirkia	20
White Kirkia	204		
White-leaved Raisin	308	False Marula	2
		Purple-pod	
Black Monkey		Cluster-leaf	11
Thorn Acacia	32	Red Bushwillow	29
Bushveld Albizia	36	Red-leaved Fig	2
Drooping Resin-tree	31	Sandpaper Raisin	30
False Marula	29	Weeping Boer-bean	25
Flaky Thorn Acacia	284	Zebra-bark Corkwood	3
Kiaat Bloodwood	166		
Large-fruit Bushwillow	288		
Purple-pod Cluster-leaf	110		
Red-leaved Fig	24		
Red Thorn Acacia	182		
Round-leaved			
Bloodwood	296		
Russet Bushwillow	300		
Sandpaper Raisin	308		
Sickle-bush	304		
Weeping Boer-bean	252		

Lebombo-ironwood, page 1

Ecozone J – Olifants Rugged Veld

ROCKY HILL		PLAINS		RIVERINE	
Shepherds-tree	34	Purple-pod		Apple-leaf	128
Tall Firethorn		Cluster-leaf	110	Natal-mahogany	232
Corkwood	186	Red Bushwillow	292	Nyala-tree	214
		Tall Firethorn		Sycamore Fig	218
Jacket-plum	274	Corkwood	186		
Large-leaved		African-wattle	90	Flame Climbing	
Rock Fig	196			Bushwillow	98
Purple-pod		Bushveld Bead-bean	39	Marula	140
Cluster-leaf	110	Flaky Thorn Acacia	284	Matumi	228
White Kirkia	204	Knob Thorn Acacia	132	River Thorn Acacia	240
Bushveld Gardenia	262	Red Spike-thorn	114	Jackal-berry	210
Leadwood		Russet Bushwillow	300		
Bushwillow	136	Sickle-bush	304		
Red Bushwillow	292	Weeping Boer-bean	252		
Russet Bushwillow	300	White-leaved			
Tamboti	222	Raisin	308		
Weeping Bushwillow	26				

Ecozone K – Stunted Knob Thorn Savannah

PLAINS		
Knob Thorn Acacia		132
Sickle-bush	304	304
African-wattle		90
Buffalo-thorn		258
Umbrella		
Thorn Acacia		80
Bushveld Bead-bean		39
Weeping Boer-bean		252
White-leaved Raisin		308

Purple pod Cluster-leaf,
page 110

Ecozone L – Mopane Shrubveld

PLAINS		DRAINAGE LINE	
Baobab	68	Fever Tree Acacia	72
Mopane	144	Mopane	144
African-wattle	90	Apple-leaf	128
Flaky Thorn Acacia	284	Bushveld Albizia	36
Jacket-plum	274	Feverberry Croton	37
Knob Thorn Acacia	132	Knob Thorn Acacia	132
Red Spike-thorn	114	Umbrella	
Tall Firethorn		Thorn Acacia	80
Corkwood	186	White-leaved Raisin	308
Bushveld Bead-bean	39	False Marula	29
Drooping Resin-tree	31	Lala-palm	76
Marula	140	Leadwood	
Round-leaved		Bushwillow	136
Bloodwood	296	Marula	140
Sickle-bush	304	Russet Bushwillow	300
Zebrawood	122	Tamboti	222
		Wild Date-palm	84

Boabab,
page 68

Ecozone M – Alluvial Plains

FLOOD PLAINS		RIVER BANKS	
Narrow-leaved		Fever Tree Acacia	72
Mustard-tree	178	Lala-palm	76
Red Spike-thorn	114	Matumi	228
Apple-leaf	128	Flame Climbing	
Bushveld Albizia	36	Bushwillow	98
Bushveld Gardenia	262	Leadwood Bushwillow	136
Leadwood		Mopane	144
Bushwillow	136	Nyala-tree	214
Mopane	144	River Thorn Acacia	240
Tall Firethorn		Sausage-tree	244
Corkwood	186	Tamboti	222
Shepherds-tree	34	Umbrella	
Umbrella		Thorn Acacia	80
Thorn Acacia	80	Water Nuxia	248
Baobab	68	Feverberry Croton	37
Fever Tree Acacia	72	Jackal-berry	210
Russet Bushwillow	300	Magic Guarri	278
Sickle-bush	304	Natal-mahogany	232
Weeping Boer-bean	252	Sickle-bush	304
Zebrawood	122	Sycamore Fig	218
		Weeping Boer-bean	252
		White-leaved Raisin	308

Ecozone N – Sandveld

SANDSTONE RIDGES		SLOPES	
Lebombo-ironwood	**170**	**African-wattle**	**90**
Pod-mahogany	**200**	**Knob Thorn Acacia**	**132**
White Kirkia	**204**	**Silver Cluster-leaf**	**148**
Red Bushwillow	292	Magic Guarri	278
Silver Cluster-leaf	148	Pride-of-De Kaap	
Tall Firethorn		Bauhinia	106
Corkwood	186	Apple-leaf	128
Zebra-bark		Leadwood	
Corkwood	38	Bushwillow	136
Black Monkey-		Red Thorn Acacia	182
orange	154	Round-leaved	
Large-fruit		Bloodwood	296
Bushwillow	288	Russet Bushwillow	300
Small False Mopane	40	Small False Mopane	40
Weeping Bushwillow	26	Sickle-bush	304
Zebrawood	122	Weeping Bushwillow	26
		Wild-pear Dombeya	27
		Zebrawood	122

Pod-mahogany,
page 200

Ecozone O – Tree Mopane Savannah

FOREST	
Mopane	**144**
Bushveld Bead-bean	39
Knob Thorn Acacia	132
Horned Thorn Acacia	270
Leadwood Bushwillow	136
Shepherds-tree	34
Tamboti	222
Umbrella Thorn Acacia	80
Zebrawood	122
Magic Guarri	278
Russet Bushwillow	300
Sickle-bush	304
Weeping Boer-bean	252
White-leaved Raisin	308

Ecozone P – Mopane / Bushwillow Woodlands

CREST		SEEPLINE/MIDSLOPE		VALLEY BOTTOM		DRAINAGE LINE	
Red Bushwillow	**292**	**Apple-leaf**	**128**	**Knob Thorn Acacia**	**132**	**Lala-palm**	**76**
African-wattle	90	**Mopane**	**144**	**Leadwood**		**Leadwood**	
Black		**Red Bushwillow**	**292**	**Bushwillow**	**136**	**Bushwillow**	**136**
Monkey-orange	154	**Silver Cluster-leaf**	**148**	**Mopane**	**144**	**Mopane**	**144**
Mopane	144			Apple-leaf	128	Apple-leaf	128
Purple-pod		**ROCKY HILL**		Long-tail Cassia	102	Jackal-berry	210
Cluster-leaf	110	**Large-leaved**		Umbrella Thorn Acacia	80	Tamboti	222
Silver Cluster-leaf	148	**Rock Fig**	**196**				
Zebrawood	122	**Tall Firethorn**		Bushveld Albizia	36	Feverberry Croton	37
		Corkwood	**186**	Flaky Thorn Acacia	284	Marula	140
Bushveld Albizia	316			Red Thorn Acacia	182	Nyala-tree	214
Marula	140	Shepherds-tree	34	Russet Bushwillow	300	Wild Date-palm	84
Small False Mopane	40	White Kirkia	204	Sandpaper Raisin	308		
White-leaved				Sickle-bush	304	**BRACK**	
Raisin	308	Bushveld Candelabra		Weeping Boer-bean	252	**Magic Guarri**	**278**
		Euphorbia	192				

Leadwood Bushwillow,
page 136

Find a tree by Ecozone or Habitat – A Six Step Guide

On pages 18 - 40 is a full description of the 16 Ecozones and the major Habitats of the Lowveld. Below are the steps you should follow every time you want to find a tree. It will soon become second nature.

1 **Decide where you are.**
In which Ecozone is this?

To identify specific trees you must first work out where you are. Turn to the Maps on pages 332 - 345, and note the Ecozone you are in. **Example: Ecozone N – Sandveld**

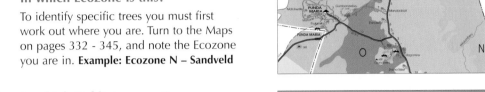

2 **In which Habitat are you?**

The descriptions on pages 20 - 25 give details of Habitats. Decide which of these applies to you.
Example: Sandstone Ridge

3 **Which trees can you find in your Ecozone and Habitat?**

On pages 41 - 46, you will find the Tree List for your Ecozone. Read this and make a note of the three or four trees you are most likely to find, and mark their pages.
Example: White Kirkia, page 204

Ecozone N – Sandveld

SANDSTONE RIDGES	SLOPES
Lebombo-ironwood170	African-wattle 90
Pod-mahogany 200	Knob Thorn Acacia132
White Kirkia 204	Silver Cluster-leaf148
Red Bushwillow 292	Magic Guarri 278
Silver Cluster-leaf148	Pride-of-De Kaap
Tall Firethorn	Bauhinia 106

4 **Create Search Images for these trees**

Look at the pictures and read the Striking Features of each of these trees. In the same way as you would create a mental picture of a blonde child, with a green shirt eating an ice-cream, imagine the Striking Features of the trees you are hoping to find.

Striking features

- It has a tall, straight, single trunk and a light green, feathery-looking, spreading canopy.
- The bark is light grey and smooth when young, and becomes flaky with corky knobs in older trees.

5 **Match Search Images to nearby trees**

Look at the larger, mature trees nearby, and see if you can find one that has similar Striking Features to any of your Search Images.

6 **Check the details**

When you find a tree, check the details more carefully. Check all the Striking Features, then read the details about the leaf, flower, pod and bark. If you have any problems with any of the terms in the text, read **"You find trees"**, pages 5 - 11.

Flowers Sprays of inconspicuous greenish-cream flowers appear on the ends of branches wih new leaves in October and November.

Fruit Thin, small, woody capsules burst open into four valves.

Trees greet you

DISTINCTIVE STRIKING FEATURES

This section of the book summarises the most distinctive of the Striking Features of each tree. When a flower, fruit, pod, leaf or bark jumps out and asks to be recognised, you simply look up the relevant page here. Page numbers of each tree are given to encourage you to look up the other Striking Features of the tree. This will enable you to recognise the tree in other areas, at other times of the year too.

The showy flowers of Wild-pear Dombeya jump out in spring, asking to be recognised.

Distinctive Striking Features

The following pages show, flowers, fruit, pods and leaves that are all very striking, or that are so distinctive you can often identify the trees on this information alone. You can use these pages as a quick reference – but it is wise to turn to the full tree description to be sure.

FLOWERS

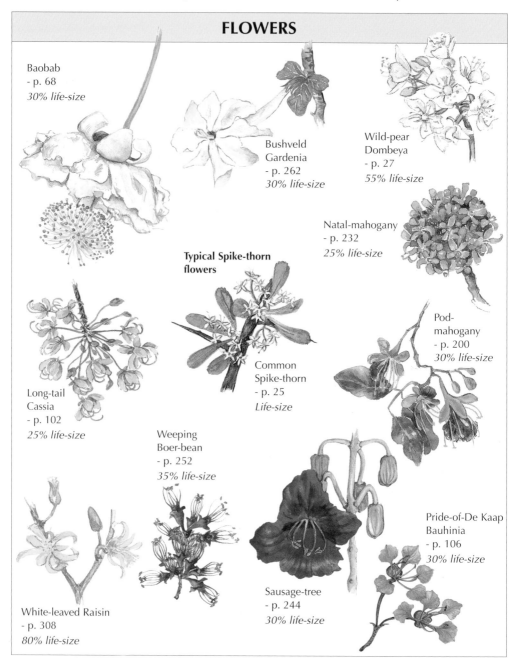

Baobab
- p. 68
30% life-size

Bushveld
Gardenia
- p. 262
30% life-size

Wild-pear
Dombeya
- p. 27
55% life-size

Natal-mahogany
- p. 232
25% life-size

**Typical Spike-thorn
flowers**

Pod-
mahogany
- p. 200
30% life-size

Long-tail
Cassia
- p. 102
25% life-size

Common
Spike-thorn
- p. 25
Life-size

Weeping
Boer-bean
- p. 252
35% life-size

Pride-of-De Kaap
Bauhinia
- p. 106
30% life-size

White-leaved Raisin
- p. 308
80% life-size

Sausage-tree
- p. 244
30% life-size

FLOWERS

SPIKES, SPRAYS, BALLS AND POWER PUFFS

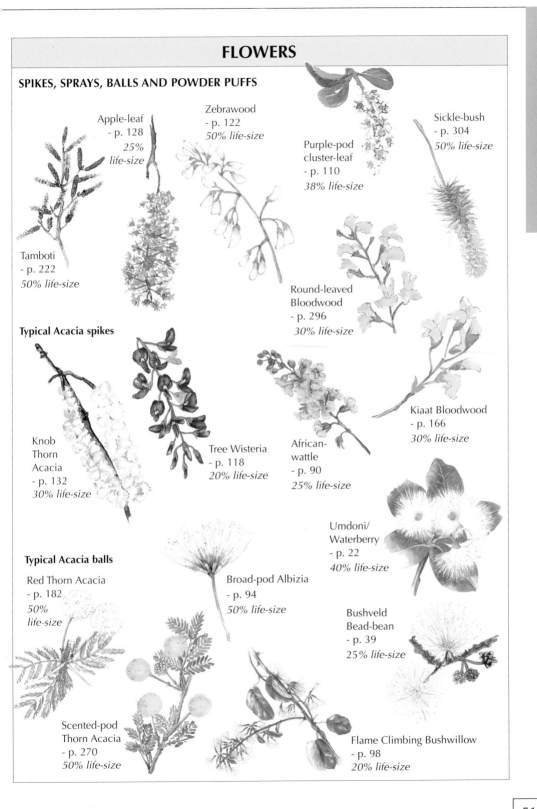

Apple-leaf
- p. 128
*25%
life-size*

Zebrawood
- p. 122
50% life-size

Purple-pod
cluster-leaf
- p. 110
38% life-size

Sickle-bush
- p. 304
50% life-size

Tamboti
- p. 222
50% life-size

Round-leaved
Bloodwood
- p. 296
30% life-size

Typical Acacia spikes

Knob
Thorn
Acacia
- p. 132
30% life-size

Tree Wisteria
- p. 118
20% life-size

African-
wattle
- p. 90
25% life-size

Kiaat Bloodwood
- p. 166
30% life-size

Umdoni/
Waterberry
- p. 22
40% life-size

Typical Acacia balls

Red Thorn Acacia
- p. 182
*50%
life-size*

Broad-pod Albizia
- p. 94
50% life-size

Bushveld
Bead-bean
- p. 39
25% life-size

Scented-pod
Thorn Acacia
- p. 270
50% life-size

Flame Climbing Bushwillow
- p. 98
20% life-size

51

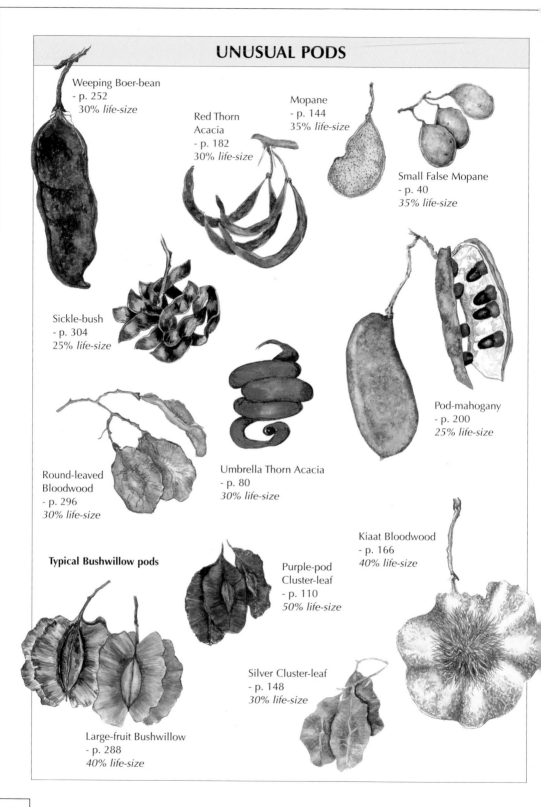

UNUSUAL PODS

Weeping Boer-bean
- p. 252
30% *life-size*

Red Thorn
Acacia
- p. 182
30% *life-size*

Mopane
- p. 144
35% *life-size*

Small False Mopane
- p. 40
35% *life-size*

Sickle-bush
- p. 304
25% *life-size*

Pod-mahogany
- p. 200
25% *life-size*

Round-leaved
Bloodwood
- p. 296
30% *life-size*

Umbrella Thorn Acacia
- p. 80
30% *life-size*

Kiaat Bloodwood
- p. 166
40% *life-size*

Typical Bushwillow pods

Purple-pod
Cluster-leaf
- p. 110
50% *life-size*

Silver Cluster-leaf
- p. 148
30% *life-size*

Large-fruit Bushwillow
- p. 288
40% *life-size*

BEAN PODS

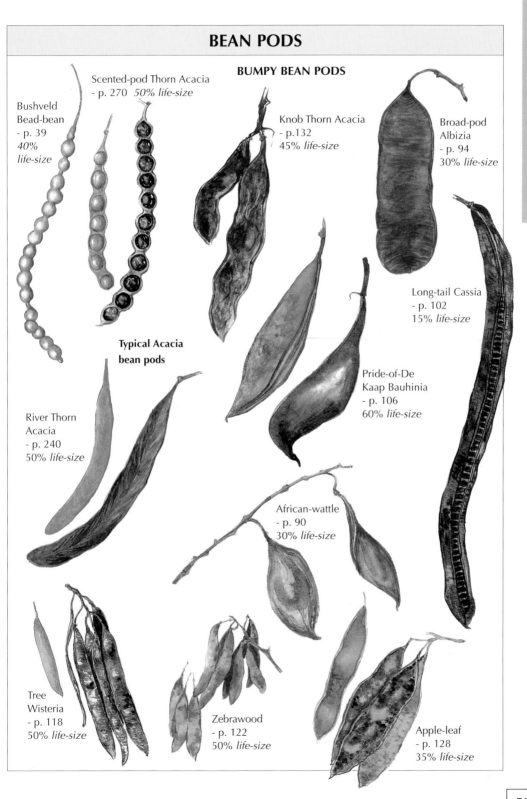

BUMPY BEAN PODS

Scented-pod Thorn Acacia
- p. 270 *50% life-size*

Bushveld
Bead-bean
- p. 39
*40%
life-size*

Knob Thorn Acacia
- p.132
45% life-size

Broad-pod
Albizia
- p. 94
30% life-size

**Typical Acacia
bean pods**

Long-tail Cassia
- p. 102
15% life-size

River Thorn
Acacia
- p. 240
50% life-size

Pride-of-De
Kaap Bauhinia
- p. 106
60% life-size

African-wattle
- p. 90
30% life-size

Tree
Wisteria
- p. 118
50% life-size

Zebrawood
- p. 122
50% life-size

Apple-leaf
- p. 128
35% life-size

UNUSUAL FRUIT

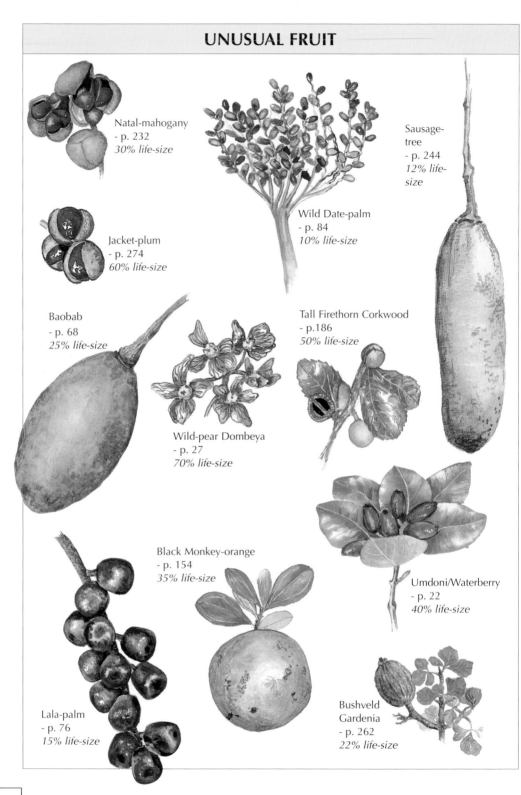

Natal-mahogany
- p. 232
30% life-size

Sausage-tree
- p. 244
12% life-size

Jacket-plum
- p. 274
60% life-size

Wild Date-palm
- p. 84
10% life-size

Baobab
- p. 68
25% life-size

Tall Firethorn Corkwood
- p.186
50% life-size

Wild-pear Dombeya
- p. 27
70% life-size

Black Monkey-orange
- p. 154
35% life-size

Umdoni/Waterberry
- p. 22
40% life-size

Lala-palm
- p. 76
15% life-size

Bushveld Gardenia
- p. 262
22% life-size

ROUND AND OVAL FRUIT

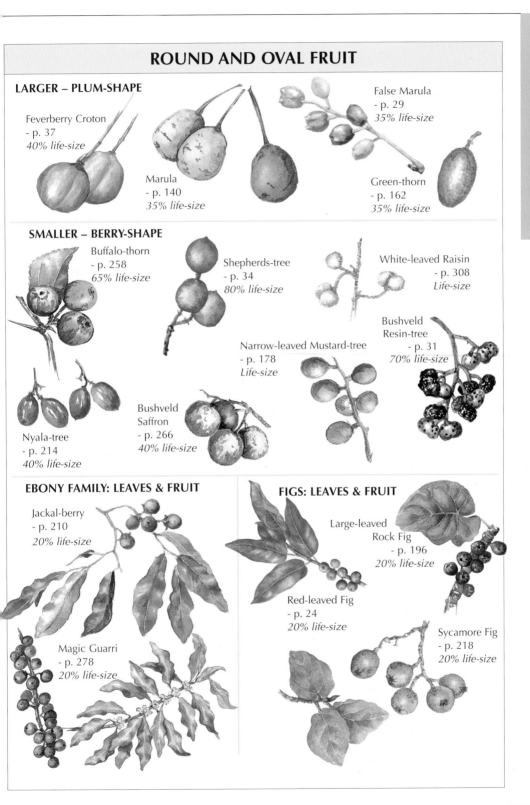

LARGER – PLUM-SHAPE

Feverberry Croton
- p. 37
40% life-size

Marula
- p. 140
35% life-size

False Marula
- p. 29
35% life-size

Green-thorn
- p. 162
35% life-size

SMALLER – BERRY-SHAPE

Buffalo-thorn
- p. 258
65% life-size

Shepherds-tree
- p. 34
80% life-size

White-leaved Raisin
- p. 308
Life-size

Bushveld
Resin-tree
- p. 31
70% life-size

Narrow-leaved Mustard-tree
- p. 178
Life-size

Nyala-tree
- p. 214
40% life-size

Bushveld
Saffron
- p. 266
40% life-size

EBONY FAMILY: LEAVES & FRUIT

Jackal-berry
- p. 210
20% life-size

Magic Guarri
- p. 278
20% life-size

FIGS: LEAVES & FRUIT

Large-leaved
Rock Fig
- p. 196
20% life-size

Red-leaved Fig
- p. 24
20% life-size

Sycamore Fig
- p. 218
20% life-size

SIMPLE LEAVES

CLUSTERED

Corkwood sp.
- p. 186
40% *life-size*

Bushveld
Gardenia
- p. 262
30%
life-size

Umdoni/
Waterberry
- p. 22
40% *life-size*

Spiny
Monkey-orange
- p. 156
(look-alike tree)
40% *life-size*

Silver Cluster-leaf
- p. 148
25% *life-size*

Bushveld Saffron
-p. 266
40% *life-size*

Jacket-plum
- p. 274
25% *life-size*

THREE-VEINED FROM THE BASE

White-leaved and
Sandpaper Raisins
- p. 308
40% *life-size*

Black Monkey-orange
- p. 154
50% *life-size*

Feverberry Croton
- p. 37 40% *life-size*

Buffalo-thorn
- p. 258
40% *life-size*

Wild-pear Dombeya
- p. 27 25% *life-size*

RIVERINE

Matumi
- p. 228
10% *life-size*

River Bushwillow
- p. 236
30% *life-size*

Water Nuxia
- p. 248
25% *life-size*

Tamboti
- p. 222
30% *life-size*

SIMPLE AND ONCE COMPOUND LEAVES

SIMPLE BUTTERFLY

ONCE COMPOUND BUTTERFLY

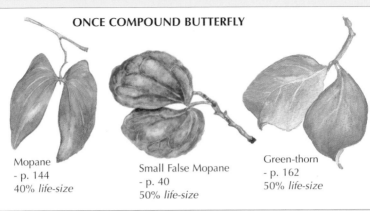

Pride-of-De
Kaap Bauhinia
- p. 106
40% *life-size*

Mopane
- p. 144
40% *life-size*

Small False Mopane
- p. 40
50% *life-size*

Green-thorn
- p. 162
50% *life-size*

ONCE COMPOUND LEAVES

HUGE

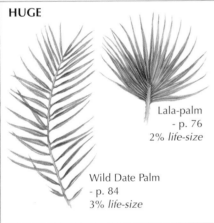

Lala-palm
- p. 76
2% *life-size*

Wild Date Palm
- p. 84
3% *life-size*

A PAIR OF LEAVES AT THE TIP

Pod-mahogany
- p. 200
25% *life-size*

Long-tail
Cassia
- p. 102
15% *life-size*

Weeping Boer-bean
- p. 252
35% *life-size*

A SINGLE LEAF AT THE TIP

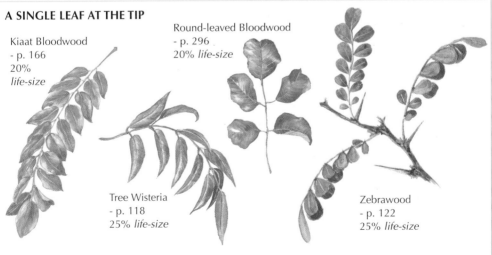

Kiaat Bloodwood
- p. 166
20%
life-size

Round-leaved Bloodwood
- p. 296
20% *life-size*

Tree Wisteria
- p. 118
25% *life-size*

Zebrawood
- p. 122
25% *life-size*

COMPOUND LEAVES

ONCE COMPOUND RIVERINE

Nyala-tree
- p. 214
20% life-size

Natal
Mahogany
- p. 232
20% life-size

Sausage-tree
- p. 244
20% life-size

Weeping Boer-bean
- p. 252
30% life-size

ONCE COMPOUND SPIRALLING AROUND TWIG TIP

False Marula
- p. 29
15% life-size

Mountain Kirkia
- p. 28
20% life-size

White Kirkia
- p. 204
20% life-size

Marula
- p. 140
15% life-size

HAND-SHAPED COMPOUND

Baobab
- p. 68
30% life-size

THREE-LEAFLET COMPOUND

Apple-leaf
- p. 128
25% life-size

TWICE COMPOUND LEAVES – ALBIZIAS AND OTHERS

Broad-pod Albizia
Albizia forbesii - p. 94

Mature tree 10 - 12 m; leaves 90 mm; feathers
are opposite and increase in size towards tip;
leaflet 9 x 2 mm; flowers white-yellow October -
December; pods russet, flat, fibrous, marked
cross-wise with fine lines (March - August)
(50 x 150 mm)

Bushveld Albizia
Albizia harveyi - p. 36

Mature tree 8 - 10 m; sickle-shaped leaves
4 - 6 mm, up to 16 feathers with numerous
tiny leaflets; flowers white, half-rounds, fluffy,
stamens up to 20 mm October - November;
pods large, pale brown, thin, flat, March -
August (180 x 20 - 30 mm)

Many-stemmed Albizia
Albizia petersiana - p. 174

Mature tree 9 m; occurs only in
Ecozone G; leaves 60 mm;
leaflet 10 x 6 mm; flowers
October - December;
pods May - June (120 x 16 mm)

African-wattle
Peltophorum africanum - p. 90

Single-stemmed tree branching low down with drooping
branches; mature trees 5 - 10 m; no thorns; large, soft,
feathery leaves (180 x 90 mm) with rounded leaflets;
abundant yellow flowers appear in sprays (November -
February); dark brown to black pods (100 x 20 mm)
appear in bunches and can be seen throughout the year

Sickle-bush
Dichrostachys cinerea - p. 304

Multi-stemmed tree or shrub (2 - 6 m); heavily intertwined
canopy; branches and twigs have long, straight, pale brown
spines (20 - 40 mm); long, fine, twice compound leaves
(30 - 200 mm) stand out against pale bark; mauve-pink
and yellow flower-spikes (40 - 60 mm) (October - January);
groups of tightly coiled, dark brown pods grow in dense
clusters (70 mm diameter) (May - September)

The art on this page is not to scale. Please refer to the text for sizes.

TWICE COMPOUND LEAVES – ACACIAS

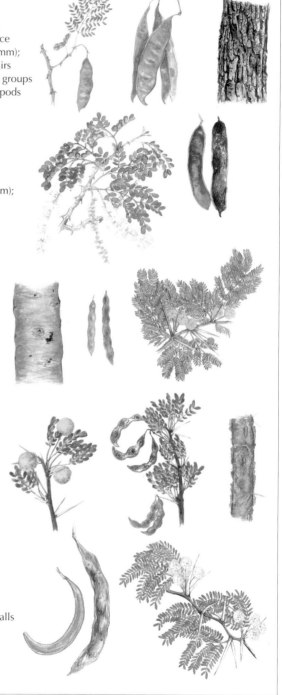

Black Monkey Thorn Acacia
Acacia burkei - p. 32

Mature trees up to 12 m; single-trunked, with umbrella-shaped to semi-circular canopy; twice compound leaves are short and stiff (25 - 70 mm); short, dark, sharply-hooked thorns grow in pairs (3 - 9 mm); white flower-spikes grow in small groups (50 - 100 x 10 - 20 mm) (October - January); pods (90 - 160 x 12 - 25 mm)

Delagoa Thorn Acacia
Acacia welwitschii - p. 158

Mature tree 15 m; occurs only in Ecozone G; leaves 40 mm; leaflet size 7 x 4 mm; paired, hooked, dark thorns fairly close together (5 mm); white flower-spikes (November - January); pods March - July (80 - 110 mm)

Fever Tree Acacia
Acacia xanthophloea - p. 72

Mature tree 10 - 15 m; yellow-green bark; leaves 100 mm; leaflet 7 x 1 mm; straight, paired thorns (80 mm); round, golden flower-balls (September - November); pods January - April, (100 x 15 mm)

Flaky Thorn Acacia
Acacia exuvialis - p. 284

Mature tree 4 - 5 m; orange-brown, flaky bark, leaving yellow under-bark; leaflet 3 - 10 x 1 - 4 mm; thorns long, straight white, paired (70 - 100 mm); yellow flower-balls October - February (most of the summer) (10 mm); pods February - May (10 x 65 mm)

Horned Thorn Acacia
Acacia grandicornuta - p. 270

Mature tree 6 - 10 m; leaves 70 mm; leaflet 3 x 9 mm; thorns long paired, can curve backwards (90 mm); white flower-balls (10 mm); October - March; pods April - July (70 x 130 mm)

TWICE COMPOUND LEAVES – ACACIAS

Knob Thorn Acacia
Acacia nigrescens - p. 132

Mature tree 8 - 18 m; knobs on bark, particularly when young; leaves 35 x 86 mm; obvious round leaflet (10 - 30 x 8 - 20 mm); thorns hooked pairs far apart (5 mm); flower-spikes August - September; pods November - April (120 x 70 mm)

Red Thorn Acacia
Acacia gerrardii - p. 182

Mature tree 5 - 10 m; leaf attachment like a sleeve covering the branchlets; slender growth-form; reddish bark; leaves 90 mm; leaflet 3 - 7 x 1 - 2 mm; thorns paired, shortish, straight, stout (10 mm); flower-balls October - February; pods November - May (80 - 160 x 6 - 16 mm)

River Thorn Acacia
Acacia robusta - p. 240

Mature trees 10 m; twice compound leaves form sleeves around branchlets (45 - 90 mm); prickly cushions at base of straight, white thorns (70 - 110 mm); white, ball-like flowers in early spring; sickle-shaped pods in bunches (70 - 160 x 13 - 30 mm) (January - August)

Scented-pod Thorn Acacia
Acacia nilotica - p. 270

Mature tree 6 - 10 m; leaves 40 mm; leaflet 1 x 4 mm; thorns long paired, arranged spirally (90 mm); yellow flower-balls October - March (12 mm); necklace-like pods, ripen during winter 15 x 200 mm

Umbrella Thorn Acacia
Acacia tortilis - p. 80

Mature tree 3 - 6 m; umbrella form of the tree; leaf 25 mm; leaflet 1 - 2 mm; thorns both straight (50 mm) and hooked (3 - 5 mm) small, white flower-balls November - December; spiral pods (125 mm) (May - June)

The art on these pages is not to scale. Please refer to the text for sizes.

SIMPLE LEAVES – BUSHWILLOWS

Flame Climbing Bushwillow
Combretum microphyllum - p. 98
Riverine creeper, on trees and shrubs;
leaves variable; flowers small with
prominent stamens, brillaint red spikes
August - November; pods, small,
September - January (20 x 20 mm)

Large-fruit Bushwillow
Combretum zeyheri - p. 288
Mature tree 5 - 15 m;
leaves 40 - 100 x 30 - 50 mm;
flowers September - November;
pods February - October;
very large fruit (50 - 100 mm)

Leadwood Bushwillow
Combretum imberbe - p. 136
Mature tree 20 m; majestic size
and shape; blocky, grey, snake-skin
bark; small leaves (35 x 15 mm);
flowers November - December;
small pods (15 mm) in autumn

Red Bushwillow
Combretum apiculatum - p. 292
Mature tree 4 - 10 m; most
common Combretum occurring on
the granites; leaves 65 x 35 mm,
twisted at the tip; flowers
September - October; pods
December - August (25 x 20 mm)

River Bushwillow
Combretum erythrophyllum - p. 236
Mature tree 5 - 12 m; bark
has irregular swellings; occurs
only along river beds; leaves
50 - 100 x 20 - 50 mm;
flowers August - November;
pods January - August,
(10 - 15 mm)

SIMPLE LEAVES – BUSHWILLOWS

Russet Bushwillow

Combretum hereroense - *p.* 300

Mature tree 3 - 5 m; Leaves small, 30 x 20 mm; flowers August - October; pods January - July; large numbers of relatively small, russet-coloured seeds, midsummer to autumn (23 x 20 mm)

Weeping Bushwillow

Combretum collinum - *p.* 26

Mature tree 4 - 12 m; leaf size varies according to rainfall (7 - 120 x 30 - 45 mm) flowers spikes (50 - 100 mm) August - October; pinkish pods (January - April) (30 - 50 x 45 mm)

SIMPLE LEAVES – CLUSTER-LEAFS

Purple-pod Cluster-leaf

Terminalia prunioides - *p.* 110

Mature tree 3 - 7 m; leaves 35 x 15 mm; strong smelling flower-spikes (65 x 20 mm) September - February; purple pods January - September (40 x 30 mm)

Silver Cluster-leaf

Terminalia sericea - *p.* 148

Mature tree 6 - 20 m; most common on granite seep-lines and sandveld; leaves 100 x 25 mm; flowers (4 mm) October - December; pods January - June (60 x 15 mm)

The art on these pages is not to scale. Please refer to the text for sizes.

BARK

RELATIVELY SMOOTH

Fever Tree Acacia - p. 72

Large-leaved Rock Fig - p. 196

Sycamore Fig - p. 218

Apple-leaf - p. 128

Black Monkey-orange - p. 154

Baobab - p. 68

SMOOTH WITH BUMPS AND/OR FISSURES

Jacket-plum - p. 274

Shepherds-tree - p. 34

Bushveld Saffron - p. 266

River Bushwillow - p. 236

SMOOTH & FLAKY

Bushveld Gardenia - p. 262

SMOOTH & FLAKY WITH SPINES OR THORNS

Flaky Thorn Acacia - p. 284

Tall Firethorn Corkwood - p. 186

Zebra-bark Corkwood - p. 38

64

BARK

COARSE; LOOKS BURNT

Jackal-berry - p. 210

COARSE & FISSURED OR ROPY

Black Monkey Thorn Acacia - p. 32

Common Spike-thorn - p. 25

River Thorn Acacia - p. 240

Silver Cluster-leaf - p. 148

ROUGH & PEELING/FLAKING

Marula - p. 140

False Marula - p. 29

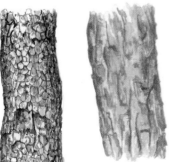

Spiny Monkey-orange - p. 156 (Look-alike tree)

Zebrawood - p. 122

ROUGH & BLOCKY

Leadwood Bushwillow - p. 136

Tamboti - p. 222

Kiaat Bloodwood - p. 166

Green-thorn - p. 162

ROUGH WITH KNOBS & THORNS

Young Knob Thorn Acacia - p. 132

Older Knob Thorn Acacia - p. 132

65

The art on these pages is not to scale. Please refer to the text for sizes.

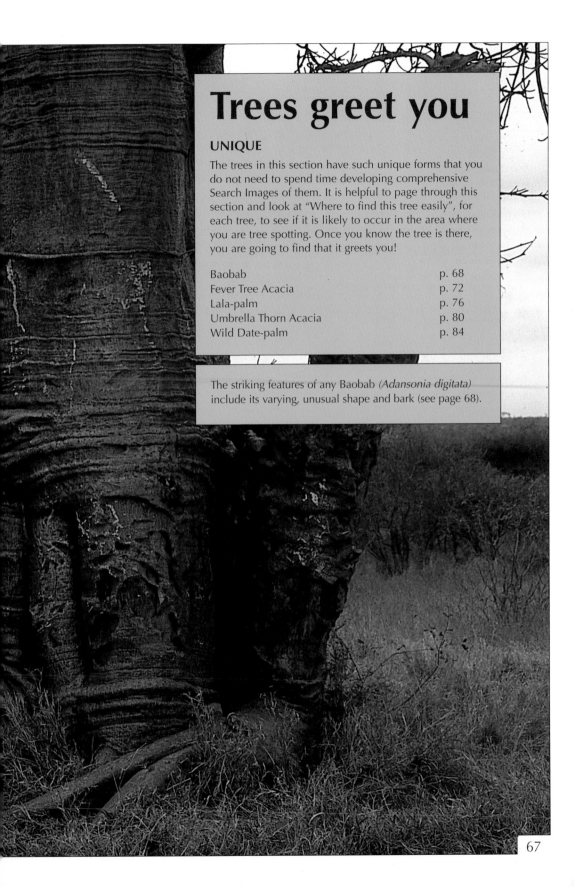

Trees greet you

UNIQUE

The trees in this section have such unique forms that you do not need to spend time developing comprehensive Search Images of them. It is helpful to page through this section and look at "Where to find this tree easily", for each tree, to see if it is likely to occur in the area where you are tree spotting. Once you know the tree is there, you are going to find that it greets you!

The striking features of any Baobab *(Adansonia digitata)* include its varying, unusual shape and bark (see page 68).

BAOBAB

Adansonia digitata

| BOMBACACEAE KAPOK FAMILY | SA Tree Number 467 |

AFRIKAANS Kremetart **N. SOTHO** Seboi **TSWANA** Mowana
TSONGA Ximuwu **VENDA** Muvhuyu

The species name **digitata** refers to the hand-shaped leaves.

Where you'll find this tree easily

The Baobab grows singly, often on small rocky
outcrops and in well-drained soils.

- It is easiest to find in Mopane/Bushwillow
  Woodlands (P).

- It can also be found in Lebombo Mountain
  Bushveld (I), on Alluvial Plains (M) and in
  Sandveld (N).

Ecozones where this tree occurs

A	E	I	M
B	F	J	N
C	G	K	O
D	H	L	P

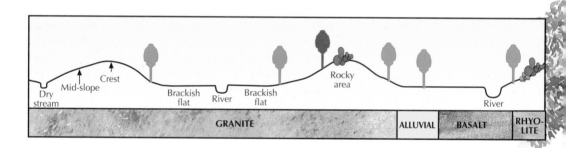

Striking features

- This gigantic tree is unmistakable.
- **Massive branches end in very thick stumps
  that look like roots, giving the tree the
  appearance of growing upside-down.**
- The bark is shiny, grey-brown and smooth,
  often dented and grooved.
- The hand-shaped compound leaves grow at
  the ends of the thick, stubby branchlets and
  twigs.

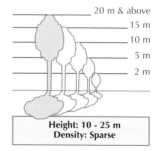

20 m & above
15 m
10 m
5 m
2 m

**Height: 10 - 25 m
Density: Sparse**

69

BAOBAB

Adansonia digitata

The trunk is huge, often with hollows deep enough for a human to hide in. Trees with a trunk circumference of 30 metres are estimated to be about 4 000 years old. The trunk decreases in girth during dry seasons and swells up again after rain.

Links with animals The tree is partly pollinated by the Straw-coloured Fruitbat *(Eidolon helvum)*. The fruit is eaten by baboon. The bark is eaten by elephant. Cattle, elephants and antelope chew on the spongy wood to relieve thirst in times of drought.

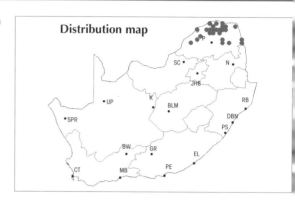

Distribution map

Human uses Fibre is made from the bark to weave baskets and hats. As the spongy wood contains a high proportion of water, humans chew on the wood to relieve thirst. There are Baobabs which have been hollowed by fire, or even by people, but the tree flourishes. The hollow trunks have been used as houses, prisons, storage barns and even water tanks. Hollow branches catch rain water and act as a reservoir that can be used by humans and animals. The bark and leaves have been used for treating malaria, dysentery, urinary disorders and mild diarrhoea. Flour is prepared from the roots. Fresh leaves are used as spinach. The fruit is edible, the creamy flesh being sucked from the pips. The pulp is rich in Vitamin C. Drink prpared from fruit pulp has been used to treat fevers and diarrhoea. Leaves are used against fever, to reduce perspiration and as an astringent. Powdered seeds are given to children as a hiccup remedy.

Gardening The Baobab can be very attractive in a large garden. It will grow best in warmer areas, on most well-drained soils. It is susceptible to frost, but is fairly drought-resistant. This tree can be grown from seed and is fairly fast-growing under warm, well-watered conditions.

Wood The wood is whitish, spongy and light and contains a high proportion of water.

70   *Amazing trunk of unusual Baobab in Kruger near Timbavati picnic site.*

It has a massive single, straight trunk with branches coming off horizontally to form a round, widely branching, sparse canopy.

Leaves   Mature leaves are hand-shaped, compound with 5 - 7 elliptic leaflets, that have smooth margins. They are grouped at the end of the branches, on long leaf-stems, that are about 120 mm in length. (Leaflet: 50 - 150 x 30 - 70 mm)

Flowers   The cup-shaped, white flowers are sweet-scented and hang downwards. They have crisp-edged petals with long protruding stamens (October and November). (120 - 240 mm)

Fruit   The characteristic, huge, oval fruit is covered by yellowish-grey, velvety hairs and hangs from the tips of branchlets and twigs. The fruit turns brown when ripe, and has a white mealy substance surrounding shiny, black pips (April to May). (100 - 120 x 200 - 240 mm)

Bark   The bark is shiny, grey-brown and smooth, often dented and grooved.

	Oct	Nov	Dec	Jan	Feb	Mar	Apr	May	Jun	Jul	Aug	Sep
Leaf	■	■	■	■	■	■	■	■				
Flower												
Fruit/Pod				■	■	■	■	■				

Seasonal changes   Deciduous. Leaves appear late in spring. Because of the massive, unique shape, these trees are easy to identify all year round.

UNIQUE
Baobab

71

FEVER TREE ACACIA

Acacia xanthophloea

Fever tree

| MIMOSACEAE ACACIA FAMILY | **SA Tree Number 189** |

AFRIKAANS Koorsboom **N. SOTHO** Mmabane, Monang, Mohlaretodi **TSONGA** Nkelenga
ZULU imHlosinga, umHlofunga, umKhanyakude, umDlovume

The species name **xanthophloea** refers to the yellow bark.

Where you'll find this tree easily

The Fever Tree Acacia grows in loose groups
of large trees.

- This tree is easiest to find on the Alluvial
  Plains (M).
- It can also be found near rivers and large streams
  in Knob Thorn/Marula Savannah (F) and in Mopane
  Shrubveld (L).

Ecozones where this tree occurs

A	E	I	M
B	F	J	N
C	G	K	O
D	H	L	P

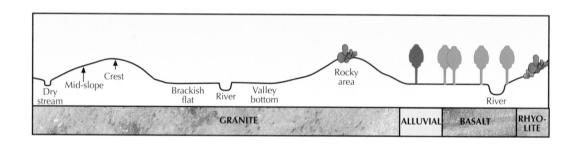

Striking features

- This tree is unique in appearance.
- **No other Acacia in this area has a trunk and
  branches that are yellow-green and covered
  in yellow powder.**
- **It has a straight, smooth, single trunk.**
- It has a sparse, roundish, spreading canopy.
- **The trunk and branches 'peel' in paper-thin
  layers.**

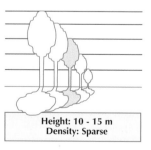

**Height: 10 - 15 m
Density: Sparse**

72

73

FEVER TREE ACACIA

Acacia xanthophloea

Links with animals The characteristic holes in the bark are caused by woodborers.

Monkeys and baboons eat the flowers, young shoots and seeds. Elephants eat the pods, leaves and branches.

Due to its proximity to permanent water, and the presence of thorns, this tree is often used by weavers to build their nests.

Human uses The bark is used for treating fevers and eye complaints. The wood is used in building.

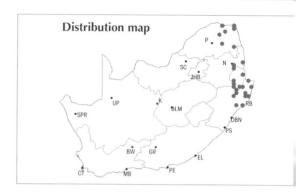

Distribution map

Gardening This ornamental tree can be very attractive in indigenous gardens in warmer areas. It needs well-watered clay soil and cannot take severe frost or drought. It can be grown from seed easily and, when well watered, is exceptionally fast-growing.

Wood The pale brown wood has a reddish tinge, and is hard and heavy (air-dry 910 kg/m^3).

Fever Trees lose leaves in winter, adding to their unique beauty

GROWTH DETAILS

The single, straight trunk is high-branching; branches come off horizontally to form a round spreading, sparse canopy.

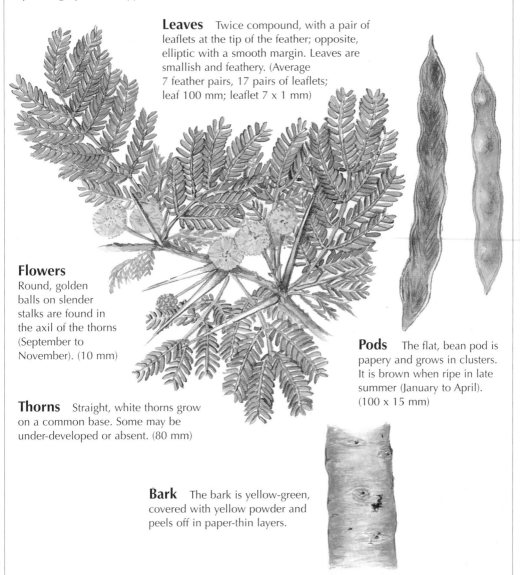

Leaves Twice compound, with a pair of leaflets at the tip of the feather; opposite, elliptic with a smooth margin. Leaves are smallish and feathery. (Average 7 feather pairs, 17 pairs of leaflets; leaf 100 mm; leaflet 7 x 1 mm)

Flowers
Round, golden balls on slender stalks are found in the axil of the thorns (September to November). (10 mm)

Thorns Straight, white thorns grow on a common base. Some may be under-developed or absent. (80 mm)

Pods The flat, bean pod is papery and grows in clusters. It is brown when ripe in late summer (January to April). (100 x 15 mm)

Bark The bark is yellow-green, covered with yellow powder and peels off in paper-thin layers.

	Oct	Nov	Dec	Jan	Feb	Mar	Apr	May	Jun	Jul	Aug	Sep
Leaf												
Flower												
Fruit/Pod												

Seasonal changes Deciduous. This tree is always easy to identify owing to the characteristic green bark and growth form.

75

LALA-PALM

Hyphaene coriacea and Hyphaene petersiana

Lala palm

ARECACEAE **PALM FAMILY**	**SA Tree Number 23/24**

AFRIKAANS Lalapalm **N. SOTHO** Mofaka, Mopalema **SISWATI** iLala **TSONGA** Nala **VENDA** Mulala **ZULU** iLala

The species name **coriacea** means thick and tough, or leathery.

Where you'll find this tree easily

The Lala-palm grows in groups along the perennial rivers of the Lowveld.

🌴 It is easiest to find this tree in Riverine areas (H).

🌴 You will also find this tree in Knob Thorn/Marula Savannah (F), on Alluvial Plains (M) and in Mopane/Bushwillow Woodlands (P).

Ecozones where this tree occurs

A	E	I	M
B	F	J	N
C	G	K	O
D	H	L	P

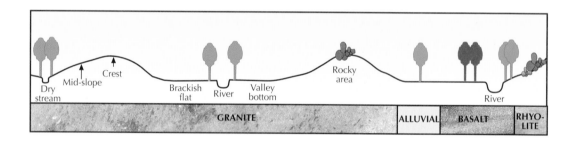

Dry stream · Mid-slope · Crest · Brackish flat · River · Valley bottom · Rocky area · River

GRANITE · ALLUVIAL · BASALT · RHYO-LITE

Striking features

- This is a typical Palm tree.
- **It has huge, hand-shaped leaves on a tall, bare, cylindrical trunk.**
- **The fruits are large, dark, shiny balls.**
- In the south of the Lowveld the Southern Lala-palm has pear-shaped fruit, and is usually a shrub.
- In the north the Northern Lala-palm has rounder fruit, and often grows into a tall single-trunked tree.

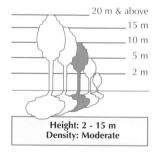

20 m & above
15 m
10 m
5 m
2 m

Height: 2 - 15 m
Density: Moderate

LALA-PALM

Hyphaene coriacea and Hyphaene petersiana

Links with animals The fruit is edible – the flesh is eaten by fruit bats and the nuts by baboon, elephant and monkey.

Human uses The white nut of the fruit is used as vegetable ivory for button-making and the carving of curios. The sap is used to brew beer. The leaves are used for thatching, mats, fibre and for making twine.

Gardening This very attractive palm grows on most soil types but requires plenty of water. It is not frost- or drought-resistant. It is slow-growing and cannot be grown from seed or cuttings.

Wood The wood is brown, spongy, light-weight and of no commercial use.

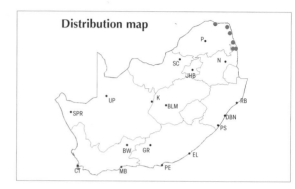

Distribution map

Look-alike tree The Wild Date-palm (*Phoenix reclinata*), page 84, is only common south of the Olifants River. The Lala-palm has hand-shaped leaves, compared with to the fern-like leaves of the Wild Date-palm.

The hand-shaped leaves of the Lala-palm are distinctive.

It has a single, straight, bare, tall trunk. Hand-shaped leaves grow directly from the main trunk to form a typical palm shape of moderate density.

Leaves Huge, bluish-green and hand-shaped. (1 300 mm)

Thorns There are hooked thorns on the leaf-stems.

Bark Bark is fibrous and shows prominent leaf scars.

(F)

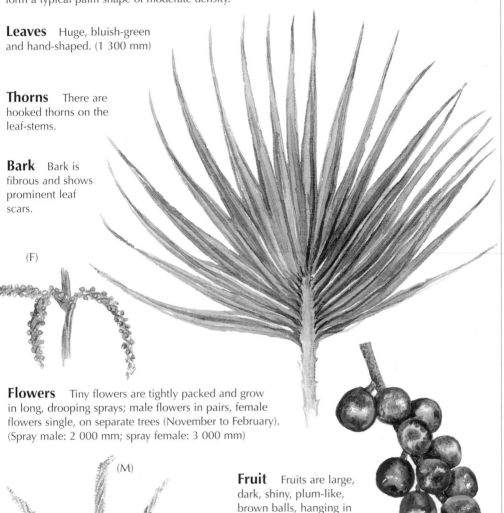

Flowers Tiny flowers are tightly packed and grow in long, drooping sprays; male flowers in pairs, female flowers single, on separate trees (November to February). (Spray male: 2 000 mm; spray female: 3 000 mm)

(M)

Fruit Fruits are large, dark, shiny, plum-like, brown balls, hanging in bunches below the leaves. They are present throughout the year. (60 mm)

UNIQUE
Lala-palm

	Oct	Nov	Dec	Jan	Feb	Mar	Apr	May	Jun	Jul	Aug	Sep
Leaf												
Flower												
Fruit/Pod												

Seasonal changes Evergreen. This tree is easy to identify throughout the year owing to its unique shape.

UMBRELLA THORN ACACIA

Acacia tortilis   Umbrella thorn

MIMOSACEAE
ACACIA FAMILY   SA Tree Number 188

AFRIKAANS Haak-en-steek, Haakdoring   **N. SOTHO** Moswaana   **SISWATI** isiThwethwe
TSONGA Nsasane   **TSWANA** Moku, Mosu   **ZULU** umSasane, isiThwethwe

The species name **tortilis** refers to the twisted pods.

Where you'll find this tree easily

Umbrella Thorn Acacia is often found in groups but larger trees also can be found growing singly.

- Umbrella Thorn Acacias are easiest to find growing in Sabie/Crocodile Thorn Thickets (D).

- This tree can be found in all other Ecozones.

Ecozones where this tree occurs

A	E	I	M
B	F	J	N
C	G	K	O
D	H	L	P

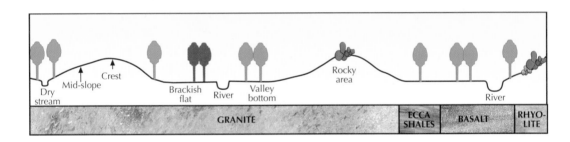

Striking features

- **This is the most striking of the Umbrella trees, with a particularly flat, thin-umbrella canopy of grey-green leaves.**
- It is a fairly low-branching, usually single-stemmed, smallish tree.
- **The leaves are tiny – amongst the tiniest of the Acacia leaves, giving the tree a fine, feathery appearance.**
- **The tightly curled pods are characteristic.**
- This tree has straight and hooked thorns which, although not always prominent, help with final identification.

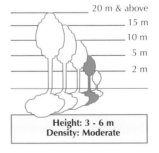

Height: 3 - 6 m
Density: Moderate

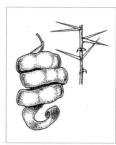

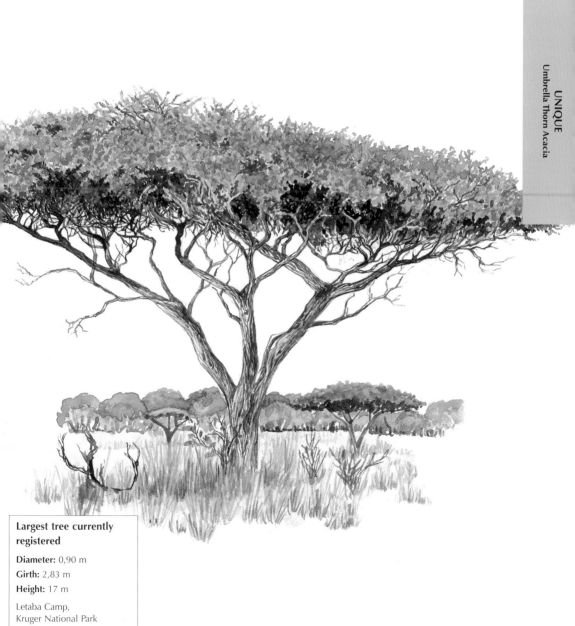

Largest tree currently registered

Diameter: 0,90 m

Girth: 2,83 m

Height: 17 m

Letaba Camp,
Kruger National Park

UMBRELLA THORN ACACIA

Acacia tortilis

Links with animals The leaves are browsed by cattle, antelope and giraffe. The pods are high in protein and are a favourite with all antelope, giraffe, monkey and baboon.

Human uses The wood is used as fuel.

Gardening This tree will grow well in most of the warmer areas, in well-watered clay soils. It is a very attractive shade tree in the indigenous garden. It is drought-resistant and can be grown from seed.

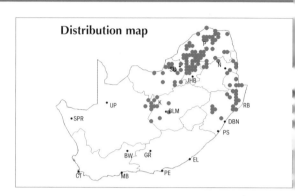

Distribution map

Wood The sapwood is whitish and soft with very obvious growth rings, while the heartwood is red.

Look-alike trees This tree can be confused with other Acacias. See page 60 - 61 for comparisons.

Young bark of the Umbrella Thorn Acacia; both straight and hooked thorns

GROWTH DETAILS

The single, straight trunk is mostly high-branching, with branches, coming off horizontally to form a moderately dense, flat, umbrella-like canopy. It does not always have the umbrella-like canopy, particularly when young, when it forms a scrubby bush with an irregular canopy.

Leaves Twice compound, opposite, elliptic, with a smooth margin. The leaves are very small even for an Acacia and are grouped at nodes. (Leaf: 25 mm; leaflet: 1 - 2 mm; feather: 13 with 19 leaflets)

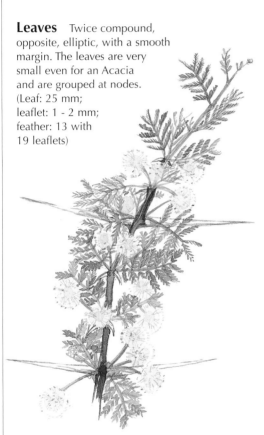

Thorns The white thorns, with a dark base and red tip, are not always obvious. Pairs of hooked and straight thorns are arranged spirally around the branchlets. Sometimes hooked or straight thorns may also form pairs on the same tree. (Straight thorn: 50 mm; hooked thorn: 3 - 5 mm)

Pods Flat, bean pods are curled up in a tight circle and hang in bunches. They ripen during May and June. (width: 8 mm; length: 125 mm)

Flowers Large numbers of white, ball-like flowers grow on old twigs. Flowers are sweet-scented and normally appear just after rain (November and December). (7 mm)

Bark The bark is grey and in older trees is deeply fissured.

	Oct	Nov	Dec	Jan	Feb	Mar	Apr	May	Jun	Jul	Aug	Sep
Leaf												
Flower												
Fruit/Pod												

Seasonal changes Deciduous. Because of the distinctive umbrella shape, mature trees can often still be recognised in winter.

WILD DATE-PALM

Phoenix reclinata

ARECACEAE	
PALM FAMILY	**SA Tree Number 22**

AFRIKAANS Wildedadelpalm   **N. SOTHO** Mopalema   **SISWATI** liLala   **TSONGA** Ncindzu, Xicindzu
VENDA Mutshema   **ZULU** iSundu

The species name **reclinata** means "bending down", and refers to the leaves.

Where you'll find this tree easily

The Wild Date-palm grows in groups, only on riverbeds along the larger rivers. It is more common south of the Olifants River.

🍃 This tree is easily found in Riverine areas (H).

Ecozones where this tree occurs

A	E	I	M
B	F	J	N
C	G	K	O
D	H	L	P

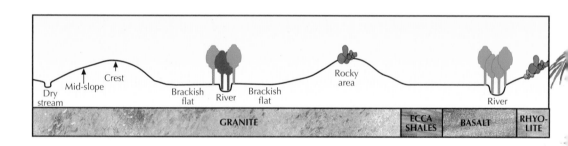

Dry stream — Mid-slope — Crest — Brackish flat — River — Brackish flat — Rocky area — River

GRANITE   ECCA SHALES   BASALT   RHYO-LITE

Striking features

- This is a reclining, multi-stemmed palm, often with no stems visible.
- **It has large, fern-like leaves which come directly off the stems.**
- It is only found on river banks and in river beds.

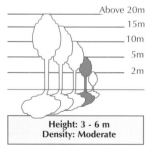

Above 20m
15m
10m
5m
2m

Height: 3 - 6 m
Density: Moderate

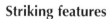

84

WILD DATE-PALM

Phoenix reclinata

Links with animals The fruit is eaten by mousebirds. The fruit, roots and leaves are eaten by elephant. The fruit and shoots are eaten by baboon and monkey. The caterpillars of the large brown butterfly, (Palm Tree Night Fighter, *Zaphotetes dysmephilai*) eat the leaves.

Human uses The fruit is edible but has little flesh. The sap is used to brew beer. The leaves are used to weave mats and hats. Fibres on the fruiting stems are used to make brushes and brooms.

Gardening This palm will grow well when generously watered in a warm garden, especially if the soil is rich. Once grown, it will produce palatable, edible fruits. It is not drought- or frost-resistant and does not grow from seed. It is particularly slow-growing.

Wood The wood is fibrous, pale-brown with darker flecks. It is light in weight (air-dry 590 kg/m^3).

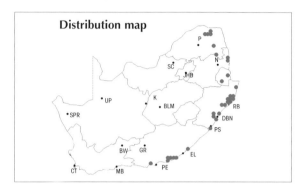

Distribution map

Look-alike tree The Lala-palm (*Hyphaene coriacea*), page 76, grows south and north of the Olifants River, while the Wild Date-palm is more common south of the river. The Lala-palm has hand-shaped leaves, in comparison to the fern-like leaves of the Wild Date-palm.

Wild Date-palms follow the course of the riverbed; here they grow near a Natal-mahogany.

GROWTH DETAILS

This tree is normally multi-stemmed. The leaves come directly off the main trunk to form an irregular, moderately dense, palm-like canopy. The trunk, when visible, displays old leaf scars.

Flowers   Male and female flowers grow on separate trees; female flowers are yellow-green; male flowers are yellow-cream. Flowers grow in bunches at the point where the young leaves join the branches. The male flowers have prominent stamens (September and October). (Single: 30 mm)

Leaves   Compound, fern-like and come off at the end of the main trunk. There are up tp 100 sharp, pointed leaflets. The lowest leaflets are reduced to spines. (1 000 - 3 000 mm)

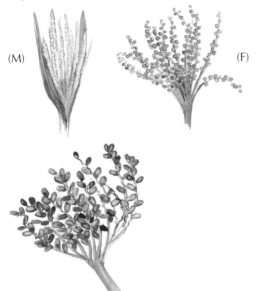

(M)   (F)

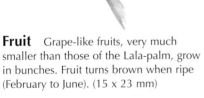

Fruit   Grape-like fruits, very much smaller than those of the Lala-palm, grow in bunches. Fruit turns brown when ripe (February to June). (15 x 23 mm)

	Oct	Nov	Dec	Jan	Feb	Mar	Apr	May	Jun	Jul	Aug	Sep
Leaf												
Flower												
Fruit/Pod												

Seasonal changes   Evergreen. This tree can be identified easily throughout the year owing to its unique shape.

Trees greet you

SEASONALLY STRIKING

These trees are particularly easy to find in certain seasons, and, on the whole, are more difficult to spot without their seasonal garb. Read through this section and check the Seasonal Grid for each tree. Also check "Where you'll find this tree easily" to be sure it occurs in the area you are tree spotting. Once you know which trees are seasonally striking in your area, you will have difficulty missing them!

Red flowers of the Flame Climbing Bushwillow *(Combretum microphyllum)* see page 98, are dramatic along a river bank, with the creeper engulfing the central branches of a very old Knob Thorn Acacia.

AFRICAN-WATTLE

Peltophorum africanum

African Weeping-wattle

**CAESALPINIACEAE
FLAMBOYANT FAMILY**

SA Tree Number 215

AFRIKAANS Huilboom   **ENGLISH** Weeping Wattle   **N. SOTHO** Mosehla   **TSONGA** Ndedze
TSWANA Mosêthla   **VENDA** Musese   **ZULU** umSehle

The species name **africanum** refers to Africa.

Where you'll find this tree easily

The African-wattle grows singly, but more than
one tree may be found growing in the vicinity.

- It is easiest to find this tree in Pretoriuskop
  Sourveld (B).
- It can also be found in most other Ecozones.

Ecozones where this tree occurs

A	E	I	M
B	F	J	N
C	G	K	O
D	H	L	P

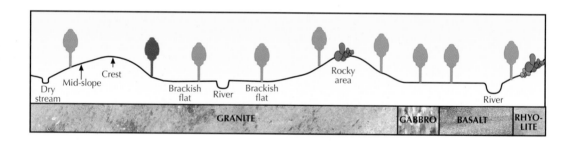

Striking features

- **This tree has striking, dull green, large, Acacia-like, soft, feathery leaves.**
- It branches low down from a stem that is often crooked, to form a spreading, irregular and untidy canopy.
- **In summer, abundant, yellow flowers amongst the large, feathery leaves are characteristic.**
- It does not have thorns.
- The mature leaves, at the tips of the branches, are often yellowish.

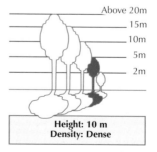

Above 20m
15m
10m
5m
2m

**Height: 10 m
Density: Dense**

90

AFRICAN-WATTLE

Peltophorum africanum

Links with animals In summer the tree is often infested with the spittle bug, *Ptyelus grossus*. The bugs' secretions drip down, causing it to 'rain' under the tree. The tree is not browsed regularly, but young shoots may be eaten by Black Rhino, elephant, giraffe and kudu.

Human uses The wood is used to make furniture, axe handles, buckets and ornaments. The wood is also used as fuel.

Gardening This decorative tree will grow in most gardens. It is sensitive to severe frost, but drought-resistant once established. It can be grown from seed and is fast-growing when planted in fertile soils and watered well.

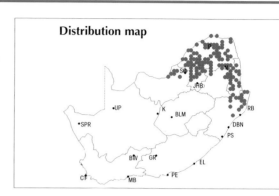
Distribution map

Wood The heartwood is reddish, close-grained and fairly hard and tough. It polishes well, and is easy to work.

Look-alike trees In the Malelane Mountain Bushveld, this tree can be confused with the Mountain Kirkia (*Kirkia wilmsii*), page 28. It can also be confused with the Acacias and Albizias listed on pages 59 - 61.

Pods and old leaves of the African-wattle stand out against a winter sky.

GROWTH DETAILS

There is usually a single, crooked stem. It branches low down with several downward curving branches forming an irregular canopy. The trunk is often obscured by drooping branchlets and leaves.

Flowers   The conspicuous, sweet-scented, bright yellow flowers grow in sprays at the ends of twigs, or in the angles formed by the leaves. The flowers have crinkled petals that are up to 20 mm in diameter. The flower stalks and the back of the petals are covered in reddish-brown hairs (September to February). (Spray: up to 150 x 80 mm) (Individual flower: up to 20 mm wide)

Leaves   The alternate, feathery, Acacia-like leaves are twice compound, with 4 - 9 pairs of feathers, and 10 - 23 pairs of leaflets. The small, soft, leaflets are silvery/dull green above, and paler below. The leaflets are oblong to almost square. The feather stalks and main vein, as well as the leaf stalk, are covered in reddish-brown hairs. (Leaf: up to 180 x 901 mm) (leaflet: 5 - 9 x 1,5 - 3 mm)

Pods   The greyish brown to dark brown pods grow in conspicuous hanging bunches. The pods are thinly woody and contain one or two seeds, which can be seen as bulges. At least a few pods can be seen on the tree for most of the year, but pods are found in much greater numbers from February to May. (pod: 40 - 100 x 12 - 20 mm)

Bark   The bark is grey and smooth on young branches, and young twigs are covered in reddish-brown hairs. The bark is brown to dark grey, to almost black, and fissured lengthways, on older branches and stems.

	Oct	Nov	Dec	Jan	Feb	Mar	Apr	May	Jun	Jul	Aug	Sep
Leaf												
Flower												
Fruit/Pod												

Seasonal changes   Deciduous. The leaves are lost late in the winter. They can be identified for most of the year, as either the leaves or pods are normally present.

BROAD-POD ALBIZIA

Albizia forbesii

Broad-pod false-thorn

MIMOSACEAE ACACIA FAMILY	SA Tree Number 154

AFRIKAANS Breëpeulvalsdoring   **TSONGA** Rinyani   **ZULU** Umnala albizia, umNala

Where you'll find this tree easily

The Broad-pod Albizia grows singly, often alongside rivers.

- It is easiest to find this tree in Riverine areas (H).
- It can also be found in Knob Thorn/Marula Savannah (F) and in Sabie/Crocodile Thorn Thickets (D).

Ecozones where this tree occurs

A	E	I	M
B	F	J	N
C	G	K	O
D	H	L	P

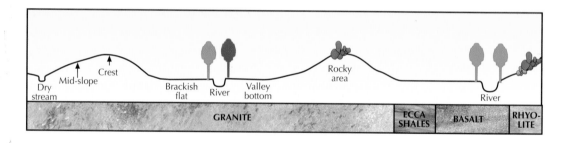

Striking features

- **The broad, russet pods are characteristic from March to September.**
- **The tree is covered by conspicuous, pin-cushion-like flowers in spring.**
- It is a tall tree with a few large branches that form a spreading canopy of feathery leaves.
- The bark is smooth and pale grey and may be broken into rectangular blocks that tend to flake.
- **Although it looks very like an Acacia, because it is an Albizia, it has no thorns.**

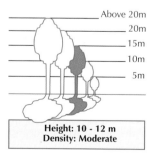

Height: 10 - 12 m
Density: Moderate

94

BROAD-POD ALBIZIA

Albizia forbesii

Links with animals Leaves and twigs are heavily utilised by elephant and other browsing game.

Human uses The wood is used for carving and as corner posts for huts. The roots were used in combination with other ingredients to create a mixture to ward off evil spirits.

Gardening This is a very attractive shade tree that grows well in most gardens. Seeds germinate easily, but the tree is not drought- or frost-resistant.

Look-alike trees The Bushveld Albizia (*Albizia harveyi*), page 36, is normally a smaller tree, and is more common on Brackish flats. The leaves are longer (150 mm), with 18 pairs of feathers and 12 - 24 very small, sickle-shaped leaflets (4 - 6 mm); pods are light brown and papery, growing in bunches that burst open on the tree.

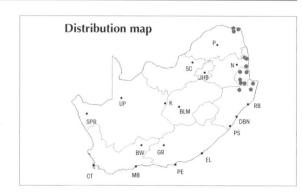

Distribution map

Wood The sapwood is pale brown and the heartwood almost black. It is quite hard and moderately heavy (air-dry 860 kg/m³). It produces a smooth finish.

A distinctive Broad-pod Albizia, on the Lower Sabie Road in Kruger, near the Sabie River bridge.

GROWTH DETAILS

This is a single-trunked, low-branching tree that branches extensively to form a moderately dense, spreading, irregular-shaped canopy.

Leaves   Twice compound leaves have a pair of feathers at the tip and are spirally arranged on young shoots. The feathers are opposite and increase in size towards the tip (4 feathers with 16 pairs of leaflets).

Leaflets are elliptic with a rounded end, but a sharp tip, with a smooth margin. A single vein is visible from above and below and splits the leaflet asymmetrically.

The leaves turn yellow before they drop in autumn. (leaf: 90 mm; leaflet: 9 x 2 mm)

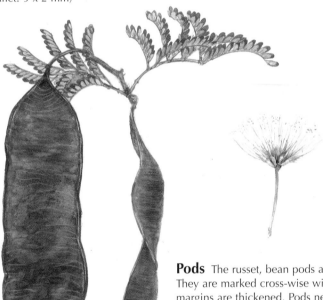

Flowers   Typical pin-cushion-like flowers of Albizias with prominent stamens, white to yellow; appear with or after the leaves (October to December). (30 mm)

Pods   The russet, bean pods are flat and fibrous. They are marked cross-wise with fine lines and the margins are thickened. Pods never open while on the tree and ripen March to September. (50 x 150 mm)

Bark   The bark is smooth and pale grey. In old trees the bark is broken into rectangular blocks that may flake off.

	Oct	Nov	Dec	Jan	Feb	Mar	Apr	May	Jun	Jul	Aug	Sep
Leaf	▨	▨	▨	▨	▨	▨	▨					
Flower	▨	▨	▨									
Fruit/Pod				▨	▨	▨	▨	▨	▨	▨	▨	▨

Seasonal changes   Deciduous. Recognisable for most of the year owing to the presence of the russet pods that stay on the tree for long periods.

97

FLAME CLIMBING BUSHWILLOW

Combretum microphyllum

Flame creeper

COMBRETACEAE BUSHWILLOW FAMILY	SA Tree Number 545

AFRIKAANS Vlamklimop   **TSONGA** Mpfunta   **VENDA** Murunda-gopokopo   **ZULU** iWapha

The species name **microphyllum** means small-leaved.

Where you'll find this climber easily

The Flame Climbing Bushwillow is a climber/scrambler that grows singly on trees in riverine vegetation.

- It is easiest to find growing in Riverine areas (H).
- This climber can be found along rivers in the Sabie/Crocodile Thorn Thickets (D), in Olifants Rugged Veld (J) and Alluvial Plains (M).

Ecozones where this climber occurs

A	E	I	M
B	F	J	N
C	G	K	O
D	H	L	P

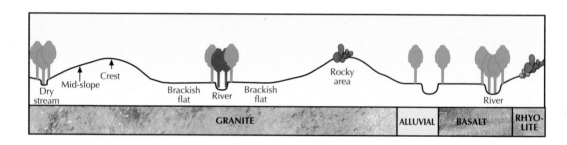

Striking features

- **The very striking, large sprays of brilliant red flowers with prominent stamens stand out amongst the riverine vegetation in spring.**
- It is a climber/scrambler normally growing up trees and shrubs.
- The pink-green, four-winged pods grow in abundance early in summer.

FLAME CLIMBING BUSHWILLOW

Combretum microphyllum

Links with animals The leaves are browsed by a variety of animals. The flowers attract sunbirds.

Human uses An extract of this plant is used to treat mentally disturbed people.

Gardening
This is a very attractive garden plant and can be very decorative in a larger garden. It needs dry winters to grow well. It is a fast grower but sensitive to frost.

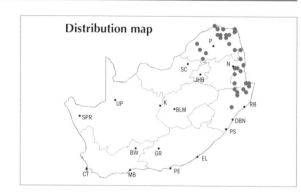

Distribution map

Look-alike climbers
The other red-flowered creeper in damp places is the Pride-of-De Kaap Bauhinia *(Bauhinia galpinii)* page 106. The flowers are more brick-red, rather than brilliant scarlet, and the leaves are noticeably butterfly; the pods are bean pod, not four winged.

100

Robust stems of the Flame Climbing Bushwillow entwined together, using a large strong riverine tree for support.

GROWTH DETAILS

This is a scrambling shrub or robust climber and is often multi-stemmed.

Flowers   The conspicuous, small, brilliant red flowers with very prominent stamens appear before the leaves and are clustered at the ends of the branches. Here they form spikes of up to 80 mm long that are held horizontally
(August to November).
(Stamen: 15 mm)

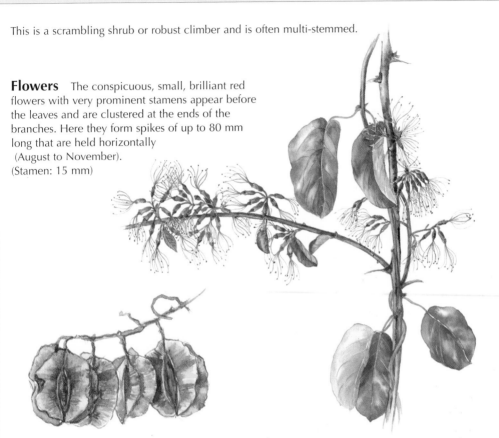

Pods   Large clusters of four-winged pods are greenish-pink when young and become straw-coloured when ripe. Pods develop quickly and may be found with the flowers (September to January). (20 x 20 mm)

Leaves   Simple, alternate or opposite leaves occur on new growth; elliptic to round. The leaf tip is normally round but may have a short point; leaf base is round and hairy especially on the underside, but becomes smoother with age. The margins are smooth; leaf stalks are velvety. (40 - 100 x 30 - 50 mm)

Bark   The bark is brown and flaking in older trees. It has long, often paired, curved woody spines that occur on the main branches.

	Oct	Nov	Dec	Jan	Feb	Mar	Apr	May	Jun	Jul	Aug	Sep
Leaf	■	■	■	■	■	■	■	■	■			
Flower	■	■									■	■
Fruit/Pod	■	■	■	■								■

Seasonal changes   Deciduous. This climber is only really easy to identify for the first time when the pods or flowers are present.

101

LONG-TAIL CASSIA

Cassia abbreviata

Sjambok pod

**CAESALPINIACEAE
FLAMBOYANT FAMILY**

SA Tree Number 212

AFRIKAANS Sambokpeul, Kersboom **ENGLISH** Long-tail cassia **N. SOTHO** Dithetlwa, Mothetlwa (Mokgwankgusha)
TSONGA Numanyama **TSWANA** Numanyama **VENDA** Muluma-nama, Munembe-nembe **ZULU** umHlambamanzi

The species name **abbreviata** means shortened.

Where you'll find this tree easily

The Long-tail Cassia grows singly.

- This tree is easiest to find in Sabie/Crocodile Thorn Thickets (D).

- It is also found growing Mixed Bushwillow Woodlands (A), Pretoriuskop Sourveld (B), in Marula Savannah (F), in Lebombo Mountain Bushveld (I) and also in Mopane/Bushwillow Woodlands (P).

Ecozones where this tree occurs

A	E	I	M
B	F	J	N
C	G	K	O
D	H	L	P

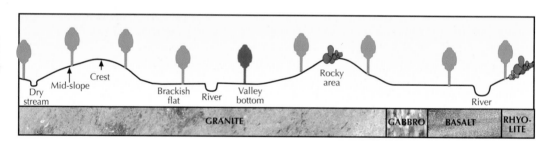

Striking features

- **Exceptionally long pods that stay on the tree for most of the year are characteristic of this tree.**
- **In early spring it is covered by masses of yellow flowers that appear before the new leaves.**
- It is a smallish tree with a slender stem and a semi-circular canopy with drooping leaves.

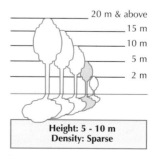

20 m & above
15 m
10 m
5 m
2 m

**Height: 5 - 10 m
Density: Sparse**

103

LONG-TAIL CASSIA

Cassia abbreviata

Links with animals The seeds are sought after by Brown-headed Parrots and Grey Louries. Young leaves are eaten by kudu.

Human uses Powdered bark has been successfully used for the treatment of bilharzia. The tree is believed to have some magical powers.

Gardening This very attractive small tree will grow well in most gardens but will be damaged by severe frost, especially when still young. It is drought-resistant. It is slow-growing and can be grown from seed easily.

Wood The sapwood is pale brown. The coarse-grained heartwood is dark brown with pale blotches, and heavy (air-dry 896 kg/m³).

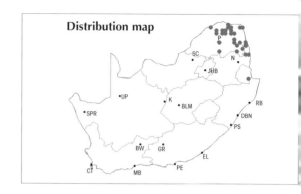

Distribution map

Look-alike trees The Tree Wisteria *(Bolusanthus speciosus)* page 118, also has long, drooping compound leaves, but they have a single leaflet at the top.

A canopy of magnificent flowers on the Long-tail Cassia, in early spring.

GROWTH DETAILS

The single, straight stem branches high up to form a semi-circular, sparse canopy of drooping leaves.

Flowers Single, yellow flowers are clustered in masses at the ends of the branches. They appear before the leaves (August to October). (30 mm)

Leaves Compound, elliptic with a smooth margin. The drooping leaves are clustered along the ends of the branches. Leaves are bright green when new in early summer, becoming darker and less striking as they mature. (Leaf: 300 mm; 9 pairs of leaflets 45 x 20 mm)

Pods Very long, cylindrical, flat bean pods appear soon after the flowers, and may take a year to ripen to dark brown. (800 x 30 mm)

Bark The bark is dark, fissured and flaking.

	Oct	Nov	Dec	Jan	Feb	Mar	Apr	May	Jun	Jul	Aug	Sep
Leaf												
Flower												
Fruit/Pod												

Seasonal changes Deciduous. This tree is without leaves from early winter until it flowers in spring. It can be identified for most of the year by its characteristic pods.

PRIDE-OF-DE KAAP BAUHINIA

Bauhinia galpinii   Pride-of-De Kaap

**CAESALPINIACEAE
FLAMBOYANT FAMILY**   **SA Tree Number 208.2**

AFRIKAANS Vlam-van-die-Vlakte   **TSONGA** Tswiriri   **TSWANA** liSololo   **VENDA** Mutswiriri
ZULU umVangatane, uiSololo, umDlondlovu

The species name **galpinii** refers to the late 19th and early 20th Century botanical collector, E.E. Galpin.

Where you'll find this woody climber easily

The Pride-of-De Kaap Bauhinia grows singly, often draped over other trees.

- It is easiest to find growing in Riverine areas (H).
- It is also found in Pretoriuskop Sourveld (B), as well as in the Sandveld (N).

Ecozones where this climber occurs

A	E	I	M
B	F	J	N
C	G	K	O
D	H	L	P

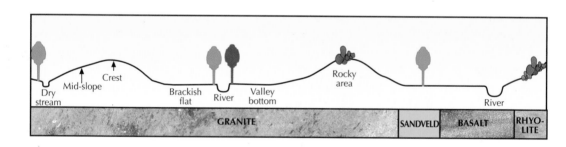

Crest · Mid-slope · Dry stream · Brackish flat · River · Valley bottom · Rocky area · River · GRANITE · SANDVELD · BASALT · RHYO-LITE

Striking features

- **The abundance of large, brick-red flowers in summer, along granite watercourses is one of the Lowveld features.**
- Bean-shaped brown pods are characteristic.
- This is a vigorous, multi-stemmed climber/scrambler, covering trees and bushes.
- **The leaves are butterfly-shaped.**

106

PRIDE-OF-DE KAAP BAUHINIA

Bauhinia galpinii

Links with animals The caterpillars of two butterflies of the genus *Deudorix*, the Brown Playboy and the Orange Barred Playboy, eat the leaves.

Human uses Branchlets are used to make baskets.

Wood The whitish-brown wood is pliable and fine-grained.

Look-alike climbers The other red-flowered climber in damp places is the Flame Climbing Bushwillow *(Combretum microphyllum)*, page 98. The flowers of the Flame Climbing Bushwillow are brilliant scarlet, and appear before the leaves; this climber only occurs along perennial rivers.

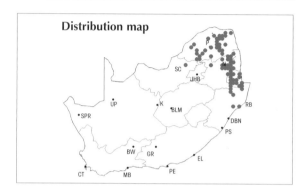

Distribution map

The red flowers of the Pride-of-de Kaap Bauhinia are conspicuous against the butterfly-shaped leaves.

GROWTH DETAILS

This is a vigorous, multi-stemmed climber, occasionally seen as a lone-standing, multi-stemmed small tree. It tends to form long, drooping, whip-like branches.

Flowers   The conspicuous, large, brick-red flowers grow in profusion. The five petals are paddle-shaped and have wavy edges (November to February). (50 - 70 mm)

Leaves   Simple, alternate and deeply lobed to form a butterfly-shaped leaf. The leaves and leaf margins are smooth; leaves are bright pale green. The veins are slightly yellow and stand out. (70 x 70 mm)

Pods   The long, flat, bean-shaped, dark brown pods are pointed, slender, hard and woody. Pods split on the tree when ripe (March to July). (80 - 100 mm)

Bark   Smooth and light brown.

	Oct	Nov	Dec	Jan	Feb	Mar	Apr	May	Jun	Jul	Aug	Sep
Leaf	▓	▓	▓	▓	▓	▓	▓	▓	▓	▓		▓
Flower		▓	▓	▓	▓							
Fruit/Pod						▓	▓	▓	▓	▓		

Seasonal changes   Deciduous to semi-deciduous. This climber is only conspicuous in summer when it is flowering.

PURPLE-POD CLUSTER-LEAF

Terminalia prunioides   Purple pod terminalia; Lowveld cluster-leaf

COMBRETACEAE **BUSHWILLOW FAMILY**	**SA Tree Number 550**

AFRIKAANS Sterkbos, Doringtrosblaar **TSONGA** Xaxandzawu **TSWANA** Mochiara, Motsiyara

Where you'll find this tree easily

The Purple-pod Cluster-leaf grows in loose groups on clay soils and sandy slopes.

- It is easiest to find this tree in Olifants Rugged Veld (J).

- You can also find it in Malelane Mountain Bushveld (C), Sabie/Crocodile Thorn Thickets (D), Mopane Shrubveld (L) and in Mopane/Bushwillow Woodlands (P).

Ecozones where this tree occurs

A	E	I	M
B	F	**J**	N
C	G	K	O
D	H	L	P

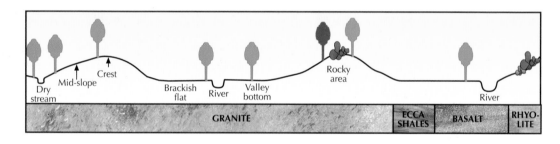

Striking features

- **The conspicuous purple pods are present for most of the summer, autumn and winter, and are the main aid to identification.**
- **During spring and summer this tree can be identified by the pungent smell of its flowers.**
- It has a drooping, spiky appearance owing to the downward-curving branchlets, irregular branching and side branches that end in spines.
- The clustered leaf arrangement is characteristic.

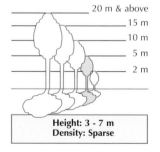

Height: 3 - 7 m
Density: Sparse

PURPLE-POD CLUSTER-LEAF

Terminalia prunioides

Links with animals The hard, green seeds are eaten by Brown-headed Parrots, baboons and monkeys. Young shoots and leaves are eaten by elephant, giraffe, kudu and impala.

Human uses The hard wood is used in the building of huts. It is also used for making axe and pick handles and as fuel.

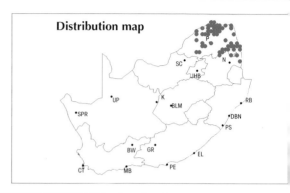
Distribution map

Gardening A very attractive tree when covered in plum-coloured pods, but the strong smell of the flowers may be overwhelming in a small garden. It also has a tendency to shrubby growth. It will grow in most soils and is fairly drought-resistant, but sensitive to frost. It grows relatively fast from seed when well watered, but it is difficult to find healthy, viable seed.

Wood The wood is brown, hard, tough and heavy (air-dry 1 120 kg/m^3).

A unusually tall example of this often bushy tree.

112

GROWTH DETAILS

This is usually a single, but sometimes a multi-trunked, low-branching tree, with many branches growing downwards to give it a drooping appearance. Side branches tend to end in spikes. The canopy is irregular, sparse and tangled.

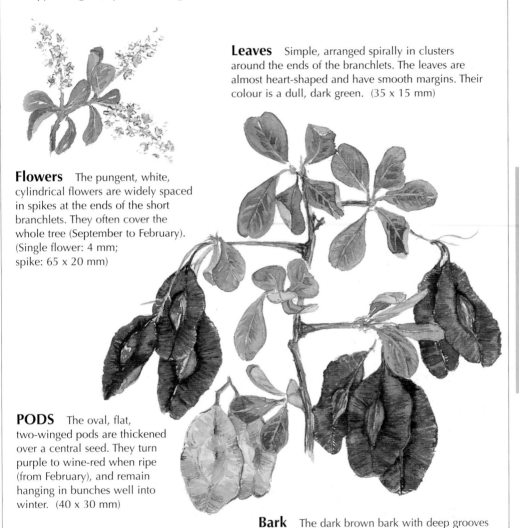

Leaves   Simple, arranged spirally in clusters around the ends of the branchlets. The leaves are almost heart-shaped and have smooth margins. Their colour is a dull, dark green. (35 x 15 mm)

Flowers   The pungent, white, cylindrical flowers are widely spaced in spikes at the ends of the short branchlets. They often cover the whole tree (September to February). (Single flower: 4 mm; spike: 65 x 20 mm)

PODS   The oval, flat, two-winged pods are thickened over a central seed. They turn purple to wine-red when ripe (from February), and remain hanging in bunches well into winter. (40 x 30 mm)

Bark   The dark brown bark with deep grooves is often obscured by the drooping branches.

	Oct	Nov	Dec	Jan	Feb	Mar	Apr	May	Jun	Jul	Aug	Sep
Leaf	▓	▓	▓	▓	▓	▓	▓	▓	▓			▓
Flower												
Fruit/Pod				▓	▓	▓	▓	▓	▓	▓	▓	▓

Seasonal changes   Deciduous to semi-deciduous. It can be recognised most of the year by the wine-red pods.

113

RED SPIKE-THORN

Gymnosporia senegalensis (Maytenus senegalensis)

Confetti Spikethorn

**CELASTRACEAE
SPIKE-THORN FAMILY**

SA Tree Number 402

AFRIKAANS Vierkantstampendoring   **ZULU** uBuhlangwe, isiHlangu, isiHlangwane

Where you'll find this tree easily

- You will find this tree easily in Knob Thorn Marula Savannah (F).
- You will also find this tree growing in Sabie/Crocodile Thorn Thickets (D), in Riverine areas (H), in Olifants Rugged Veld (J) and on Alluvial Plains (M).

Ecozones where this tree occurs

A	E	I	M
B	F	J	N
C	G	K	O
D	H	L	P

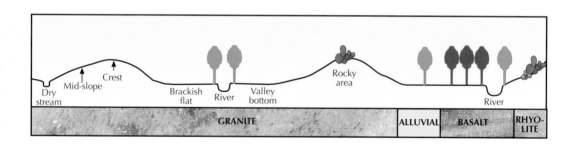

Dry stream · Mid-slope · Crest · Brackish flat · River · Valley bottom · Rocky area · River

GRANITE   ALLUVIAL   BASALT   RHYO-LITE

Striking features

- **It is evergreen and very conspicuous in Ecozone F in winter.**
- This is an untidy, sparse, multi-stemmed shrub.
- Young branches and twigs are red.
- It branches into many long, thin, whitish-grey branchlets and twigs that curve downwards.
- Grey-green leaves grow towards the tips of twigs, and give an overall whitish-grey appearance.
- Long, thin spines may carry leaves.
- **Abundant, small, white flowers smell sweet.**

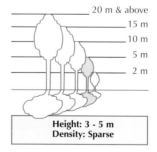

20 m & above
15 m
10 m
5 m
2 m

**Height: 3 - 5 m
Density: Sparse**

115

RED SPIKE-THORN

Gymnosporia senegalensis (Maytenus senegalensis)

Links with animals The leaves are eaten by elephant, kudu, giraffe and impala. The fruit is eaten by birds. The bark and leaves are eaten by Black Rhino.

Human uses The fruit is edible. Extracts of the roots and thorns can treat colds and coughs. Extracts of the tree can treat snakebite. The twigs were used to start fires by using friction.

Gardening Trees can be grown from seed. Trees grow slowly and are drought-resistant but sensitive to frost.

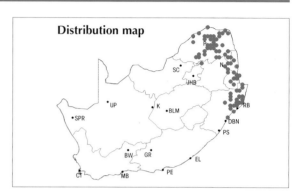

Distribution map

Wood The yellowish-white wood is hard, straight-grained and durable. It is of little commercial use except, perhaps, as box wood.

Look-alike tree This tree can be confused with the Common Spike-thorn *(Gymnosporia buxifolia)*, page 25. The Common Spike-thorn is normally single-stemmed with very coarse bark, shown in this photograph. The Red Spike-thorn is mostly multi-stemmed with smooth, reddish bark. The flowers of the Red Spike-thorn are sweet-smelling, while the flowers of the Common Spike-thorn have an offensive smell.

This coarse bark of the Common Spike-thorn distinguishes it from the Red Spike-thorn.

GROWTH DETAILS

This shrub is multi-stemmed and seldom develops into a fully grown tree. The stems are short and crooked. Branches come off haphazardly to form a tangled, sparse, irregularly shaped canopy. Many branches and twigs curve downwards, with the leaves towards the tips. Young twigs and branches are red.

Leaves Simple, narrow, elliptic leaves are arranged alternately in clusters on short side branchlets or on the spikes. They are usually leathery and bluish-grey. The leaves are very finely serrated and the tip is rounded. (20 - 120 x 40 - 60 mm)

Flowers Conspicuous male and female flowers grow on separate trees. The white star-shaped flowers grow in clusters at the base of the leaves. The flowers are sweetly scented (May to September). (4 - 6 mm; cluster 40 mm)

Fruit The berry-like fruit is reddish when ripe. The fruit is a two-lobed capsule (August to February). (2 - 6 mm)

Thorns The long, sharp, thin spines may be absent on some branches. (40 mm)

Bark The bark is grey and smooth.

	Oct	Nov	Dec	Jan	Feb	Mar	Apr	May	Jun	Jul	Aug	Sep
Leaf	■	■	■	■	■	■	■	■	■	■	■	■
Flower												
Fruit/Pod	■	■	■	■	■						■	■

Seasonal changes Evergreen. They are easiest to identify in winter, being one of the few green trees away from the rivers, in basalt areas.

TREE WISTERIA

Bolusanthus speciosus

FABACEAE
PEA FAMILY   **SA Tree Number 222**

AFRIKAANS Vanwykshout   **N. SOTHO** Mogohlo   **SWAZI** umHohlo   **TSONGA** Mpfimbahongonyi
VENDA Mukumba, Muswinga-phala   **ZULU** umHonhlo

The species name **speciosus** means beautiful.

Where you'll find this tree easily

The Tree Wisteria grows singly, but other trees will be found in the vicinity.

- It is easiest to find growing in Thorn Veld (E).

- It is also to be found in Mixed Bushwillow Woodlands (A), Pretoriuskop Sourveld (B), as well as in Marula Savannah (F) and Delagoa Thorn Thickets (G).

Ecozones where this tree occurs

A	E	I	M
B	F	J	N
C	G	K	O
D	H	L	P

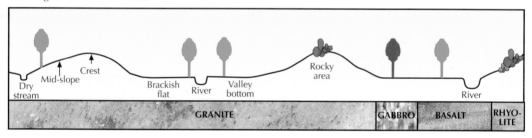

Dry stream / Mid-slope / Crest / Brackish flat / River / Valley bottom / Rocky area / River

GRANITE   GABBRO   BASALT   RHYO-LITE

Striking features

- **This tree can be easily identified by bunches of violet and white, pea-like flowers in September and October.**
- It is a very upright, narrow tree, branching low down but with the main branches growing upwards, almost parallel to one another.
- Branchlets and twigs are thin and bear the leaves towards their tips.
- The leaves are light in weight, and grow on thin twigs. They are tilted inwards, exposing both the bright green upper-surfaces and paler under-surfaces, creating a twinkling effect in the wind.
- The bark is deeply grooved and brown to dark brown.
- In Kruger its occurrence on gabbro soils (Ecozone E) will help with identification.

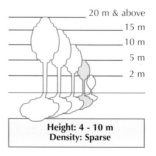

20 m & above
15 m
10 m
5 m
2 m

Height: 4 - 10 m
Density: Sparse

119

TREE WISTERIA

Bolusanthus speciosus

Links with animals Baboons and monkeys eat the flower buds but otherwise it is seldom utilised.

Human uses The wood is termite-resistant, and has been used for wagons, yokes, axe handles, fence poles and furniture.

Gardening This is a very attractive garden tree and will grow well in most soil types. It grows fast in sandy soils. It can be grown easily from seed and once established is fairly drought- and frost-resistant.

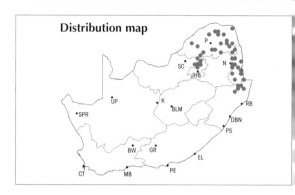

Distribution map

Wood The sapwood is thin and bright yellow. The heartwood is pale to dark brown, hard, strong and heavy (air-dry 930kg/m³).

Look-alike tree Long-tail Cassia (*Cassia abbreviata*), page 102, also has long, drooping, compound leaves, but its leaves have a pair of leaflets at the tip.

Baboons eating the flower buds in late winter

GROWTH DETAILS

This is a low-branching, fairly straight-stemmed tree with the main branches growing upwards. The branchlets and twigs grow outwards, bearing the leaves towards their ends to form a sparse, narrow canopy and then droop.

Flowers   Bunches of purple, pea-like flowers appear with, or before, the new leaves (September to October). (Spray 200 mm)

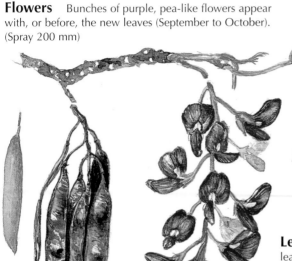

Leaves   Compound, with a single leaflet at the tip and 5 - 6 pairs of opposite, or almost opposite, leaflets. Leaflets narrowly elliptic to slightly sickle-shaped, with a smooth margin. Thei central vein is slightly off-centre and the tip is curled. The leaves are shiny, bright green above and paler below with an obvious yellow central vein. Young leaves are covered by fine hairs but older leaves are smooth. (Leaf: 250 mm; leaflet: 70 x 10 mm)

Pods   The flat, narrow, papery pods are pale brown but become almost black with age. They hang in clusters and do not split on the tree. Pods have sharp points at both ends (ripen November to March). (70 - 100 x 10 mm)

Bark   The bark is pale to dark brown and is deeply fissured and grooved, especially in older trees.

	Oct	Nov	Dec	Jan	Feb	Mar	Apr	May	Jun	Jul	Aug	Sep
Leaf												
Flower												
Fruit/Pod												

Seasonal changes   Deciduous. This tree can be identified even in the dry period by its spindly shape and deeply grooved bark.

121

ZEBRAWOOD

Dalbergia melanoxylon   Zebrawood Flat-bean

FABACEAE
PEA FAMILY   SA Tree Number 232

AFRIKAANS Sebrahout   **TSONGA** Shilutsi, Shipalatsi   **TSWANA** Mokelete   **VENDA** Muhuluri
ZULU umPhingo

Where you'll find this tree easily

The Zebrawood grows in groups often on road verges.

🌳 It is easy to find this tree growing in Knob Thorn/Marula Savannah (F).

🌳 This tree can also be found growing in most other Ecozones.

Ecozones where this tree occurs

A	E	I	M
B	F	J	N
C	G	K	O
D	H	L	P

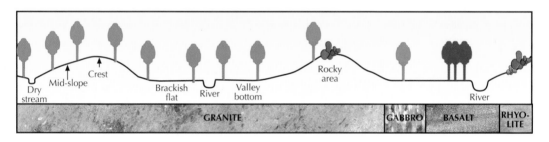

Dry stream | Mid-slope | Crest | Brackish flat | River | Valley bottom | Rocky area | River

GRANITE | GABBRO | BASALT | RHYO-LITE

Striking features

- **Masses of tiny, greenish-white, scented, pea-shaped flowers cover these trees in summer.**
- **The papery, pea-like pods can be seen on the tree for long periods from March to July.**
- It is a multi-stemmed shrub or tree with a densely branched and intertwined, V-shaped canopy.
- Thick spines stand out at right angles from the branches, branchlets and younger stems, bearing leaves and flowers.
- The bark in young branches is pale grey while the bark of older trees is rough and peels off in long strips.
- **The once compound leaves are soft and droopy.**

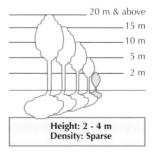

20 m & above
15 m
10 m
5 m
2 m

Height: 2 - 4 m
Density: Sparse

122

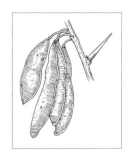

123

ZEBRAWOOD

Dalbergia melanoxylon

Links with animals Elephant favour the roots. Leaves are eaten by giraffe, impala and kudu.

Human uses The roots are used to treat headaches and toothache. The roots and wood are used to make jewellery such as earrings and brooches.

Gardening Not a very attractive garden plant except when flowering. It grows well from seed but grows slowly.

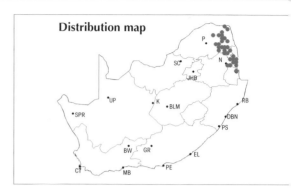

Distribution map

Wood The sapwood is narrow and off-white to bright yellow. The heartwood is black, sometimes with brown striations. It is hard, being even heavier than Leadwood Bushwillow, finely textured and heavy (air-dry 1 280 kg/m^3).

Look-alike trees Because of its compound leaves, spines and pods, it can be confused with small Acacias. The leaves however are once compound, and the flower is pea-shaped. This distinguishes this tree from Acacias and Albizias, compared on pages 59 - 61.

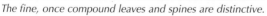

The fine, once compound leaves and spines are distinctive.

GROWTH DETAILS

This is a multi-stemmed tree with the stems often intertwined, branching profusely to form a dense, roundish, woody canopy. Branches have thick spines, which are modified shoots that bear the leaves and flowers.

Pods   The flat, papery, oblong pods grow in bunches, are slightly swollen over the seeds, and are pointed at both ends. They are pale brown when young, but grey-brown to black when mature. They do not split open and may be seen on the tree for long periods (March to July). (50 x 13 mm)

Leaves   Compound, dark green leaves arranged alternately. Leaves consist of 6 - 13 leaflets, opposite to alternate, with a single leaf at the tip. Leaflets elliptic with notched tips and smooth margins. The leaves turn yellow in autumn. (Leaf: 90 mm; leaflet: 15 - 25 mm)

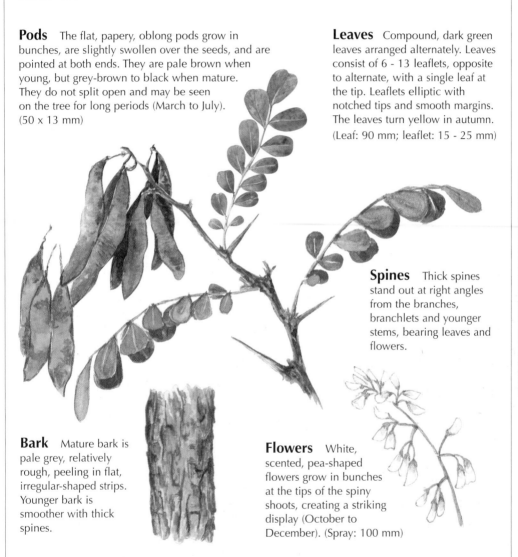

Spines   Thick spines stand out at right angles from the branches, branchlets and younger stems, bearing leaves and flowers.

Bark   Mature bark is pale grey, relatively rough, peeling in flat, irregular-shaped strips. Younger bark is smoother with thick spines.

Flowers   White, scented, pea-shaped flowers grow in bunches at the tips of the spiny shoots, creating a striking display (October to December). (Spray: 100 mm)

	Oct	Nov	Dec	Jan	Feb	Mar	Apr	May	Jun	Jul	Aug	Sep
Leaf	▓	▓	▓	▓	▓	▓						
Flower												
Fruit/Pod						▓	▓	▓	▓	▓		

Seasonal changes   Deciduous. The leaves turn yellow in autumn. The spiny growth form and bark of trunk and branches will help with identification even when no leaves are present.

125

Find trees by Ecozone

BIG SIX

Wherever you stop in the Lowveld you have a very good chance of seeing at least one, if not more, of the following trees. The trees in this section are chosen because they are generally either the tallest, or the most common trees. To avoid confusion while looking for your first few Ecozone trees, do not stop too near a river, dry stream or rocky area, or too close to the change-over from one Ecozone to another. In these places the distribution of trees is not specifically reliable for that Ecozone.

Silver Cluster-leafs *(Terminalia sericea)* grow in groups on the mid-slopes of granite Ecozones, and are the dominant tree in Ecozone B (see page 148).

APPLE-LEAF

Philenoptera violacea (Lonchocarpus capassa)   **Rain Tree**

FABACEAE **PEA FAMILY**	**SA Tree Number 238**

AFRIKAANS Appelblaar   **N. SOTHO** Lengana   **SISWATI** isHomuhomu   **TSONGA** Mbhandzu, Mbandu
TSWANA Mohota   **VENDA** Mufhanda   **ZULU** umBandu, umPhandu, isiHomohomo

The species name **capassa** is the Mozambique vernacular name meaning 'of no value'.

Where you'll find this tree easily

The Apple-leaf grows singly along perennial rivers.
Groups of smaller trees can also be found further
from rivers in higher rainfall areas, or where the
soil is waterlogged.

- It is easiest to find this tree in Riverine
  areas (H).

- You will also find this tree growing in most
  other Ecozones.

Ecozones where this tree occurs

A	E	I	M
B	F	J	N
C	G	K	O
D	H	L	P

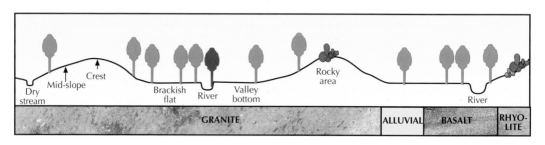

Striking features

- The meandering, single, smooth, bare trunk is
  high-branching and is whitish-grey.
- The tree has a sparse, irregularly shaped
  canopy with branches clearly visible between
  the leaves.
- **The large, pale grey-green, leathery leaves are
  individually visible even from a distance of
  30 metres.**
- **Bunches of pale lilac/purple flowers are
  conspicuous in late spring and early summer.**

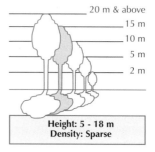

Height: 5 - 18 m
Density: Sparse

129

APPLE-LEAF

Philenoptera violacea (Lonchocarpus capassa)

Links with animals The tree may be infected with aphids (Froghopper, *Ptyelus grossus*) which excrete a sweet foam that drips down to form a wet patch on the ground. Hence the old name 'Rain Tree'.

The leaves are not very palatable, but in the absence of other food young leaves are eaten by giraffe, eland, kudu, elephant, impala and steenbok. Elephants also eat the branches – in some areas this tree is known as the 'Elephant Tree'.

Human uses The wood provides poles for building, pestles for pounding grain, pots and axe handles.

Gardening The unusual shape of this tree can make it an interesting addition to the garden. It will grow in most soil types, is fairly drought-resistant but not resistant to frost. It grows slowly and can be grown easily from seed.

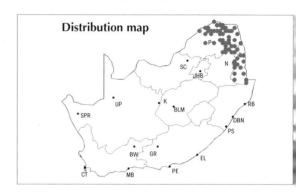

Distribution map

Wood The sapwood is off-white. The orange-brown heartwood is hard and dense with a straight, fairly close grain. It has prominent annual rings (air-dry 770 kg/m³).

130   *Apple-leaf trees have a distinctive meandering growth pattern.*

GROWTH DETAILS

The single, high-branching, meandering, smooth, whitish-grey trunk divides into only a few main branches. These come off in various directions to form an irregular, sparse canopy.

Pods   Pale green to pale brown, flat-winged, bean pods grow in large, conspicuous bunches from January. Pods stay on the tree long after they ripen in late summer. (120 x 25 mm)

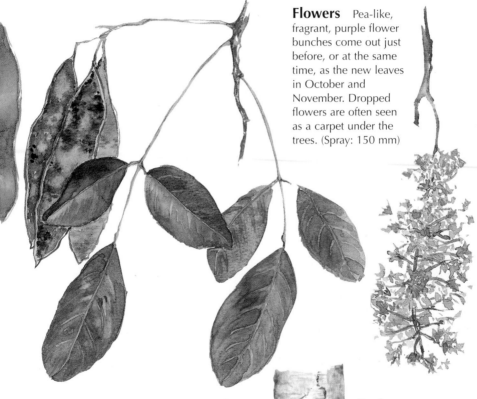

Flowers   Pea-like, fragrant, purple flower bunches come out just before, or at the same time, as the new leaves in October and November. Dropped flowers are often seen as a carpet under the trees. (Spray: 150 mm)

Leaves   The compound leaf has 1 to 2 pairs of opposite leaflets with a much larger leaflet at the tip. The pale grey-green leaves are very hairy when young and become leathery when older. (Leaf: 150 mm; leaflet: 60 x 35 mm)

Bark   The bark is white-grey and smooth when young, and rougher when older.

	Oct	Nov	Dec	Jan	Feb	Mar	Apr	May	Jun	Jul	Aug	Sep
Leaf												
Flower												
Fruit/Pod												

Seasonal changes   Deciduous to semi-deciduous. This is one of the few trees that usually has leaves in winter. Brown pods make identification easy in late summer and early winter.

KNOB THORN ACACIA

Acacia nigrescens

Knob thorn

MIMOSACEAE **ACACIA FAMILY**	**SA Tree Number 178**

AFRIKAANS Knoppiesdoring   **N. SOTHO** Mogaya   **TSONGA** Nkaya   **TSWANA** Mokala, Mokôba
VENDA Mukwalo   **ZULU** umKhaya, umBhebe, isiBambapala

The species name **nigrescens** means 'black' and probably refers to the pods.

Where you'll find this tree easily

Larger Knob Thorn Acacias grow singly near rivers, but there are often more than one in an area. Smaller, mature Knob Thorns grow in dense groups in clay soils.

 Large trees are easiest to find in Riverine areas (H), as well as in Knob Thorn/Marula Savannah (F).

 Smaller Knob Thorns are easily found throughout Stunted Knob Thorn Savannah (K).

This tree can also be found in all the granite, gabbro and basalt Ecozones.

Ecozones where this tree occurs

A	E	I	M
B	F	J	N
C	G	K	O
D	H	L	P

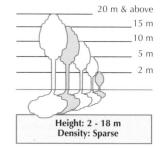

20 m & above
15 m
10 m
5 m
2 m

Height: 2 - 18 m
Density: Sparse

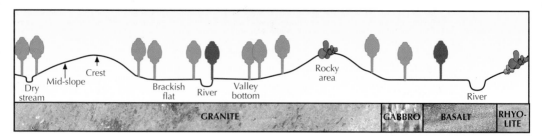

Crest · Dry stream · Mid-slope · Brackish flat · River · Valley bottom · Rocky area · River

GRANITE · GABBRO · BASALT · RHYO-LITE

Striking features

- This is an upright thorn tree, with a straight, single trunk that branches high up.
- It has a sparse, round, but relatively narrow canopy.
- **There are woody knobs on the trunks of young trees, and on large, young branches of older trees.**
- The leaflet is large for an *Acacia*, giving the impression of a butterfly-type leaf.
- **In spring and early summer, the Knob Thorn Acacia is the only tree to have masses of white flower spikes and no leaves.**

132

Largest tree currently registered

Diameter: 0,97 m

Girth: 3,05 m

Height: 13 m

Nwanedi Resort,
Northern Province

133

KNOB THORN ACACIA

Acacia nigrescens

Links with animals This tree is vulnerable to animal damage. It is often attacked, and may even be killed, by woodborers. The tree seldom re-grows after being pushed over, or otherwise damaged, by elephants.

The flowers are eaten by baboon, monkey and giraffe. Leaves and shoots are eaten by kudu, elephant and giraffe. Giraffe also eat the pods. Holes in the trunk and branches provide nesting sites for birds. White-backed Vultures often nest on top of these trees.

Human uses The wood is used for fence posts and also for walking sticks and knobkieries (fighting sticks). Poles are planted in the ground to act as lightning conductors. The bark is used for tanning.

Gardening This tree will grow well in most gardens. It likes warm conditions, is susceptible to frost but is fairly drought-resistant. The tree tends to drop thorny twigs, which will be a disadvantage in family gardens. It can be grown from seed easily, but grows very slowly.

Look-alike trees It can be confused with other Acacias. See pages 60 - 61 for comparisons.

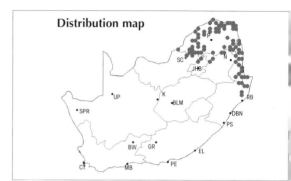

Distribution map

Wood The heartwood is yellow-brown and the sapwood is yellow. The wood has an irregular grain, is difficult to saw, and planes well to a smooth finish. It turns readily and varnishes satisfactorily, but does not hold nails well.

Knob Thorn Acacias dominate many Ecozones; they are at their most dramatic in early spring.

GROWTH DETAILS

This tree has a single, straight trunk that branches to form a moderate, irregular canopy.

Leaves The twice compound, opposite leaves have pale green leaflets that are almost round and have a smooth margin. There are 1 - 3 feather pairs, each feather consisting of 1 - 2 pairs of leaflets, each pair resembling a butterfly leaf. (Leaf: 35 x 80 mm; leaflet: 10 - 30 x 8 - 25 mm)

Flowers From late June to early July the tree has a plum-coloured sheen from the developing flower-buds. They open to form a spectacular creamy-white display covering the leafless trees in spring (July to September). The sweet-scented flower-spikes grow in clusters of 2 - 3 at the leaf-buds. Flowers are most abundant after good, late summer rains. (80 - 100 mm)

Thorns Downward-curving, hooked thorns grow on characteristic protruding knobs on the thicker branches and young trunks. Smaller, hooked thorns grow in pairs on branchlets and twigs. (5 - 10 mm)

Pods The flat bean pods hang down in clusters. They change from pale green to brown as they ripen. Pods never open on the trees but break up on the ground (December to June). (110 - 140 x 20 mm)

Bark The bark is dark brown, rough and deeply fissured lengthwise, revealing yellowish under-bark. Younger branches and trees have paler bark and have the characteristic knobs with hooked thorns.

	Oct	Nov	Dec	Jan	Feb	Mar	Apr	May	Jun	Jul	Aug	Sep
Leaf												
Flower												
Fruit/Pod												

Seasonal changes Deciduous. The leaves turn yellow before they fall in autumn. The knobs are still visible in winter making it easy to find.

135

LEADWOOD BUSHWILLOW

Combretum imberbe   *Leadwood*

COMBRETACEAE
BUSHWILLOW FAMILY   **SA Tree Number 539**

AFRIKAANS Hardekool   **PEDI** Motswiri   **SISWATI** umMono, imPondozendhlovu   **TSONGA** Mondzo
TSWANA Motswere   **VENDA** Muheri   **ZULU** umBondwe omnyama

The species name **imberbe** refers to the hairless leaves.

Where you'll find this tree easily

The Leadwood Bushwillow grows singly, in
the open basalt plains, and often along rivers and
large drainage lines.

* It is easiest to find this tree in Knob Thorn and
  Marula Savannah (F).

* This tree can also be found in most other
  Ecozones.

Ecozones where this tree occurs

A	E	I	M
B	F	J	N
C	G	K	O
D	H	L	P

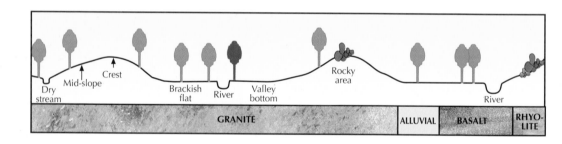

Striking features

* This is a very tall, high-branching, majestic tree.
* The sparse foliage has a yellow tinge
  throughout the year.
* **The pale grey bark, which breaks up into
  small, regular blocks (like snake-skin),
  is characteristic.**
* Mature trees often have dead, bare branches
  and twigs.
* **It has characteristic, small, four-winged pods.**

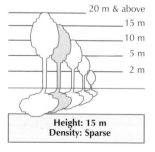

Height: 15 m
Density: Sparse

BIG SIX
Leadwood Bushwillow

Largest tree currently registered

Diameter: 1,40 m
Girth: 4,40 m
Height: 20 m

B G Bronn, 24 Kruis Road, ('Korthoek') Dist. Ellisras

137

LEADWOOD BUSHWILLOW

Combretum imberbe

This tree grows very slowly, forming exceptionally hard wood. Dead trees take a long time to decay, and often become well-known landmarks. Some of these have been carbon-dated at over one thousand years old.

Links with animals The leaves are eaten by giraffe, kudu, elephant and impala.

Human uses As the wood burns slowly and forms good coals, it is highly sought-after as cooking fuel. However, to protect our trees, wood fires are discouraged. The calcium-rich ash is used as a whitewash on houses. The flowers are used in a cough mixture, and smoke from the burning leaf is inhaled to relieve coughs and colds. The leaves and fruit are believed to have mystical powers. Trees damaged by elephants or other animals usually recover well.

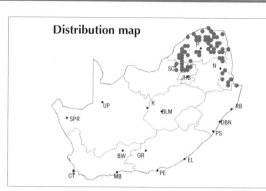

Distribution map

The wood is used for ornaments but is difficult to work, rapidly blunting and breaking tools. It is termite- and borer-proof.

Gardening The Leadwood Bushwillow will grow in most well-drained gardens. It is fairly drought-resistant, but could be damaged by frost. It can easily be grown from seed, but is extremely slow-growing. The seeds are thought to be poisonous.

Wood The heartwood is dark brown, hard and very heavy, (air-dry 1 200 kg/m³), whilst the sapwood is thin and yellowish.

Look-alike trees While young, this tree can be confused with other Bushwillows. See page 62-63 for comparisons.

Gnarled, snakeskin bark on an ancient trunk of Leadwood Bushwillow

138

It has a single, straight trunk that branches high up, with branches growing both horizontally and upwards. The canopy is wide-spreading and sparse.

Leaves   The simple, opposite leaves are broadly elliptic to oval with a wavy margin. The tip and the base of the leaf are rounded to broadly tapering. The leaves are characteristically grey-green to yellow-green, with silvery scales, are leathery and without hairs. (25 - 80 x 10 - 30 mm)

Flowers   The creamy to creamy-yellow flowers are sweet-smelling. The long, slender spikes grow in the angle formed by the leaf or at the ends of branches (November to March). (Flower spikes: 40 - 80 x up to 15 mm)

Pods   The pod is four-winged and is characteristic of the bushwillow family. It is small for the size of the tree and is yellowish-green, drying to pale brown. The pod often drops just after it has ripened in autumn (February to June). (15 - 19 mm diameter)

Bark   The pale grey bark, which breaks up into small, regular blocks (like snake-skin), is characteristic.

	Oct	Nov	Dec	Jan	Feb	Mar	Apr	May	Jun	Jul	Aug	Sep
Leaf	▓	▓	▓	▓	▓	▓	▓	▓				▓
Flower		░	░	░	░	░						
Fruit/Pod					▓	▓	▓	▓				

Seasonal changes   Deciduous. Leaves turn yellow-brown before falling in winter. The majestic growth form and characteristic pale grey, snake-skin bark make identification possible throughout the year.

139

MARULA

Sclerocarya birrea

ANACARDIACEAE
MANGO FAMILY

SA Tree Number 360

AFRIKAANS Maroela   **N. SOTHO** Morula   **SISWATI** umGana   **TSONGA** Nkanyi   **TSWANA** Morula
VENDA Mufula   **ZULU** umGanu

The species name **birrea** is based on the common name of the tree "birr" in Senegal and Gambia.

Where you'll find this tree easily

The Marula tree grows singly throughout the Lowveld.

- This tree is most common, and can most easily be found in Knob Thorn and Marula Savannah (F).
- It can also be found along rivers and large streams of Ecozones A, B, C, D, E, F, H, I, J, P.

Ecozones where this tree occurs

A	E	I	M
B	F	J	N
C	G	K	O
D	H	L	P

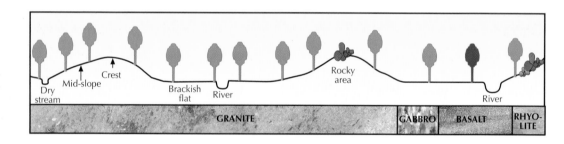

Striking features

- This is a single-trunked, high-branching tree with a characteristic semi-circular canopy.
- **The bark often peels in conspicuous, characteristic, rounded depressions, exposing the smooth pink-brown under-surface.**
- Leaves hang from the end of thickened twigs that stand out, like stubby fingers, in winter.
- **Marula fruit are often seen under the female trees during January and February.**

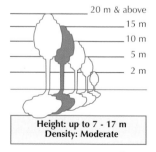

20 m & above
15 m
10 m
5 m
2 m

Height: up to 7 - 17 m
Density: Moderate

Largest tree currently registered

Diameter: 1,33 m

Girth: 4,18 m

Height: 19 m

N G Kerk Kranspoort
Mission Station,
Dist. Soutpansberg

141

MARULA

Sclerocarya birrea

Links with animals The caterpillars of eight species of butterfly eat the leaves. Several types of parasitic plants grow on the Marula.

The fruit is eaten by a wide variety of animals such as elephant, monkey, baboon, kudu, duiker, impala and zebra. The foliage and bark are eaten by elephant.

Human uses Water that is stored in large quantities in the roots is tapped in times of drought. The fruit is very tasty, and rich in Vitamin C. It is used to make beer, jelly and jam. Seed kernels are rich in oil and protein. The bark is traditionally used for the treatment of malaria. The tree plays an important part in marriage rituals, and has an integral role in fertility rites. The Marula is particularly sacred in the Lowveld.

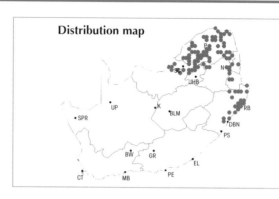

Distribution map

Wood The heartwood is pinky-red. Sometimes patches of darker colour are seen. It turns well.

Look-alike trees The False Marula (*Lannea schweinfurthii*), page 29, has bark that peels in large patches or strips, not like the small, round depressions of the Marula.

The leaflets of the compound leaf of the False Marula are brighter green (not blue-green), and are slightly rounder than those of the Marula. The False Marula leaf usually consists of only 1 - 3 pairs of leaflets, with a terminal, larger leaflet.

See the comparisons of various once compound leaves on the Distinctive Striking Features, pages 57 - 58.

In the winter Marulas are very easy to identify with their bare, short, stubby twigs.

GROWTH DETAILS

It has a single, straight trunk which branches high up into a few bare, main branches. These grow slightly upwards and horizontally to form a moderately dense, round to semi-circular canopy.

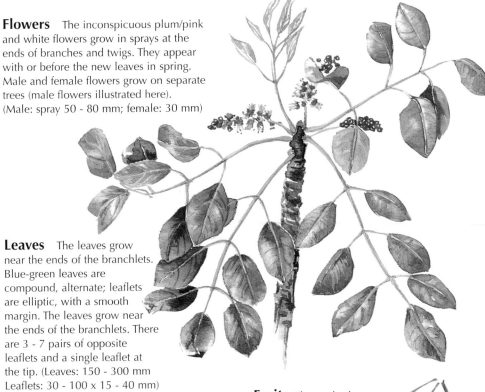

Flowers The inconspicuous plum/pink and white flowers grow in sprays at the ends of branches and twigs. They appear with or before the new leaves in spring. Male and female flowers grow on separate trees (male flowers illustrated here). (Male: spray 50 - 80 mm; female: 30 mm)

Leaves The leaves grow near the ends of the branchlets. Blue-green leaves are compound, alternate; leaflets are elliptic, with a smooth margin. The leaves grow near the ends of the branchlets. There are 3 - 7 pairs of opposite leaflets and a single leaflet at the tip. (Leaves: 150 - 300 mm Leaflets: 30 - 100 x 15 - 40 mm)

Bark The bark often peels in conspicuous, characteristic, rounded depressions exposing the smooth, pink-brown under-surface.

Fruit The oval, plum-sized fruit ripens from January to March. The fruit drops when it is still green and ripens on the ground. Each fruit has two to three seeds, and their holes can be seen in the central woody stones (Visible November to March). (40 mm)

(F)

	Oct	Nov	Dec	Jan	Feb	Mar	Apr	May	Jun	Jul	Aug	Sep
Leaf												
Flower												
Fruit/Pod												

Seasonal changes Deciduous. The shiny leaves turn yellow-green before they drop and the trees have long periods without leaves. However, the characteristic bark and the stubby twigs are very striking, making identification very easy in winter.

MOPANE

Colophospermum mopane

**CAESALPINIACEAE
FLAMBOYANT FAMILY**

SA Tree Number 198

AFRIKAANS Mopanie   **N. SOTHO** Mopane   **SISWATI** Mophne   **TSONGA** Nxanatsi   **VENDA** Mupani
ZULU umZololo

The species name **mopane** is derived from the local name for the tree.

Where you'll find this tree easily

The Mopane tree grows in large, uniform
groups north of the Olifants River.

- This tree is easily found in Mopane
  Shrubveld (L), in Tree Mopane Savannah (O)
  and in Mopane/Bushwillow Woodlands (P).

- It is also to be found in the northern parts of
  the Lebombo Mountain Bushveld (I) as well
  as in Olifants Rugged Veld (J).

Ecozones where this tree occurs

A	E	I	M
B	F	J	N
C	G	K	O
D	H	L	P

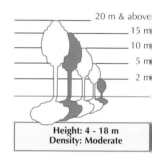

20 m & above
15 m
10 m
5 m
2 m

**Height: 4 - 18 m
Density: Moderate**

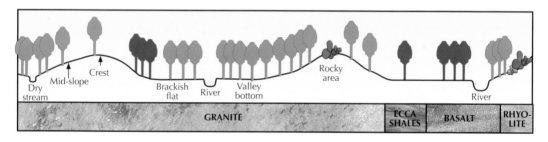

Dry stream   Mid-slope   Crest   Brackish flat   River   Valley bottom   Rocky area   River

GRANITE   ECCA SHALES   BASALT   RHYO-LITE

Striking features

- **The Mopane covers vast areas, as far as the
  eye can see, with few other shrubs or trees
  between them.**
- When large, the tree has a single, straight
  trunk and is high-branching, with a narrow
  canopy.
- Shrubs are multi-stemmed with a V-form,
  and a round, poorly developed canopy.
- **The butterfly leaf is characteristic.**

144

MOPANE

Colophospermum mopane

Links with animals The leaves are not very palatable but are eaten by elephant. Fallen leaves are eaten by almost all animals during drought periods. Scale-insects that infect the leaves are eaten by baboon. Holes in the trunk provide nesting sites for birds and small mammals.

Human uses The wood produces good coals when burned. Extracts of the wood are used to treat venereal diseases. The bark is used for tanning. Mopane worms that feed on the leaves are an important source of protein.

Distribution map

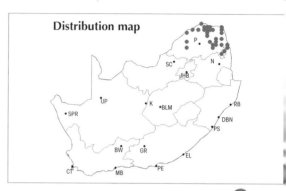

Wood The sapwood is yellow to light brown. The dark-red heartwood is very hard and heavy (air-dry 1250 kg/m³). It is durable and termite resistant.

Look-alike tree In the northern part of Kruger this tree can be confused with the Small False Mopane (*Guibourtia conjugata*), page 40, which also has a pair of opposite leaflets with five veins from the base. Leaflets are smaller, and the edges are more wavy than those of Mopane. The flowers are creamy, and the pods are close to being circular.

A tall Mopane tree in bright winter foliage

GROWTH DETAILS

Large Mopane trees often occur among the stunted form. The large Mopane tree is single-trunked and high-branching. Branches grow upwards to form a narrow, moderately dense canopy.
The shrub form is multi-stemmed and low-branching. Branches grow upwards in a V-form and the shrub has a round, poorly developed canopy.

Flowers
Inconspicuous greenish flowers grow in sprays at the ends of the branches (December to January).

Pods The flattened, oval, leathery kidney-shaped pods are covered by glands that make them sticky. Pods turn pale brown when ripe from April to June. (50 x 20 mm)

Leaves Compound, opposite; typical butterfly shape with a smooth margin; a minute third "leaflet" can be seen between the butterfly wings; veins radiate from the butterfly join. They have an aromatic smell. Reddish new leaves; mature leaves turn yellow-gold during autumn. (80 x 35 mm)

Bark The bark is fissured lengthways.

	Oct	Nov	Dec	Jan	Feb	Mar	Apr	May	Jun	Jul	Aug	Sep
Leaf	■	■	■	■	■	■	■					
Flower			■	■								
Fruit/Pod						■	■	■	■			

Seasonal changes Deciduous. This tree has rich yellow and brown colours in autumn. It is bare throughout the winter. The new leaves that appear in early summer have a red tinge.

SILVER CLUSTER-LEAF

Terminalia sericea

**COMBRETACEAE
BUSHWILLOW FAMILY**

SA Tree Number 551

AFRIKAANS Vaalboom   **N. SOTHO** Mogônônô, Moletsa-nakana   **TSONGA** Nkonono
TSWANA Mogonono   **VENDA** Mususu   **ZULU** amaNgwe-amphlophe

The species name **sericea** refers to the soft, silvery, hairy leaves.

Where you'll find this tree easily

The Silver Cluster-leaf grows in loose groups on the seeplines of granite crests.

- This tree is easiest to find in Pretoriuskop Sourveld (B).

- It can also be found in Mixed Bushwillow Woodlands (A), in Malelane Mountain Bushveld (C), in Sandveld (N) and in Mopane/Bushwillow Woodlands (P).

Ecozones where this tree occurs

A	E	I	M
B	F	J	N
C	G	K	O
D	H	L	P

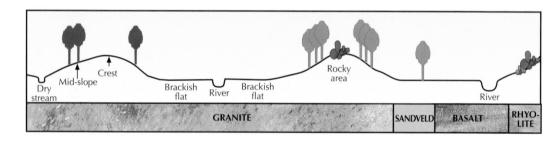

Striking features

- This is a silvery-blue, upright, single-trunked tree.
- **The branches leave the trunk at different levels to form distinct, horizontal layers.**
- The simple leaves are clustered towards the tips of slender branchlets and twigs.
- The young leaves have silver hairs, giving the tree a characteristic silver shine.
- The rough, dark bark is deeply fissured lengthways.
- The two-winged pods are red to brown and remain on the tree for long periods.

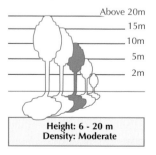

Height: 6 - 20 m
Density: Moderate

148

149

SILVER CLUSTER-LEAF

Terminalia sericea

Links with animals Although the nutritional value is low, leaves and young shoots are eaten by elephant, giraffe, kudu and impala. Dry leaves on the ground are eaten by wildebeest. The branches are eaten by elephant and giraffe.

Human uses The wood is used for fence poles, household goods, firewood and axe handles. The gum is eaten. Extracts of the bark are used as an antidote to poisons, and for tanning. Root extracts are used as a remedy for stomach disorders and diarrhoea, as well as for eye lotions and to treat pneumonia. Bark is used to treat diabetes and wounds.

Gardening This tree grows well in deep, sandy soils and may be an attractive addition to gardens. It is fairly frost- and drought-resistant and is difficult to grow from the few undamaged seeds that may be found.

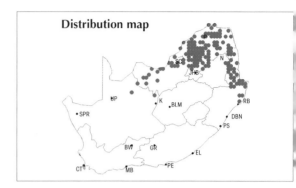

Distribution map

Wood The wood is yellow, hard and close-grained. It is strong and elastic, and termite- and borer-proof when properly seasoned. The wood is quite difficult to work.

Silver Cluster-leaf trees have a distinctive shape; the branches tend to layer horizontally.

The branches are low down, leaving the trunk horizontally, to form a moderately dense, spreading canopy.

Leaves   The simple, spirally arranged leaves are clustered towards the tips of slender branchlets. They are elliptic with a broadly tapering tip, that tends to be pointed, and a narrowly tapering base. The pale green to grey silvery-green leaves are leathery and have a smooth margin. The young leaves are covered in silky, silvery hairs, giving the tree an overall silver-blue appearance. (55 - 120 x 13 - 45 mm)

Flowers   The inconspicuous, very pungent, cream to yellow flowers grow on spikes that are found in the angle made by the leaf (September to January). (Spike: up to 70 mm long; individual flower: 4 mm diameter)

Pods   The two-winged pods grow in bunches at the ends of branchlets and twigs. They are pink to red when mature, later drying to brown. The pods may remain on the tree until the next flowering season (January to June). (25 - 60 x 15 - 25 mm)

Bark   The bark is rough and dark grey or brown, and is deeply fissured lengthways on older branches and trunks. The branchlets are dark brown or purplish, and flake in rings and strips, to reveal light brown underbark. Young twigs are covered in fine, silvery hairs.

	Oct	Nov	Dec	Jan	Feb	Mar	Apr	May	Jun	Jul	Aug	Sep
Leaf												
Flower												
Fruit/Pod												

Seasonal changes   Deciduous. Although this tree is without leaves for most of the winter, the horizontal, branching growth form is characteristic and makes identification easy. In summer the new leaves with their silvery hairs further assist identification.

Find trees by Ecozone

ECOZONE SPECIALISTS

Most trees included in this book are common in many areas of the Lowveld. However those in this chapter have been chosen because they are relatively selective, and grow in only one or two Ecozones.

Delagoa Thorn Acacia (*Acacia welwitschii*) is the dominant Acacia in Ecozone G; here the tree has flowers, typically on the top of the canopy (see page 158).

BLACK MONKEY-ORANGE

Strychnos madagascariensis

LOGANIACEAE **WILD ELDER FAMILY**	**SA Tree Number 626**

AFRIKAANS Swartklapper, Botterklapper   **N. SOTHO** Mookwane   **TSONGA** Nkwakwa
ZULU umGuluguza

The species name **madagascariensis** means from Madagascar.

Where you'll find this tree easily

The Black Monkey-orange grows singly on
well-drained soils.

- This tree can most commonly be found in
  Pretoriuskop Sourveld (B).

- It can also be found in Mixed Bushwillow Woodlands
  (A), in Malelane Mountain Bushveld (C), in Sandveld
  (N) and in Mopane/Bushwillow Woodlands (P).

Ecozones where this tree occurs

A	E	I	M
B	F	J	N
C	G	K	O
D	H	L	P

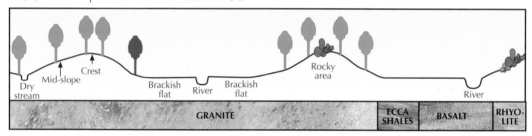

Striking features of Monkey-oranges

- **Big, rounded, orange-like fruit with
  a very hard skin is characteristic.**
- Many of the species have spines.
- Leaves are simple and opposite and are
  not attached by an obvious leaf-stem.

Striking features of this tree

- **The conspicuous, orange-sized, round fruit is
  blue-green for most of the year, becoming
  bright orange-yellow when ripe.**
- It is a multi-stemmed shrub or short tree, with
  a heavily-branched, irregular, flattish canopy.
- The leaves are clustered on the ends of short,
  thick twigs.
- The bark of the younger branches and trees is
  pale grey with white and dark grey patches,
  while the older branches are darker and
  rougher.
- Knobbly side shoots resemble spines.

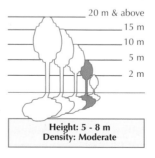

Height: 5 - 8 m
Density: Moderate

154

155

BLACK MONKEY-ORANGE

Strychnos madagascariensis

Links with animals Leaves are eaten by duiker, kudu, impala, steenbok, nyala and elephant. The fruit is eaten by baboon, monkey, bushpig, nyala and eland.

Human uses The fruit pulp is edible but the seeds are avoided as they are a purgative. In India a *Strychnos* species is used to prepare strychnine.

Gardening This tree can be grown easily from seed and will grow fairly fast when cultivated. It is sensitive to frost.

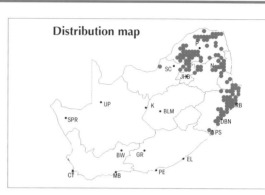

Distribution map

Wood The finely textured wood is strong and resistant. It is durable, difficult to plane and saw; not suitable for bending but polishes well.

Look-alike tree The Spiny Monkey-orange *(Strychnos spinosa)*, has slender, paired, slightly curved, woody spines at the base of the shiny, simple, opposite leaves (15 - 90 x 12 - 75 mm). Bark is rough, peeling or flaking; the fruit is large (120 mm) and turns yellow-brown when ripe.

156

Black Monkey-orange fruit, in winter, on knobbly branches with lichen

This is a very variable tree. It may be single-stemmed with a grooved and dented stem, or (more often) multi-stemmed, branching low-down. Many thin branchlets and twigs come off the main branches irregularly, to form a spreading canopy, giving it a thick matted appearance. Many side branches tend to emerge at right angles. Knobbly side shoots of 10 - 30 mm resemble spines.

Fruit   The big, round, fleshy, orange-like fruit is characteristic. It has a hard, woody shell. The fruit may take a long time to ripen to yellow-orange, and fruit may still be present into the next flowering season. Large seeds are tightly packed inside the shell, and each seed is covered by yellow pulp (March to August). (70 - 120 mm)

Leaves   The leaves are simple and opposite or are clustered at the tips of thick, knobbly twigs. Broadly elliptic leaves are velvety, shiny, blue-green above and paler below. The margins are smooth with a round tip and a wedge-shaped base. Leaves have 3 - 5 veins radiating from the base with two secondary veins that run parallel to the margin. (Leaf: 20 - 90 x 10 - 60 mm)

Flowers   Small, inconspicuous, greenish-yellow, trumpet-shaped flowers grow in small clusters at the base of the leaves on the old wood. Flowers tend to appear only after good rains (November to December). (8 - 10 mm diameter)

Bark   The bark is light grey and smooth.

	Oct	Nov	Dec	Jan	Feb	Mar	Apr	May	Jun	Jul	Aug	Sep
Leaf												
Flower												
Fruit/Pod												

Seasonal changes   Deciduous. The leaves turn yellow in autumn. It is possible to identify this tree all year round if fruit is present.

DELAGOA THORN ACACIA

Acacia welwitschii   Delagoa thorn

**MIMOSACEAE
ACACIA FAMILY**   SA Tree Number 163

AFRIKAANS Delagoa-doring

Where you'll find this tree easily

The Delagoa Thorn Acacia can only be found
growing in loose groups of large trees.

🌿 It is easiest to find in Delagoa Thorn
Thickets (G).

Ecozones where this tree occurs

A	E	I	M
B	F	J	N
C	G	K	O
D	H	L	P

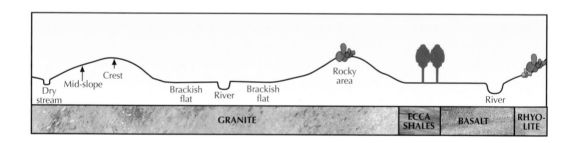

Striking features

- **Identification is primarily by Ecozone distribution – Ecozone G.**

- It has a single, crooked trunk.

- It is a low-branching thorn tree with typical Acacia leaves, flowers, pods and hooked thorns.

- **Prominent white twigs are visible through the foliage.**

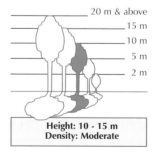

Height: 10 - 15 m
Density: Moderate

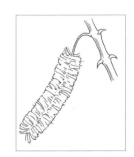

159

DELAGOA THORN ACACIA

Acacia welwitschii

Links with animals This is a favourite food of the giraffe.

Gardening This is not an attractive garden plant and will need specific clay soils to flourish. It is fairly drought-resistant, but is sensitive to low temperatures. It is a slow-growing tree that can be grown from seed.

Wood The wood is hard and heavy (air-dry 960 kg/m³). The sapwood is yellow-brown while the heartwood is black. It is difficult to saw and is not insect-proof.

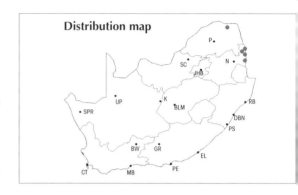

Distribution map

Look-alike trees This can be confused with other Acacias. See pages 60 - 61 for comparisons. It is most easily confused with the Black Monkey Thorn Acacia (*Acacia burkei*), page 32, the bark of which is more yellow.

The typical layered, triangular shape of Delagoa Thorn Acacias are easily recognised in Ecozone G.

160

GROWTH DETAILS

The single, crooked trunk is low-branching, with branches leaving the main stem horizontally to form a wide-spreading canopy. Large branches are formed high up, and here the leaves grow in layers.

Leaves Compound, with a pair of leaflets at the top of each feather, opposite, elliptic with a smooth margin. Medium to big for an Acacia. (2 - 5 feather pairs, 40 mm; 8 pairs of leaflets each 7 x 4 mm)

Thorns Pairs of hooked, dark thorns are fairly close to one another. (5 mm)

Flowers White flower spikes are normally only visible at the top of the canopy (November to January). (70 x 10 mm)

Pods Narrow, long, flat, bean pods are deep wine-red, changing to purple-green, and finally to brown-black when ripe. They are usually only visible at the top of the tree, as those lower down are eaten. Ripen late autumn and winter (March to July). (80 - 110 mm)

Bark The bark is coarse and fissured, light grey with yellow grooves that run lengthways.

	Oct	Nov	Dec	Jan	Feb	Mar	Apr	May	Jun	Jul	Aug	Sep
Leaf												
Flower												
Fruit/Pod												

Seasonal changes Deciduous. This tree may be recognised in winter by its Ecozone distribution, its growth form, and by the prominent white twigs.

GREEN-THORN

Balanites maughamii

**BALANITACEAE
GREEN-THORN FAMILY**

SA Tree Number 251

AFRIKAANS Groendoring **SWAZI** umNununu **TSONGA** Nnulu **ZULU** umNulu, uGobandlovu

Where you'll find this tree easily

The Green-thorn commonly grows singly, but large trees may be found surrounded by groups of smaller, young trees.

- It is easiest to find in Sabie/Crocodile Thorn Thickets (D).
- It can also be found in Thorn Veld (E).

Ecozones where this tree occurs

A	E	I	M
B	F	J	N
C	G	K	O
D	H	L	P

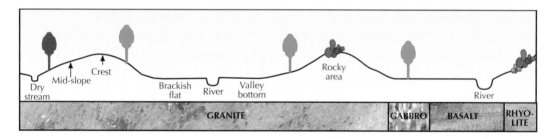

Striking features

- **The specific distribution in Ecozone D makes identification easy.**
- **It is a very high-branching tree with a deeply multi-fluted trunk and smooth, grey bark.**
- **It has zigzag twigs and branchlets that grow outwards to give it an overall thorny look.**
- Young trees often surround older mature trees and give the trunk a multi-stemmed, untidy, thorny appearance.
- The canopy in very old trees is umbrella-like. It remains V-shaped in some quite large, mature trees.
- **The forked spines are green with brown tips.**
- The compound two leaflet leaves are characteristic; leaflets are broadly elliptic to almost round, with a central vein that is slightly off centre.

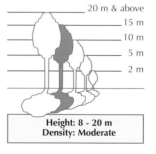

**Height: 8 - 20 m
Density: Moderate**

162

163

GREEN-THORN

Balanites maughamii

Links with animals Baboon, monkey, impala, kudu, duiker, warthog, porcupine and steenbok eat the fruit. Elephant eat the young shoots.

Human uses The fruit can be eaten. Although harmless to humans, it can kill snails, tadpoles and fish, and has been used to control bilharzia snails. The kernels are rich in fine, colourless oil, like olive oil, and are burned for torches. Bark soaked in water is used for a refreshing bath. Extract of the bark is used to induce vomiting.

Gardening This tree can be grown from seed and will grow in most gardens. Its abundant thorns make it unsuitable for the family garden.

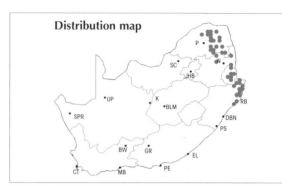

Distribution map

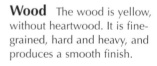

Wood The wood is yellow, without heartwood. It is fine-grained, hard and heavy, and produces a smooth finish.

Newly fallen fruit can be found beneath Green-thorns for several months of the year.

It is a very high branching tree with a characteristic trunk that is deeply fluted and buttressed. Branchlets have a zig-zag pattern. There are often upward-growing side branches on the trunk, giving a narrow V-shaped canopy. Very old trees spread into a wide umbrella.

Fruit The big, oval, plum-like fruit is pale brown and covered with fine hairs. The flesh is thin and bitter. It appears from November to January, and is yellowish when ripe from May. Ripe fruit is dropped with the stem attached, from May to July. (30 - 50 x 20 - 30 mm)

Spines The spines are usually, but not always, forked and very prominent, especially on sterile branches where they may have 2 - 3 prongs. The fruiting branches have thinner, straight thorns. Thorns are green with brown tips. On older branches the thorns are grey-brown.

Flowers Small, inconspicuous, scented, star-shaped flowers are covered by velvety hairs. The tree only flowers every second or third year (July to October). (20 mm)

Bark The bark is grey and smooth in young trees. In older trees it is rough and breaks into small, irregular blocks.

Leaves Compound, with two leaflets; broad and elliptic with smooth margins; central vein is slightly off-centre; leaves finely hairy when young; green to buff-green. (60 - 80 x 50 - 70 mm)

	Oct	Nov	Dec	Jan	Feb	Mar	Apr	May	Jun	Jul	Aug	Sep
Leaf	▓	▓	▓	▓	▓	▓	▓	▓	▓	▓	▓	▓
Flower	▓									▓	▓	▓
Fruit/Pod		▓	▓	▓	▓	▓	▓	▓	▓	▓		

Seasonal changes Evergreen or deciduous, depending on its locality. Trees near rivers tend to be evergreen. Owing to the presence of leaves most of the year, and the unique growth form, particularly of the trunk, it can be identified throughout the year.

KIAAT BLOODWOOD

Pterocarpus angolensis

Wild Teak

FABACEAE
PEA FAMILY

SA Tree Number 236

AFRIKAANS Kiaat **N. SOTHO** Morôtô **N. SOTHO** Mmilo (Morôtô) **TSONGA** Mvhangazi, Murotso
TSWANA Mokwa **VENDA** Mutondo **ZULU** umVangazi, umBilo

The species name **angolensis** refers to Angola.

Where you'll find this tree easily

The Kiaat Bloodwood grows singly on well-drained soils in areas with rainfall above 500 mm.

- It is easy to find this tree growing in Pretoriuskop Sourveld (B).
- This tree can also be found growing in Malelane Mountain Bushveld (C).

Ecozones where this tree occurs

A	E	I	M
B	F	J	N
C	G	K	O
D	H	L	P

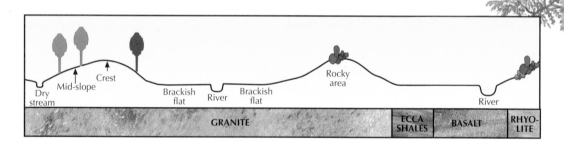

Striking features

- **The specific distribution in higher rainfall areas only, particularly Ecozone B, makes identification easy.**
- This is a large, striking, single-trunked tree with a few large branches growing upwards and outwards, bearing the leaves very high up to form an umbrella-like canopy.
- The tree has a feathery, drooping foliage.
- **The pods are characteristic and conspicuous, especially when the leaves have dropped.**
- The bark of the trunk and large branches is dark brown to black. When sections flake off there are lighter under-bark patches.

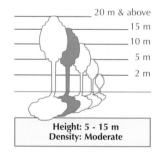

| 20 m & above |
| 15 m |
| 10 m |
| 5 m |
| 2 m |

Height: 5 - 15 m
Density: Moderate

166

KIAAT BLOODWOOD

Pterocarpus angolensis

Links with animals The leaves are eaten by elephant and kudu. Baboon eat the young pods. The seeds are eaten by baboon, monkey and tree squirrel. Elephant often push the trees over.

Human uses The wood is excellent for making furniture and curios. It is also used for canoes and building. The red gum and sap are used as a dye. The sap is used to cure cuts and sores.

Gardening It is extremely difficult to grow from seed, but it can be grown from cuttings taken in spring. It grows slowly on most soil types and is not frost-resistant.

Wood The wood is medium-hard. It varies greatly in weight and colour, but in general the sapwood is off-white to yellow, and the heartwood is light brown to dark reddish-brown.

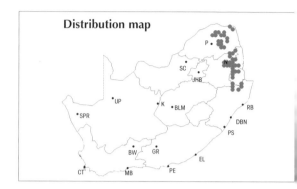

Distribution map

Look-alike trees See the comparisons of various once compound leaves on the Distinctive Striking Features, pages 57 - 58.

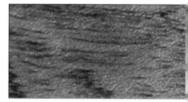

168 *The wide-spreading canopy of the large Kiaat Bloodwood makes it an attractive and distinctive tree in Ecozone B.*

GROWTH DETAILS

This is a single-trunked, high-branching tree with a few large branches growing upward and out-wards, bearing the leaves very high up to form a moderately dense, flat-to-umbrella-shaped canopy with drooping leaves.

Pods   Distinctive pods have a central seed case covered by long, stiff bristles, surrounded by a single, round, flat, papery plate. They grow singly or in bunches on long twigs. The pods ripen in late summer (February to August) and remain on the tree long after the leaves have fallen. (80 - 150 mm diameter)

Leaves   The leaves are compound and the leaflets are alternately arranged, with a single leaflet at the tip. There are 4 - 25 pairs of leaflets. The leaflets are elliptic with a prominent twisted tip and smooth margin. The leaves are shiny dark green above and have fine hairs below. They are droopy, hang down, and turn yellow before dropping early in winter. Young leaflets are soft and covered in brown hairs. (Leaf: up to 380 mm; leaflets: 20 - 70 x 25 - 45 mm)

Flowers   The striking, orange-yellow, sweet-scented, pea-shaped flowers are found in abundance in branched sprays, usually on older, darker branches. The flowers appear before, or with, the new leaves, and the flowering period lasts 2 - 3 weeks (August to November). (Spray: 100 - 200 mm long; Individual flower: 10 - 20 mm long)

Bark   The bark is dark grey to dark brown, and in very old trees it may be black. It is rough, and is fissured or cracked into lengthways sections. Red sap oozes out when the bark is damaged, and young twigs are smooth and grey and covered with hairs.

	Oct	Nov	Dec	Jan	Feb	Mar	Apr	May	Jun	Jul	Aug	Sep
Leaf												
Flower												
Fruit/Pod												

Seasonal changes   Deciduous. The tree can be identified easily in all seasons by its specific Ecozone preference, characteristic form and the presence of the pods for most of the year.

169

ECOZONE SPECIALISTS
Kiaat Bloodwood

LEBOMBO-IRONWOOD

Androstachys johnsonii

EUPHORBIACEAE	
EUPHORBIA FAMILY	**SA Tree Number 327**

AFRIKAANS Lebombo-ysterhout, Wildekweper   **SWAZI** ubukhunku   **TSONGA** Nsimbitsi
ZULU uBukhunku, umBitzani

Where you'll find this tree easily

The Lebombo-ironwood is mostly found in loose groups, but larger trees may be found growing singly.

- It is easiest to find this tree in Lebombo Mountain Bushveld (I).

- It can also be found growing in Sandveld (N).

Ecozones where this tree occurs

A	E	**I**	M
B	F	J	**N**
C	G	K	O
D	H	L	P

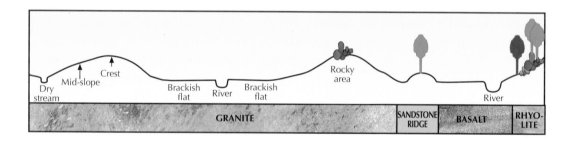

Striking features

- **The specific distribution only in Ecozones I and N makes identification easy.**
- This tree grows in large, uniform groups on the crests of hills and mountains.
- It is a single-stemmed upright tree with a sparse, grey-green canopy.
- The canopy is narrow and almost pointed, especially from a distance.
- The young branches and twigs are angular.
- The simple leaf arrangement of pairs of opposite leaves at right angles to the pairs above and below, is distinctive.
- **Edges of the leaves curl under in dry conditions.**

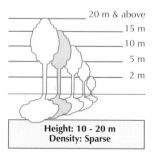

Height: 10 - 20 m
Density: Sparse

ECOZONE SPECIALISTS
Lebombo-ironwood

LEBOMBO-IRONWOOD

Androstachys johnsonii

Links with animals The leaves are eaten by a variety of game.

Human uses The wood is used for sleepers, fence posts, flooring and building. Lebombo-ironwood was used in the construction of the first huts in Punda Maria and Shingwedzi rest camps.

Gardening This is not a very attractive tree. It will grow easily but slowly from seed. It is drought-resistant but not frost-resistant.

Wood The sapwood is pale while the heartwood is dark. It is hard, durable and termite-resistant.

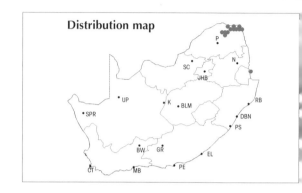

Distribution map

A forest of Lebombo-ironwoods on a sandstone ridge on the Mahonie Loop in Kruger.

GROWTH DETAILS

A single-stemmed, upright tree, with a narrow canopy formed by slender branches. Young branches and twigs are angular and their stems are covered by dense, silvery-white hairs. Side branches are initially paired, but one of the pair may die off later.

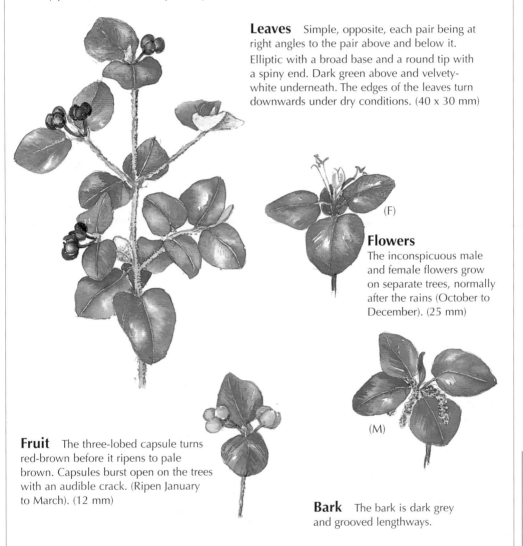

Leaves   Simple, opposite, each pair being at right angles to the pair above and below it. Elliptic with a broad base and a round tip with a spiny end. Dark green above and velvety-white underneath. The edges of the leaves turn downwards under dry conditions. (40 x 30 mm)

(F)

Flowers
The inconspicuous male and female flowers grow on separate trees, normally after the rains (October to December). (25 mm)

(M)

Fruit   The three-lobed capsule turns red-brown before it ripens to pale brown. Capsules burst open on the trees with an audible crack. (Ripen January to March). (12 mm)

Bark   The bark is dark grey and grooved lengthways.

	Oct	Nov	Dec	Jan	Feb	Mar	Apr	May	Jun	Jul	Aug	Sep
Leaf												
Flower												
Fruit/Pod												

Seasonal changes   Evergreen. This tree may look very wilted in the dry season. It is possible to identify it throughout the year by its growth form and the presence of leaves.

MANY-STEMMED ALBIZIA

Albizia petersiana   Many-stemmed false-thorn; Nala tree

MIMOSACEAE
ACACIA FAMILY   **SA Tree Number 153**

AFRIKAANS Meerstamvalsdoring   **TSONGA** Nnala   **ZULU** umNala

Where you'll find this tree easily

The Many-stemmed Albizia grows in groups.

It can only be found in Delagoa Thorn Thickets (G).

Ecozones where this tree occurs

A	E	I	M
B	F	J	N
C	G	K	O
D	H	L	P

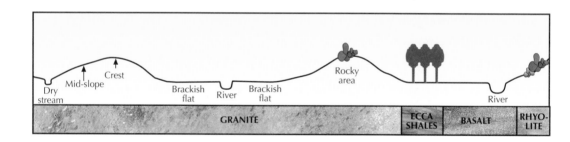

Striking features

- **The specific distribution only in Ecozone G makes identification easy.**

- It is a moderately dense, multi-stemmed, V-shaped tree.

- **In mature trees each stem is thick, like those of a single-trunked tree.**

- Twice compound leaves form a dark green canopy, with reddish leaves in spring, and yellow leaves in autumn.

- The bark is smooth and grey with a yellow tinge, and peels in narrow, flat strips.

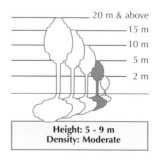

Height: 5 - 9 m
Density: Moderate

174

175

MANY-STEMMED ALBIZIA

Albizia petersiana

Links with animals The leaves are eaten by kudu, impala and elephant. The pods are eaten by giraffe, and the shoots by elephant.

Human uses The wood is generally not used because most trees are infected with woodborers.

Gardening This is not a general garden tree, as it needs specific clay soils. It is fairly drought-resistant, but susceptible to frost. This tree can be grown from seed easily, but is slow-growing.

Wood The sapwood is pale brown while the heartwood is yellow to dark brown. It is fairly hard and heavy (air-dry 830 kg/m³).

Look-alike trees This tree can be confused with other Albizias. See page 59, for comparisons.

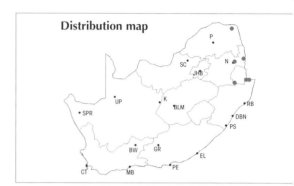
Distribution map

An early spring view when a Many-stemmed Albizia has pods, but is almost leafless, Knob Thorn Acacia nearby in flower

GROWTH DETAILS

It is multi-stemmed and low-branching, with branches growing upwards to form a V-shaped canopy of moderate density.

Flowers These are not the typical powder-puff of most Albizias. Inconspicuous flowers, white with prominent red stamens, appear after the leaves. (October to December). (30 mm diameter)

Pods Long flat, green, bean pods ripen in autumn to brown. (March to June) (120 x 16 mm)

Bark The bark is smooth and grey with a yellow tinge, and peels in narrow, flat strips.

Leaves Twice compound leaves have a pair of leaflets at the tip of each feather, and a pair of feathers at each leaf tip; leaflets are opposite, broadly elliptic to heart-shaped. The leaves are larger than those of most common Acacia species. They are red when young, turning dark green when mature and yellow in autumn. (Leaf: 60 mm; leaflet: 10 x 6 mm)

	Oct	Nov	Dec	Jan	Feb	Mar	Apr	May	Jun	Jul	Aug	Sep
Leaf												
Flower												
Fruit/Pod												

Seasonal changes Deciduous. This tree is without leaves for most of the winter and spring. Owing to its very specific Ecozone distribution and characteristic shape, this tree is easily identified all year round.

177

NARROW-LEAVED MUSTARD-TREE

Salvadora australis   **Transvaal mustard tree**

SALVADORACEAE
MUSTARD FAMILY   **SA Tree Number 621**

AFRIKAANS Smalblaarmosterdboom, Leeubos   **ZULU** umPheme, iChithamuzi

The species name **australis** means southern.

Where you'll find this tree easily

The Narrow-leaved Mustard-tree grows in groups
on the floodplains of the Shingwedzi and
Levuvhu rivers.

- This tree can be found growing on the Alluvial
  Plains (M).

Ecozones where this tree occurs

A	E	I	M
B	F	J	N
C	G	K	O
D	H	L	P

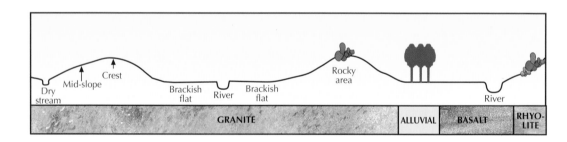

Striking features

- **The specific distribution only in Ecozone M
  makes identification easy.**
- **This small tree or shrub is pale bluish-grey.**
- It is multi-stemmed and sprawling, and
  grows in large groups.
- The branches often hang on the ground.

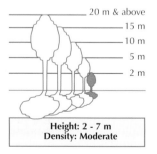

Height: 2 - 7 m
Density: Moderate

NARROW-LEAVED MUSTARD-TREE

Salvadora australis

Links with animals The fruit is readily eaten by impala, elephant and kudu. The leaves are eaten by browsers – often heavily browsed in the dry season.

Human uses Leaf extracts are used to treat eye ailments.

Gardening This is not really a garden tree, but it is evergreen and will grow in clay soils. It is probably not frost-resistant, but is fairly drought-resistant. It is not known whether it can be grown from seed, and it appears to be slow-growing.

Wood The pale brown wood is fairly hard and fine-grained.

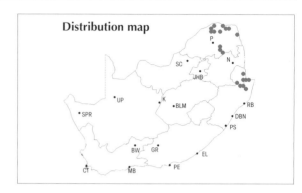

Distribution map

Although relatively low and bushy, these trees are so common that they are easy to recognise in Ecozone M.

GROWTH DETAILS

This multi-stemmed shrub has very short, grooved stems. The branches come off in an overall down-ward pattern to form an irregular, moderately dense canopy. Branchlets are covered with a pale green, furry layer.

Leaves Simple, opposite, elliptic to round, with a smooth margin. The slender leaves are thick, fleshy and covered with fine, soft, blue-grey hairs. (45 x 10 mm)

Flowers Sprays of inconspicuous, small, yellow-green flowers grow at the end of branches and at the base of the upper leaves (August to September). (2 mm)

Fruit Round to oval, berry-like, pale greenish-pink fruit often grows in profusion. The fruit is covered with fine hair, and ripens during November and December. (5 mm)

Bark The bark is light grey, with darker flecks that may break up into irregular blocks.

	Oct	Nov	Dec	Jan	Feb	Mar	Apr	May	Jun	Jul	Aug	Sep
Leaf												
Flower												
Fruit/Pod												

Seasonal changes Evergreen. This tree is therefore easy to identify throughout the year.

RED THORN ACACIA

Acacia gerrardii   Red Thorn

MIMOSACEAE
ACACIA FAMILY   **SA Tree Number 167**

AFRIKAANS Rooidoring   **N. SOTHO** Mooka   **SWAZI** siNga   **TSWANA** Moki   **VENDA** Muunga
ZULU umPhuze, umNgampunzi

The species name **gerrardii** is in honour of the English botanist, W.T. Gerrard, who collected the first specimen in KwaZulu-Natal.

Where you'll find this tree easily

The Red Thorn Acacia often grows as a single tree. On the basalts it grows in groups of smaller trees.

- It is easiest to find in groups in Knob Thorn/Marula Savannah (F).

- It can also be found in all the granite Ecozones A,B,C,D and P; as well as Lebombo Mountain Bushveld (I), Delagoa Thorn Thickets (G) and Thorn Veld (E).

Ecozones where this tree occurs

A	E	I	M
B	F	J	N
C	G	K	O
D	H	L	P

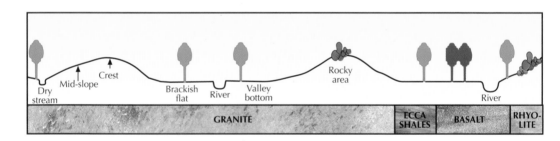

Crest — Mid-slope — Dry stream — Brackish flat — River — Valley bottom — Rocky area — River

GRANITE — ECCA SHALES — BASALT — RHYOLITE

Striking features

- **The specific distribution makes identification easy in Ecozone F.**

- This is a single-stemmed, slender Acacia, with reddish bark on younger branches and trees.

- **The leaves seem to be attached directly to the large branches, forming a continuous green sleeve that covers the entire length of most branches.**

- The canopy is sparse and often flattened on one side.

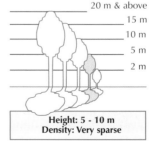

20 m & above
15 m
10 m
5 m
2 m

Height: 5 - 10 m
Density: Very sparse

182

183

RED THORN ACACIA

Acacia gerrardii

Links with animals The pods and young shoots are eaten by baboon. The bark and leaves are eaten by Black Rhino. The foliage and pods are eaten by giraffe, duiker, kudu and steenbok.

Human uses The bark contains astringent chemicals called tannins. It is used for medicinal purposes because of this property. The inner bark is used to make twine.

Gardening This can be an attractive addition to the indigenous garden and will grow in most gardens. It grows well from seed but is slow-growing. The tree will take some frost, and is drought-resistant.

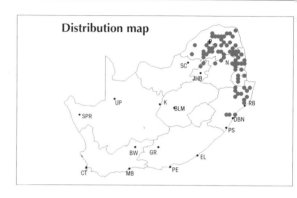

Distribution map

Wood The wood is off-white with a brown tinge and coarse-grained. It is quite hard and heavy (air-dry 900 kg/m³).

Look-alike trees This tree can be confused with other Acacias. See pages 60 - 61 for comparisons.

184   *The leaves of the Red Thorn Acacia form a sleeve along the branches and branchlets.*

GROWTH DETAILS

This is a single-stemmed, high-branching tree with a sparse, irregular canopy formed by a few upward-growing branches.

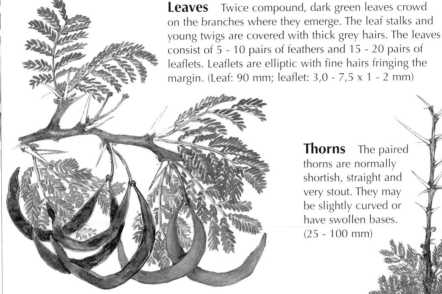

Leaves   Twice compound, dark green leaves crowd on the branches where they emerge. The leaf stalks and young twigs are covered with thick grey hairs. The leaves consist of 5 - 10 pairs of feathers and 15 - 20 pairs of leaflets. Leaflets are elliptic with fine hairs fringing the margin. (Leaf: 90 mm; leaflet: 3,0 - 7,5 x 1 - 2 mm)

Thorns   The paired thorns are normally shortish, straight and very stout. They may be slightly curved or have swollen bases. (25 - 100 mm)

Pods   The sickle-shaped, flat pods are covered by fine, grey hairs and grow in bunches. The fruit ripens from December to May, and bursts open while still on the tree. (80 - 160 x 6 - 16 mm)

Flowers   Conspicuous, round, creamy-white, sweet-scented flower-balls are crowded at the nodes, next to the thorns, amongst the leaves (October to February). The flower-ball stalks are long (30 mm) and covered with hairs. (10 - 20 mm)

Bark   The bark of the trunk and branches in older trees is dark grey to reddish. It is smooth and seamed crosswise in young trees. In older trees and branches the bark is reddish and deeply fissured or wrinkled, exposing a rusty under-layer.

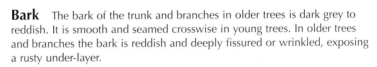

	Oct	Nov	Dec	Jan	Feb	Mar	Apr	May	Jun	Jul	Aug	Sep
Leaf	▓	▓	▓	▓	▓	▓	▓	▓				
Flower												
Fruit/Pod			▓	▓	▓	▓	▓	▓				

Seasonal changes   Deciduous. The spindly form, bark colour and texture make identification possible even in winter.

185

TALL FIRETHORN CORKWOOD

Commiphora glandulosa   **Tall common corkwood**

**BURSERACEAE
MYRRH FAMILY**   **SA Tree Number 285.1**

AFRIKAANS Grootdoringkanniedood   **TSONGA** Xifati   **TSWANA** Morôka   **VENDA** Mutalu   **ZULU** iMinyela

The species name **glandulosa** refers to the glandular hairs on the flowers and flower-stalks.

Where you'll find this tree easily

The Tall Firethorn Corkwood grows singly on well-drained soils and in rocky areas.

🌿 This tree is easy to find in Olifants Rugged Veld (J).

🌿 This tree can also be found in most other Ecozones.

Ecozones where this tree occurs

A	E	I	M
B	F	J	N
C	G	K	O
D	H	L	P

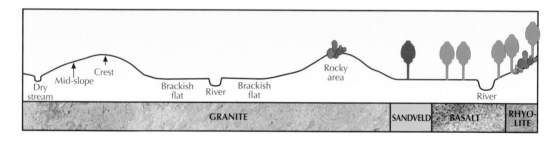

Striking features of Corkwoods

- **Corkwoods have robust, fleshy stems and branches with conspicuous, often peeling, papery bark exposing a shiny under-surface.**
- Some Corkwoods have single, while others have compound, leaves; many have spines, and the fruit is normally berry-like.

Striking features of this tree

- This tree is single-stemmed, branching profusely to form a roundish canopy.
- **The bark peels in small, straw-coloured, papery strips to expose a shiny, green under-surface.**
- The stem is obviously fleshy.
- The branchlets come off at right angles from the main stem and branches, and end in spines, giving the tree a spiky appearance.
- **The simple leaves are characteristically clustered at the base of the spines.**

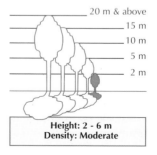

Height: 2 - 6 m
Density: Moderate

186

187

TALL FIRETHORN CORKWOOD

Commiphora glandulosa

Links with animals The fruit is eaten by yellowbilled hornbills. Young shoots and leaves are eaten by duiker and elephant.

Human uses The wood is used to make cups and buckets, and is sometimes made into other household utensils. Most Corkwoods produce aromatic resins and gums.

Gardening This tree can be planted to form a hedge. It grows fast from seed and easily from cuttings. It is fairly frost-resistant and very drought-resistant.

Look-alike trees Firethorn Corkwood *(Commiphora pyracanthoides)* is very similar, but multi-stemmed with grey-green, flaky bark; simple leaves (75 x 32 mm), may be three-leaflet compound; clustered spine-tipped side branches. The Zebra-bark Corkwood *(C. viminea)*, page 38, occurs in the far northern areas of Kruger; simple leaves have a toothed edge at top third (45 x 25 mm); leaves clustered in rosettes; bark of older trees peels in horizontal bands, with streaks of grey, corky bark in between.

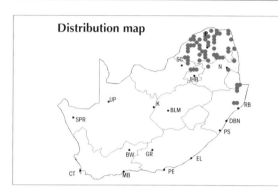

Distribution map

Wood The grey-white wood is very soft and coarsely textured.

Typical young leaves, spikes and bark of a Tall Firethorn Corkwood

GROWTH DETAILS

This is a single-stemmed tree that branches low-down to form a roundish canopy. The branches are stiff and arching and tend to hang down. The branchlets come off at right angles from the main stem and branches, and end in spines, giving the tree a spiky appearance. The young twigs are often red.

Leaves   The leaves are usually simple and found in clusters in rosette-like groups on short, spiny branchlets. The young leaves, however, are often 3-leaflet, with a big terminal and two smaller leaflets. Leaves are elliptic to broadly elliptic, with a broadly tapering tip that may be pointed, and a tapering base; they have a toothed margin. They are bright green to grey green above and paler green below. The central- and side-veins are yellow and clearly visible on the upper surface. (30 - 75 x 20 - 35 mm)

Spines   Branchlets often end in hard spines, and there are sometimes single spines that grow on the main stem or branches.

Flowers   The inconspicuous, small, slender pink to reddish, trumpet-like flowers grow in cluster-like groups on short side-branchlets. Similar female and male flowers are found on separate trees (September to October).

Fruit   The berry-like fruit is round to egg-shaped and red-green to brown when ripe. The fruit splits open to expose black and red seeds (February to April). (13 x 10 mm)

Bark   The bark is typical of many Corkwoods. It varies from grey to yellow, or sometimes even reddish, but is usually yellow-green. It peels in small, papery flakes to expose a grey-green, shiny, oily under-surface.

	Oct	Nov	Dec	Jan	Feb	Mar	Apr	May	Jun	Jul	Aug	Sep
Leaf												
Flower												
Fruit/Pod												

Seasonal changes   Deciduous. The characteristic bark and growth form of this tree makes identification possible throughout the year.

189

Find trees by Easy Habitat

ROCKY FOUR

Some trees thrive despite both the limited space and water available in Rocky Areas. Rock-lovers can often be found on Plains, or on Mountain Slopes, but always with their roots in amongst boulders or on large stones.

Rocky areas create an ideal habitat for specific trees like this Large-leaved Rock Fig *(Ficus abutilifolia)*, see page 196.

BUSHVELD CANDELABRA EUPHORBIA

Euphorbia cooperi   **Transvaal candelabra tree**

EUPHORBIACEAE
EUPHORBIA FAMILY   **SA Tree Number 346**

AFRIKAANS Noorsdoring   **N. SOTHO** Mohlotla   **SISWATI** umHlonhlo, umHlohlo
TSONGA Konde, Xihaha, Nhlohlo   **VENDA** Tshikonde-ngala   **ZULU** umPhapha euphorbia, umPhapha, umHlonhlo

The genus name **Euphorbia** is in honour of Euphorbus, physician to the King Juba of Mauritania, first century

Where you'll find this tree easily

The Bushveld Candelabra Euphorbia grows singly
in Rocky Areas, and there is often more than one
tree in the vicinity.

- It is easy to find this tree growing in the
  Lebombo Mountain Bushveld (I).

- You can also find this tree in Pretoriuskop
  Sourveld (B), in Malelane Mountain Bushveld
  (C) and in Sabie/Crocodile Thorn Thickets (D).

Ecozones where this tree occurs

A	E	I	M
B	F	J	N
C	G	K	O
D	H	L	P

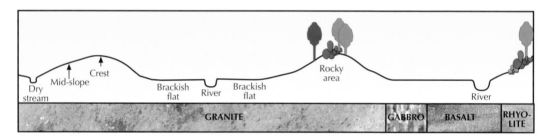

Striking features

- This is an evergreen tree with no obvious
  leaves.
- The straight, tall, bare trunk and top
  branches form a candelabra shape.
- The branches do not split again, unlike the
  Naboom Euphorbia *(Euphorbia ingens)*
  (see diagram page 194).
- Old, dead branches hang underneath the
  crown.
- **It has paired thorns on the edges of the
  angular branches.**
- **Branches are tightly constricted, forming
  a string of heart-shaped segments.**
- Holes of previous branch attachments are
  visible on the trunk.

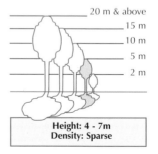

Height: 4 - 7m
Density: Sparse

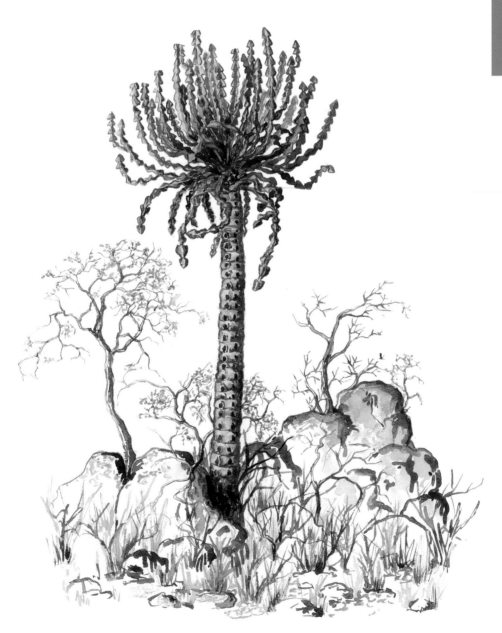

BUSHVELD CANDELABRA EUPHORBIA

Euphorbia cooperi

Links with animals Baboons eat the soft fruit and flowers. Doves eat the seeds.

Human uses The white, milky latex is an irritant to humans and animals. It is used to stupefy fish, making it possible to catch them by hand.

Gardening This tree can be used effectively in large, rocky, well-drained gardens of the drier areas, although its spines and irritant latex make it unsuitable for a family garden. It is susceptible to frost but very drought-resistant. It is slow-growing and can be grown from seed or cuttings.

Wood The wood is of no commercial use. It is white, light in weight, soft and fibrous.

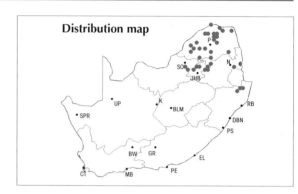

Distribution map

Look-alike trees The Rubber-hedge Euphorbia *(Euphorbia tirucalli)* page 30, has long, thin, finger-like branches. The Lebombo Euphorbia *(Euphorbia confinalis)*, page 33, has heart-shaped, segmented branches. Individual branches form many side branches that originate at the same level. The Naboom Euphorbia *(Euphorbia ingens)*, has thick, straight branches with slightly constricted, long, angular segments with virtually no thorns on the segments

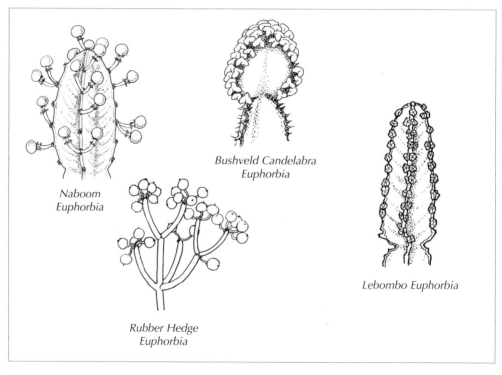

*Naboom
Euphorbia*

*Bushveld Candelabra
Euphorbia*

*Rubber Hedge
Euphorbia*

Lebombo Euphorbia

GROWTH DETAILS

The single, straight trunk is high-branching. The branches grow upwards to form a sparse candelabra-like canopy.

Fruit   The capsule-like fruit matures from green to red, and bursts open on the tree, flinging the individual seeds several metres. (10 mm)

Leaves   No visible "leaves".

Flowers   The inconspicuous, yellow-green flowers are not true flowers. They are arranged in three parallel rows, with several male flowers and one female flower per cyathium ('flower') (May to August). (4 mm)

Thorns   There are paired thorns on the edges of the angular branches. (5 - 15 mm)

Bark   The bark shows lesions of old branch attachments.

	Oct	Nov	Dec	Jan	Feb	Mar	Apr	May	Jun	Jul	Aug	Sep
Leaf												
Flower												
Fruit/Pod												

Seasonal changes   Owing to its characteristic form, this tree can be identified easily throughout the year.

LARGE-LEAVED ROCK FIG

Ficus abutilifolia

MORACEAE
MULBERRY FAMILY

SA Tree Number 63

AFRIKAANS Grootblaarrotsvy **N. SOTHO** Monokane **TSONGA** Xirhomberhombe **TSWANA** Momelantsweng
VENDA Tshikululu **ZULU** imPayi

The species name **abutilifolia** refers to the fact that the leaves resemble those of the genus Abutilon.

Where you'll find this tree easily

The Large-leaved Rock Fig grows singly in rocky areas.

- It is easiest to find this tree in the Sabie/Crocodile Thorn Thickets (D).
- You can also find this tree in most other Ecozones.

Ecozones where this tree occurs

A	E	I	M
B	F	J	N
C	G	K	O
D	H	L	P

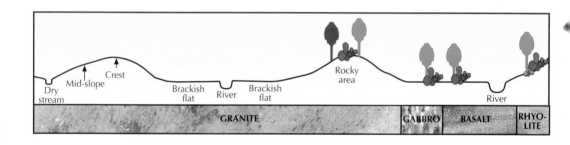

Striking features

- **It has a gnarled, yellow-white, smooth trunk with papery bark that peels off.**
- Conspicuous white roots are visible, spreading over the rock face.
- **The large leaves are smooth, heart-shaped and large with prominent veins.**

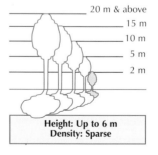

20 m & above
15 m
10 m
5 m
2 m

Height: Up to 6 m
Density: Sparse

197

LARGE-LEAVED ROCK FIG

Ficus abutilifolia

Links with animals Baboon, monkey, bushbuck, duiker, nyala and bushpig eat the fruit.

Human uses The tasty fruit is a valued food. Bark extracts are taken as strengthening tonics by men.

Gardening This tree can be used very effectively in a rocky garden. It is not frost-resistant but can withstand drought. It can be grown from cuttings and, although slow-growing, it responds well to watering in well-drained soils.

Wood The wood is light and tough. It is pale brown with a yellowish tint.

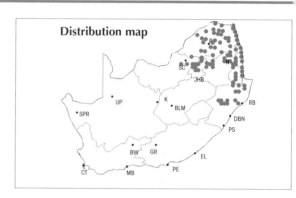

Distribution map

Look-alike tree The Red-leaved Fig *(Ficus ingens)*, page 24, is also common in Rocky Areas. The leaves are long and thin (60 - 150 x 30 - 100 mm), and new leaves are bright red. The small figs (10 - 13 mm) are dull red when ripe.

Look for the white roots growing over rocks on many Rocky Areas in the Lowveld.

GROWTH DETAILS

The single, crooked trunk branches low down at irregular angles to form a sparse canopy. All parts of the tree contain copious amounts of white latex.

Leaves   The large, simple leaves are spirally arranged or alternate, and they have a smooth margin that may be wavy. The leaves are heart-shaped to round, with a pointed tip which can be rounded. The base is distinctly, deeply lobed. Leaves are dark green above and paler below. The veins are clearly visible on both surfaces and are pale red-brown to yellow. The central vein stands out underneath. The leaf stems are long, varying from 25 to 170 mm. (Leaf: 60 -160 x 80 - 250 mm)

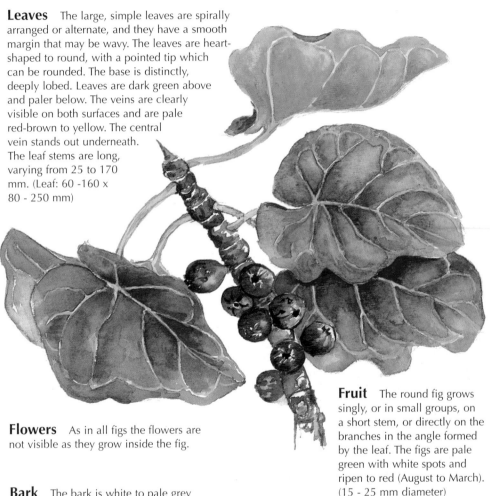

Fruit   The round fig grows singly, or in small groups, on a short stem, or directly on the branches in the angle formed by the leaf. The figs are pale green with white spots and ripen to red (August to March). (15 - 25 mm diameter)

Flowers   As in all figs the flowers are not visible as they grow inside the fig.

Bark   The bark is white to pale grey and smooth, and on older branches and trunks often flakes or peels in layers. The trunk is often twisted.

	Oct	Nov	Dec	Jan	Feb	Mar	Apr	May	Jun	Jul	Aug	Sep
Leaf												
Flower												
Fruit/Pod												

Seasonal changes   Semi-deciduous. It can be identified throughout the year by the characteristic growth form and bark colour.

199

POD-MAHOGANY

Afzelia quanzensis

CAESALPINIACEAE
FLAMBOYANT FAMILY

SA Tree Number 207

AFRIKAANS Peulmahonie   **SISWATI** umKholikholi   **TSONGA** Nxenhe   **VENDA** Mutokota
ZULU umHlakuva, umShamfuthi

The species name **quanzensis** refers to the Cuanza River in Angola.

Where you'll find this tree easily

The Pod-mahogany usually grows singly, often
on small rocky outcrops or well-drained soils.

🌿 It is easiest to find in the Sandveld (N).

🌿 It can also be found growing in Mixed
Bushwillow Woodlands (A) and, in Lebombo
Mountain Bushveld (I).

Ecozones where this tree occurs

A	E	I	M
B	F	J	N
C	G	K	O
D	H	L	P

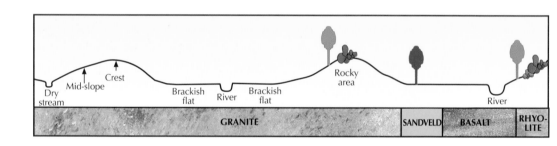

Striking features

- The habitat preference of this tree helps with
  identification.
- This is a large, prominent tree with a long,
  bare trunk and huge umbrella-like canopy.
- There are large, glossy leaves.
- **Black and red seeds are conspicuous when
  the pods burst open from April.**

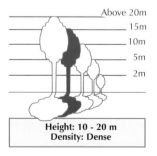

Above 20m
15m
10m
5m
2m

Height: 10 - 20 m
Density: Dense

200

POD-MAHOGANY

Afzelia quanzensis

Links with animals The leaves are eaten by elephant and duiker. The bark and shoots are eaten by elephant, and the fallen flowers are eaten by all antelope. The caterpillars of *Charaxes* butterflies eat the leaves.

Human uses The seeds are used to make necklaces. The wood is used for carpentry, wagons, railway sleepers and canoes. The roots are used for the treatment of eye ailments, bilharzia and pneumonia.

Gardening This ornamental shade tree can be very attractive in the garden, preferring well-drained soils. It is fairly drought-resistant once established, but is very sensitive to frost. This tree can be grown from seed, but is slow-growing.

Wood The sapwood is pale brown. The heartwood is dark, reddish brown with paler blotches. It is hard and heavy (air-dry 890 kg/m³).

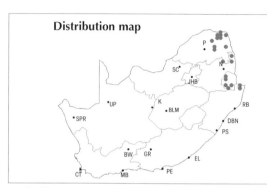

Distribution map

Look-alike trees See the comparisons of various once compound leaves on the Distinctive Striking Features, pages 57 - 58.

202

In Ecozones A, I, and N the Pod-mahogany is a striking, distinctive tree in Rocky Areas.

GROWTH DETAILS

The single, straight trunk is high-branching. The branches grow horizontally to form an umbrella-like, dense canopy.

Flowers   Conspicuous flowers, each with a single red petal and prominent stamens, grow on the ends of branches and stand upright amongst the drooping leaves. The flowers seldom form a striking display, as buds do not all open at the same time during October and November. (50 mm)

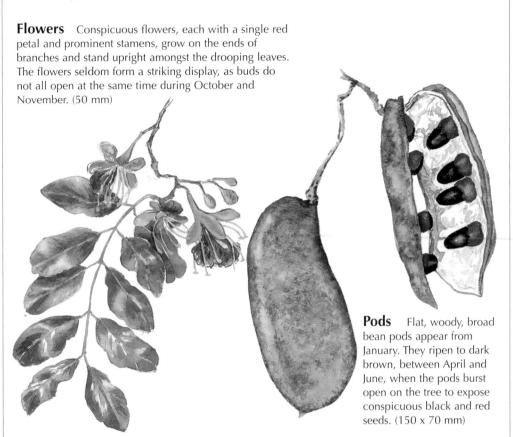

Pods   Flat, woody, broad bean pods appear from January. They ripen to dark brown, between April and June, when the pods burst open on the tree to expose conspicuous black and red seeds. (150 x 70 mm)

Leaves   Compound, alternate, with a pair of leaflets at the tip. Leaflets are elliptic with a wavy margin. The shiny, dark green leaves are coppery-red when new in spring. (Leaf: 150 - 400 mm; 4 - 7 pairs of leaflets: 55 x 30 mm)

Bark   In younger trees, the bark is mostly smooth and pale grey. In older trees it is dark grey and flakes off in irregular blocks.

	Oct	Nov	Dec	Jan	Feb	Mar	Apr	May	Jun	Jul	Aug	Sep
Leaf	■	■	■	■	■	■						■
Flower	■	■										
Fruit/Pod				■	■	■	■	■				

Seasonal changes   Deciduous. In spring the copper-coloured, glossy foliage stands out amongst the other trees. In its specific habitat, the size of the tree and the umbrella-like canopy will help with identification in winter.

203

WHITE KIRKIA

Kirkia acuminata

White seringa

SIMAROUBACEAE **TREE OF HEAVEN FAMILY**	**SA Tree Number 267**

AFRIKAANS Witsering **N. SOTHO** Modumela **TSONGA** Mvumayila **TSWANA** Modumela
VENDA Mubvumela **ZULU** umSila-omhlophe, umSilinga

The species name **acuminata** refers to the sharp, pointed leaflets.

Where you'll find this tree easily

The White Kirkia grows singly on sandstone ridges, rocky and sandy areas, but you will often find more than one growing in the vicinity.

- You will find this tree easily in Sandveld (N).
- You will also find this tree in the Lebombo Mountain Bushveld (I), Olifants Rugged Veld (J) in Mopane Shrubveld (L) and in Mopane/Bushwillow Woodlands (P).

Ecozones where this tree occurs

A	E	I	M
B	F	J	N
C	G	K	O
D	H	L	P

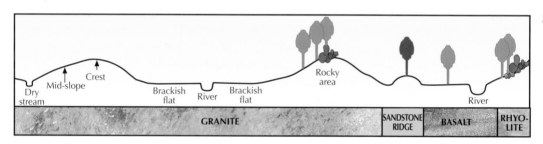

Striking features

- This is a common tree on rocky ridges.
- It has a tall, straight, single trunk.
- **This tree has a light green, fine-leaved and feathery-looking, spreading canopy.**
- The bark is light grey and smooth when young, and becomes flaky with corky knobs in older trees.
- Spectacular in autumn, the leaves turn brilliant gold and red.

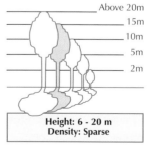

Height: 6 - 20 m
Density: Sparse

205

WHITE KIRKIA

Kirkia acuminata

Links with animals Game dig up the roots in times of drought.

Human uses Water-laden roots may be used as a source of drinking water. The wood is used for furniture and to make household goods such as bowls.

Gardening A very attractive tree, especially in autumn and spring when the leaves are very colourful. It will only grow well in well-drained soils, such as rocky outcrops in larger gardens. It is drought-resistant but not frost-resistant. It can be grown from seeds and cuttings and is fairly fast-growing when well-watered.

Wood The sapwood is light grey to whitish, and the heartwood is narrow and dark coppery to greenish-brown with dark wavy markings.

Look-alike trees See the comparisons of various once compound leaves on the Distinctive Striking Features, pages 57 - 58.

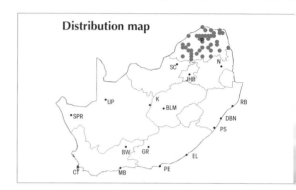

Distribution map

Spectacular autumn colours make this one of the most beautiful trees in Rocky Areas in the Lowveld

GROWTH DETAILS

It has a single, straight trunk with horizontal branches that form a sparse, spreading canopy.

Leaves The compound leaves are spirally arranged and clustered at the ends of bluntly-tipped branchlets, and have long leaf stems (50 - 100 mm). The leaf consists of 6 - 17 pairs of opposite or alternate leaflets and a leaflet at the tip. The leaflets are elliptic and have a narrowly tapering tip and a rounded base that is asymmetrically attached to the leaflet stem. The leaflets have a finely toothed margin and are bright lime-green to dark green. The leaves turn to splendid golden and red colours in autumn. The leaf stalk is 50 - 100 mm long. (Leaf: 200 - 450 mm; leaflet: 20 - 83 x 10 - 29 mm)

Fruit The small, light brown woody capsule is divided into four sections (valves) and grows in bunches. When the capsule opens, each section contains one seed. The fruit may remain on the tree for long periods, some until the next flowering season (January to September). (15 x 5 mm)

Flowers The greenish-cream to creamy-white flowers grow on long stems (up to 110 mm) in branched sprays at the ends of branchlets or in the angle formed by the leaf (October to November). (Spray: up to 200 mm long, including the flower stem)

Bark The bark is white to light grey and smooth. On older trees the bark may become rougher and break up into small, irregular blocks. The branchlets have visible leaf scars, and the trunk and older branches often have conspicuous dark, corky knobs.

	Oct	Nov	Dec	Jan	Feb	Mar	Apr	May	Jun	Jul	Aug	Sep
Leaf	■	■	■	■	■	■	■	■				
Flower	■	■										
Fruit/Pod				■	■	■	■	■	■	■	■	■

Seasonal changes Deciduous. The leaves have beautiful autumn colours. There is a long period without leaves in winter when it is more difficult to identify. New reddish leaves appear in spring.

207

Find trees by Easy Habitat

EASY RIVER TRUNKS

Many Lowveld rivers are spectacular because of the dramatic line of trees along their banks. These four trees are easily recognised because they have such distinctive trunks.

The trunks of Jackel-berry, Sycamore Fig and Marula make identification easy.

JACKAL-BERRY

Diospyros mespiliformis   Ebony Jackal-berry

EBENACEAE **EBONY FAMILY**	**SA Tree Number 606**

AFRIKAANS Jakkalsbessie **ENGLISH** Transvaal ebony   **N. SOTHO** Dithetlwa   **SISWATI** umToma
TSONGA Ntoma   **TSWANA** Mokochong   **VENDA** Muchenje   **ZULU** umThoma

Where you'll find this tree easily

The Jackal-berry grows singly along rivers
and on termite mounds in higher rainfall areas.

● This tree can be easily found in Riverine
  areas (H).

● It can also be found along larger streams of most
  other Ecozones, and away from rivers in Ecozone B.

Ecozones where this tree occurs

A	E	I	M
B	F	J	N
C	G	K	O
D	H	L	P

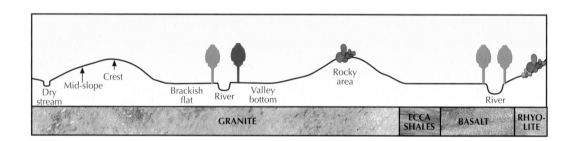

Striking features

- This is a big tree with a dense, dark green,
  roundish, spreading canopy.
- The single, massive trunk is usually gnarled
  or fluted.
- **The trunk divides into a few large branches
  that spread out close to their origin. Each
  branch is itself very thick and trunk-like.**
- The bark is black-grey, looking as though the
  tree has been burnt; bark is rough and often
  deeply grooved.
- **The leaves and fruit are characteristic.**

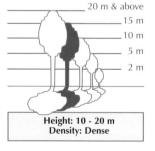

Height: 10 - 20 m
Density: Dense

211

JACKAL-BERRY

Diospyros mespiliformis

Links with animals Fruit on the tree is eaten by Green Pigeons, Brown-headed Parrots, Grey Hornbills and Purple-crested Louries. Monkey and baboon also eat fruit off the tree. Fallen fruit is eaten by kudu, impala, nyala and jackal. The leaves are eaten by elephant, kudu and eland.

Human uses The wood is used to make furniture and household articles such as pestles for grinding maize. The fruit is edible. Fruit, leaves and roots contain tannins and have medicinal uses in the treatment of wounds and against internal parasites. Extracts of various parts of the tree have antibiotic properties.

Gardening This very attractive shade tree can enhance any big garden. It will grow best in well-drained soils. This tree cannot take severe frost and needs to be well watered. It grows slowly but easily from seed.

Look-alike trees This tree can be confused with the Tamboti *(Spirostachys africana)* page 222, which has very dark distinctive blocky bark, and small, simple leaves with toothed edges. Tambotis often grow in groups, and young trees have pale bark and spines (see page 23).

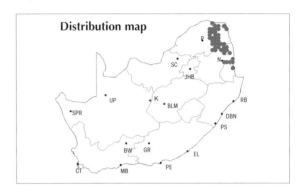

Distribution map

Wood The sapwood is pale. The heartwood is dark-brown, fine-grained, hard and heavy (air-dry 850 kg/m³).

Young Jackal-berry trees with old, yellow leaves; along a river in September

GROWTH DETAILS

The single, gnarled trunk is high-branching. Huge branches leave the main trunk horizontally to form a wide-spreading, dense, round canopy.

Leaves   Simple, alternate, elliptic with a conspicuous, closely waved margin. Dark green above and paler green below. Young leaves are reddish, whilst old are yellowish. (80 x 30 mm)

Flowers   Inconspicuous, fragrant, creamy-white flowers appear after the leaves (October to December). Male and female flowers grow on different trees. (12 mm)

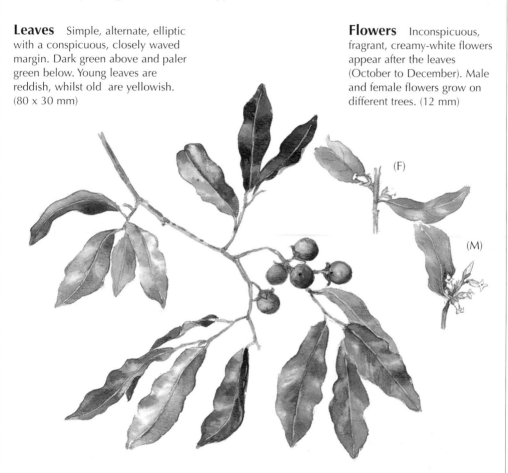

(F)

(M)

Fruit   Round, green berries take up to a year to ripen and are therefore often present in large numbers. They turn yellow when ripe during September and October. (20 mm)

Bark   The bark is black-grey, looking as though the tree has been burnt; it is rough and often deeply grooved.

	Oct	Nov	Dec	Jan	Feb	Mar	Apr	May	Jun	Jul	Aug	Sep
Leaf	■	■	■	■	■	■	■	■	■	■		■
Flower	■	■	■									
Fruit/Pod	■			■	■	■	■	■	■	■	■	■

Seasonal changes   Deciduous. However, this tree is seldom without leaves, as new leaves appear at the same time as the old ones fall. New young leaves are reddish when they appear in spring; old leaves are yellow and brown.

213

NYALA-TREE

Xanthocercis zambesiaca

FABACEAE	
PEA FAMILY	**SA Tree Number 241**

AFRIKAANS Njalaboom   **TSONGA** Nhlahu   **TSWANA** Motha

Where you'll find this tree easily

The Nyala-tree grows singly on alluvial soils of the larger rivers as well as in deep, sandy soils. It is more common in the north.

- It is easiest to find this tree growing in Riverine areas (H).

- You can also find this tree growing along rivers and larger streams of the Sabie/Crocodile Thorn Thickets (D) and Alluvial Plains (M).

Ecozones where this tree occurs

A	E	I	M
B	F	J	N
C	G	K	O
D	H	L	P

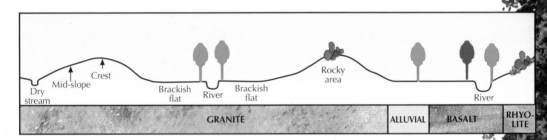

Striking features

- This is a large, dense, evergreen, riverine tree that branches low down.
- The massive trunk often appears to be composed of multiple stems buttressed together.
- **The trunk is gnarled and crooked with clusters of leaves growing directly from the trunk.**
- **The relatively small, compound leaves are not easily, individually, distinguished from a distance of 30 metres.**

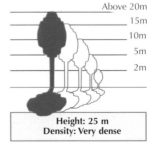

Above 20m
15m
10m
5m
2m

Height: 25 m
Density: Very dense

215

NYALA-TREE

Xanthocercis zambesiaca

Links with animals The fruit is eaten by a wide variety of birds, as well as by monkey and baboon. Elephant and buck eat fruit that has fallen to the ground.

Human uses The fruits are edible when fresh, and are used to make a porridge when dried.

Gardening An ornamental shade tree that grows well in clay soils in large gardens, it is not frost- or drought-resistant. It can be grown from seed but is a slow grower.

Look-alike trees Riverine trees with compound leaves can be confused with one another. See the comparisons of various once compound leaves on the Distinctive Striking Features, pages 57 - 58.

Distribution map

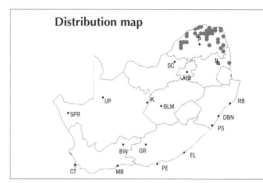

Wood The wood is white, hard and heavy.

The massive, dramatic skeleton of the Nyala-tree is visible through new spring leaves.

GROWTH DETAILS

It has a single, gnarled trunk branching low down. Branches come off horizontally and droop at the ends to form a wide-spreading, round, dense canopy. Clusters of leaves grow directly from the trunk.

Leaves Compound, with a single leaflet at the tip, alternate, oval, with smooth margins. The leaves are dark green and shiny. There are up to 7 pairs of leaflets with a terminal leaflet. (Leaf: 120 mm; leaflet: 55 x 20 mm)

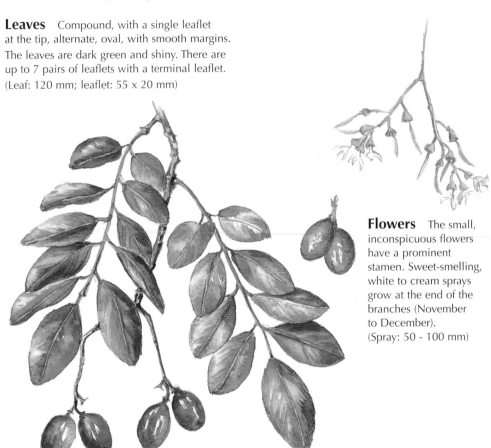

Flowers The small, inconspicuous flowers have a prominent stamen. Sweet-smelling, white to cream sprays grow at the end of the branches (November to December). (Spray: 50 - 100 mm)

Fruit The grape-like fruits are green and turn dark brown from March. They stay on the tree until the following spring. (25 x 20 mm)

Bark The bark is dark grey tinged with yellow. It tends to be rough and does not peel, but is cracked into small, irregular squares.

	Oct	Nov	Dec	Jan	Feb	Mar	Apr	May	Jun	Jul	Aug	Sep
Leaf												
Flower												
Fruit/Pod												

Seasonal changes Evergreen to semi-deciduous. This tree can be recognised throughout the year.

217

SYCAMORE FIG

Ficus sycomorus

Common cluster fig

MORACEAE	
MULBERRY FAMILY	**SA Tree Number 66**

AFRIKAANS Sycomorusvy **N. SOTHO** Motoro, Magoboya **TSONGA** Nkuwa **VENDA** Muhuyu-lukuse
ZULU umNcongo, umNconjiwa, umKhiwane

The term **sycomorus** is derived from the Greek word meaning fig-mulberry.

Where you'll find this tree easily

The Sycamore Fig grows singly along perennial rivers.

- It is easiest to find this tree along rivers in the Sabie/Crocodile Thorn Thickets (D).

- You can also find this tree in Pretoriuskop Sourveld (B), and along rivers of the Knob Thorn/Marula Savannah (F) and in Olifants Rugged Veld (J).

Ecozones where this tree occurs

A	E	I	M
B	F	J	N
C	G	K	O
D	H	L	P

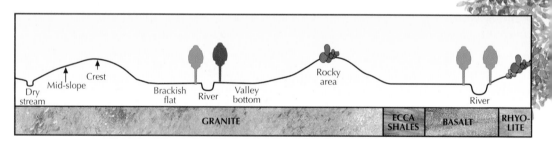

Striking features

- This is a very large tree seen on the banks of rivers with permanent water.
- **The yellow-pinkish, smooth bark has peeling, papery sections.**
- There is a fluted, relatively short but massive trunk, often buttressed and gnarled.
- The canopy is wide with pale branches clearly visible between the leaves, even to the edges of the tree.
- **Figs grow in heavily branched masses on the trunk and main branches.**

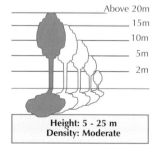

Height: 5 - 25 m
Density: Moderate

219

SYCAMORE FIG

Ficus sycomorus

Links with animals The fruit is eaten off the tree by baboon, monkey and bushbaby. Bushpig, warthog, rhino and many antelope pick up fallen fruit. The fruit is the favourite food of Green Pigeons, Brown-headed Parrots, hornbills, barbets and rollers.

Human uses The trunk is used to make drums such as those seen at the Skukuza restaurant.

Wood The sapwood is grey and the heartwood is yellow-brown. It is a rare wood, not suitable for turned articles, but varnishes well.

Look-alike trees All figs have similarities that can be confusing. The Sycamore Fig in the Lowveld is almost always on river banks, or occasionally on an old termite mound, and is often massive; the yellow-pink-green tinge to the bark is distinctive.

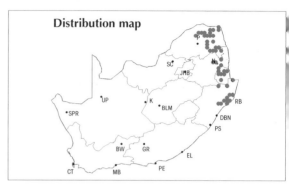

Distribution map

220

A handsome giant Sycamore Fig, along a river bank

It has a single, fluted or buttressed, relatively short trunk that branches low down. The horizontal branches form a moderately dense, wide-spreading canopy.

Leaves   Simple, clustered around the branchlets. The almost round leaves are thin, hard and hairy and rough like a cat's tongue. (80 x 50 mm)

Flowers   Flowers grow inside the fruit and are not visible – this is a feature of all figs.

Fruit   The plum-like fruit, which grows in dense clusters on the main stem and thick branches, is green to yellow-brown, turning pinkish when ripe. Fruit ripens throughout the year and trees can produce up to four crops annually. (30 mm)

Bark   The bark is smooth and peels in small papery patches to expose a pinkish, yellowish or greenish under-surface.

	Oct	Nov	Dec	Jan	Feb	Mar	Apr	May	Jun	Jul	Aug	Sep
Leaf	■	■	■	■	■	■	■	■	■	■	■	■
Flower												
Fruit/Pod	■	■	■	■	■	■	■	■	■	■	■	■

Seasonal changes   Evergreen to semi-deciduous. In years with even minimal rainfall, this tree does not lose all its leaves at once. The leaves turn yellow and fall throughout the year.

TAMBOTI

Spirostachys africana

EUPHORBIACEAE
EUPHORBIA FAMILY

SA Tree Number 341

AFRIKAANS Tambotie **N. SOTHO** Morekuri (Modiba) **SISWATI** umThombotsi, umThombothi
TSONGA Ndzopfori **TSWANA** Morukuru **VENDA** Muonze **ZULU** umThombothi, iJuqa, uvBanda

The species name **africana** means of Africa.

Where you'll find this tree easily

The Tamboti tree grows singly along the rivers, as well as in dense groups of smaller trees in the brack areas.

- This tree can most easily be found in mixed Bushwillow Woodlands (A) and in Riverine areas (H).
- It can also be found in most other Ecozones.

Ecozones where this tree occurs

A	E	I	M
B	F	J	N
C	G	K	O
D	H	L	P

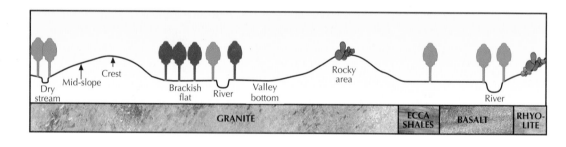

Striking features

- This tree has a straight, upright, single, bare trunk.
- There is a dense, rounded, narrow canopy.
- **The bark is characteristically dark to black, thick, rough and neatly cracked into regular rectangles.**
- Old, red leaves are often visible among the mature, green leaves.
- It is often in groups of a few big trees growing fairly close together along a river or stream.

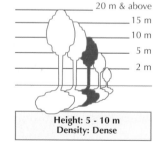

Height: 5 - 10 m
Density: Dense

Largest tree currently registered

Diameter: 1,85 m

Girth: 5,81 m

Height: 13 m

S van Schalkwyk, Diepkuil,
Dist. Thabazimbi

TAMBOTI

Spirostachys africana

Small amounts of a poisonous, extremely irritant, milky latex are produced when branches are broken.

Links with animals The fruit is eaten by Crested Guineafowl, francolin and doves. Black Rhino eat young branches. Dry, fallen leaves are eaten by Vervet Monkey, kudu, nyala and impala.

Human uses The very valuable wood produces exceptional furniture. The poisonous latex is used to stupefy fish, making them easier to catch, but can cause severe illness if the wood is used to fuel cooking fires.

Gardening This tree can be very attractive in a large garden. It is fairly drought- and frost-resistant. It grows well from seed but slowly.

Look-alike trees The bark is as dark as that of the Jackal-berry (*Diospyros mespiliformis*), page 210. Jackal-berry bark looks burnt and is irregularly coarse. Tamboti bark is also very dark, but the blocks are neat, regular rectangles.

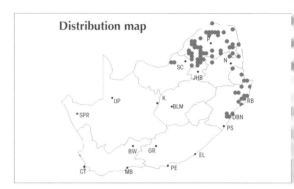

Distribution map

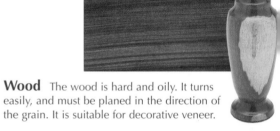

Wood The wood is hard and oily. It turns easily, and must be planed in the direction of the grain. It is suitable for decorative veneer.

Tamboti often grow in groups along edges of smaller rivers and streams

GROWTH DETAILS

The single, straight trunk is high-branching with branches growing upwards to form a narrow, dense canopy. Young trees may have multiple trunks and spines of up to 150 mm.

Leaves Simple, alternate, spiral, elliptic leaves have a finely serrated margin. Red leaves are often visible among the green leaves throughout the year. (50 x 25 mm)

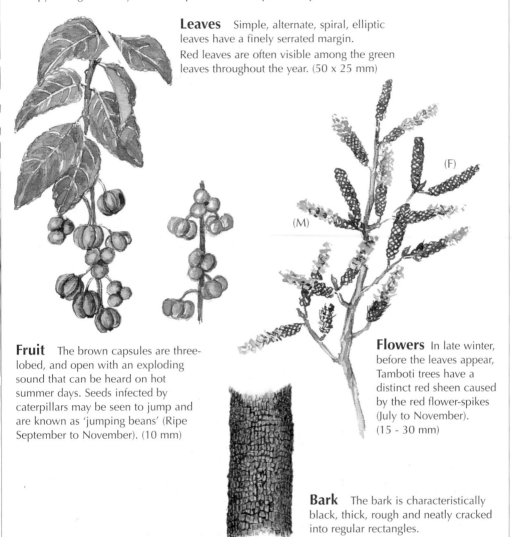

(F)

(M)

Fruit The brown capsules are three-lobed, and open with an exploding sound that can be heard on hot summer days. Seeds infected by caterpillars may be seen to jump and are known as 'jumping beans' (Ripe September to November). (10 mm)

Flowers In late winter, before the leaves appear, Tamboti trees have a distinct red sheen caused by the red flower-spikes (July to November). (15 - 30 mm)

Bark The bark is characteristically black, thick, rough and neatly cracked into regular rectangles.

	Oct	Nov	Dec	Jan	Feb	Mar	Apr	May	Jun	Jul	Aug	Sep
Leaf	■	■	■	■	■	■	■					■
Flower	■	■								■	■	■
Fruit/Pod	■	■										■

Seasonal changes Deciduous to evergreen, depending on where it grows. Leaves turn red before dropping in winter and the fresh new leaves in spring are pale green. The bark is characteristic making identification possible even when no leaves are present.

225

Find trees by Easy Habitat

EASY RIVER CANOPIES

The trees along Lowveld rivers grow spectacularly large, and they are often crowded together. None-the-less, once you have learnt to recognise the Big Six, these seven trees have distinctive foliage that should make clear Search Images easy to develop.

This Sausage-tree, along the Sabie River, cannot be mistaken for any other tree because of the presence of the distinctive fruit, and the stiff once compound leaves.

MATUMI

Brèonadia salicina

RUBIACEAE **GARDENIA FAMILY**	**SA Tree Number 684**

AFRIKAANS Mingerhout **SISWATI** umHlume **TSONGA** Mhlume **VENDA** Mut u-lume
ZULU umFala, umHlume

The species name **salicina** means having leaves like a willow.

Where you'll find this tree easily

The Matumi grows in rocky areas in rivers.

- It is easiest to find this tree in Riverine areas (H).
- This tree can also be found growing near the larger streams of the Sabie/Crocodile Thorn Thickets (D), in Olifants Rugged Veld (J) and on Alluvial Plains (M).

Ecozones where this tree occurs

A	E	I	M
B	F	J	N
C	G	K	O
D	H	L	P

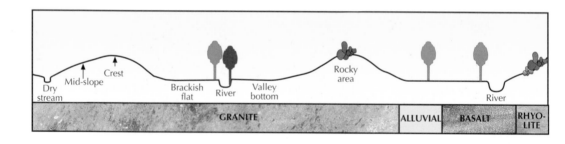

Striking features

- **This single-trunked tree overhangs large, flowing rivers and is easy to identify whether small or huge.**
- It has an irregular, narrow canopy of fresh, shiny, green leaves.
- **Leaves are thin and lancet-shaped, and are crowded at the end of the branches.**
- The leaves tend to grow upwards like the leaves of a pineapple.

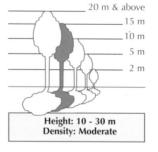

Height: 10 - 30 m
Density: Moderate

229

MATUMI

Breonadia salicina

Human uses The bark is used for stomach complaints. The wood is used for flooring, boats, canoes and furniture. It is also used for building huts and cattle kraals.

Gardening The ornamental Matumi needs very well-watered soils as found along large ponds or streams. It is not frost- or drought-resistant. It can be grown from seed in coarse sandy soils, and will grow fairly fast.

Wood The wood is yellowish with brown markings and has an oily smell. It is very hard, fine-grained and heavy (air-dry 1 026 kg/m³).

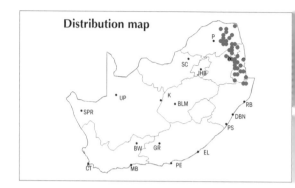

Distribution map

Matumis are conspicuous growing right on the edges of rivers, often in Rocky Areas.

230

GROWTH DETAILS

Unlike many other trees in this book, this tree is easy to identify, even when small and young. The single, straight trunk often branches high up – the branches tend to grow upwards to form a moderately dense, irregular, narrow crown. The tree may also branch low down to form a wide-spreading, irregular canopy.

Leaves Simple, narrow, elliptic, with a smooth margin. Crowns of four leaves clustered at the ends of branches tend to grow upwards. The leathery leaf is green above and light green below while new leaves are pale yellow-green.
(175 x 35 mm)

Flowers Inconspicuous, small, light yellow balls of little flowers grow in the leaf origin from November to March. (20 mm)

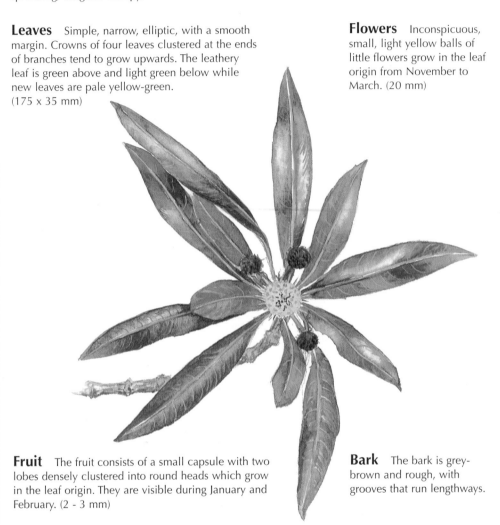

Fruit The fruit consists of a small capsule with two lobes densely clustered into round heads which grow in the leaf origin. They are visible during January and February. (2 - 3 mm)

Bark The bark is grey-brown and rough, with grooves that run lengthways.

	Oct	Nov	Dec	Jan	Feb	Mar	Apr	May	Jun	Jul	Aug	Sep
Leaf												
Flower												
Fruit/Pod												

Seasonal changes Evergreen. This tree does not lose its leaves in winter and can be identified throughout the year.

231

NATAL-MAHOGANY

Trichilia emetica

MELIACEAE
MAHOGANY FAMILY

SA Tree Number 301

AFRIKAANS Rooiessenhout   **N. SOTHO** Mmaba   **SISWATI** umKhuhlu   **TSONGA** Nkuhlu
TSWANA Mosikiri   **VENDA** Mutshikili, Mutuhu   **ZULU** umKhuhlu, uMathunzini, iGwolo

The term **emetica** refers to the bark being used to induce vomiting.

Where you'll find this tree easily

The Natal-mahogany grows singly along the larger rivers.

- This tree can most commonly be found in Riverine areas (H).
- It can also be found along rivers and larger streams of the Sabie/Crocodile Thorn Thickets (D), Knob Thorn/Marula Savannah (F), Olifants Rugged Veld (J) and on Alluvial Plains (M).

Ecozones where this tree occurs

A	E	I	M
B	F	J	N
C	G	K	O
D	H	L	P

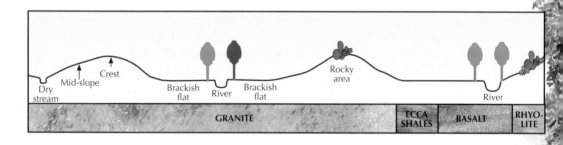

Striking features

- **This large tree is striking even from afar because its dense, deep green, glossy foliage allows virtually no branching to be visible from the outside.**
- This is a sturdy, single-trunked, low-branching tree with a rounded canopy.
- **The leaf shape and seeds are characteristic.**

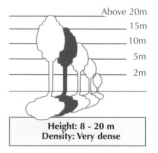

Above 20m
15m
10m
5m
2m

Height: 8 - 20 m
Density: Very dense

Largest tree currently registered

Diameter: 1,36 m
Girth: 4,27 m
Height: 14 m

J Nell
Brakspruit,
Dist. Barberton

233

NATAL-MAHOGANY

Trichilia emetica

Links with animals Baboon, monkey and nyala eat the fruit. Seeds are eaten by Crowned, Grey and Trumpeter Hornbills. Fish such as barbel eat seeds that fall into the water. Kudu and giraffe eat the young leaf shoots. The caterpillars of several species of butterfly eat the leaves.

Human uses The wood is used to make furniture, fish-floats, dugout canoes and musical instruments. The bark is used for medicinal purposes. The seeds are poisonous, and oil is extracted from the seeds.

Gardening This dense, evergreen, ornamental tree provides good shade in a garden. It will grow best in fertile soils, and is not frost- or drought-resistant; can be grown easily from seed or cuttings; will grow fast when well-watered. If seeds are used, plant while still fresh.

Wood The colour varies from pinkish-brown to brownish-grey to yellow. It holds nails well and planes smoothly. Though not suitable for turning, it polishes well and varnishes readily.

Distribution map

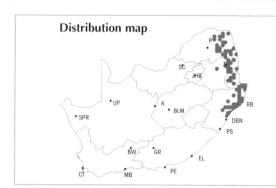

Look-alike trees
Riverine trees with compound leaves can be confused with one another. See the comparisons of various once compound leaves o the Distinctive Striking Features, pages 57 - 58.

The exceptionally dark, dense and evenly round canopy makes the Natal-mahogan
easy to recognise along river

GROWTH DETAILS

It has a single, straight trunk, high-branching to form a very dense, rounded canopy.

Leaves The large, alternate, compound leaves are crowded towards the ends of branchlets and twigs. They have 3 - 5 pairs of leaflets, with a single leaflet at the tip. The leaflets are dark green above and slightly paler below with brownish hairs, particularly along the 13 -16 side veins. Leaflets are elliptic with a tapering, rounded tip and base. They are opposite or sub-opposite, with the lower pair smaller than the rest. New leaves are shiny, red-brown, and turn very bright lime-green before darkening. (Leaf: 350 - 500 mm; end leaflet: 150 - 160 x 55 mm)

Fruit The dry, grey-green, capsules grow in bunches. When mature the capsule bursts open to show striking black seeds wrapped in bright red pulp   (November to April). (45 x 30 mm)

Flowers Small, green, sweet-smelling, trumpet-shaped flowers appear in dense sprays at the ends of the branches (August to October). (16 mm)

Bark The bark is dark brown, fairly smooth, but becoming slightly grooved in older trees.

	Oct	Nov	Dec	Jan	Feb	Mar	Apr	May	Jun	Jul	Aug	Sep
Leaf												
Flower												
Fruit/Pod												

Seasonal changes Evergreen. Owing to the intense green of the leaves, and the density of the foliage, this tree stands out amongst other riverine trees all year round.

235

RIVER BUSHWILLOW

Combretum erythrophyllum

COMBRETACEAE
BUSHWILLOW FAMILY

SA Tree Number 536

AFRIKAANS Riviervaderlandswilg   **N. SOTHO** Modibo   **TSWANA** Modubunoka, Mokhukhu
VENDA Muvuvhu, Mugwiti   **XHOSA** umDubu   **ZULU** umBondwe, umDubu

The term **erythrophyllum** refers to the red colour of the leaf in autumn.

Where you'll find this tree easily

The River Bushwillow grows in groups along the
perennial rivers.

- It is easiest to find this tree growing in Riverine
  areas (H).
- It is most common in the riverine areas of the
  Sabie/Crocodile Thorn Thickets (D).

Ecozones where this tree occurs

A	E	I	M
B	F	J	N
C	G	K	O
D	H	L	P

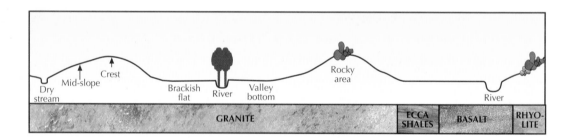

Striking features

- It is usually a multi-stemmed tree with several
  thick, often-crooked stems growing upright, or
  spreading.
- **The trunk and larger branches tend to meander,
  and old stems are often bumpy with irregular
  swellings, like cellulite.**
- The bark is smooth, pale yellowish and grey-
  brown, and flakes in irregular patches to expose
  rich, apricot coloured under-bark.
- **It has typical, four-winged, bushwillow pods.**
- In the outer canopy new shoots are perpendicular.
  They carry pairs of simple, opposite leaves
  growing upright in a tight V-shape.

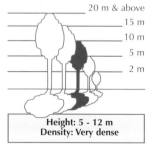

Height: 5 - 12 m
Density: Very dense

Largest tree currently registered

Diameter: 1,21 m
Girth: 3,80 m
Height: 16 m

WGF Neetling, Riverside Estate, Dist. Pretoria

RIVER BUSHWILLOW

Combretum erythrophyllum

Links with animals This is not a very palatable tree, but leaves are eaten by giraffe and elephant. Pied Barbets seem to be one of the few bird species that eat the seeds.

Human uses The wood is used for timber. The seeds are poisonous.

Gardening It is very attractive, fast-growing garden plant that grows well from seed. It is fairly frost-resistant after about two years.

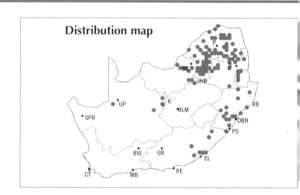

Distribution map

The lumpy trunk of an older, bigger River Bushwillow looks like cellulite on fat thighs!

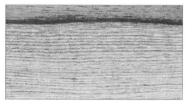

Wood The yellow wood has a straight grain, turns well ands is suitable for carving.

Look-alike trees The Water Nuxia *(Nuxia oppositifolia)* page 248 has simple elliptic leaves, but they are narrower, and the top one third is toothed and wavy.

GROWTH DETAILS

This is a multi-stemmed tree with several thick, often-crooked stems growing upright, or spreading. The branches are low down and they form a very dense, irregular canopy of long, drooping branches, often covering the stem and hanging over the water.

Flowers Roundish spikes of small, inconspicuous, cream to yellow-green, sweet-scented flowers appear just after the new leaves (August to November). (20 x 10 mm)

Leaves Simple; generally opposite towards the ends of new branches, but may form clusters. Narrow and elliptic with a sharp tip. The margins are smooth.
New leaves are shiny, yellow-green that deepens to darker shiny-green as the leaf matures. Leaves are slightly hairy underneath and they turn red in autumn. (50 - 100 x 20 - 50 mm)

Pods Abundant, small, four-winged pods turn light brown when ripe from January, and often stay on the tree until the next flowers appear in August. (10 - 15 mm)

Bark The bark is smooth on a lumpy trunk; grey to greenish with patches of orange under-bark, stems often covered by foliage in smaller trees, and then not clearly visible.

	Oct	Nov	Dec	Jan	Feb	Mar	Apr	May	Jun	Jul	Aug	Sep
Leaf	■	■	■	■	■	■	■	■	■			
Flower	░	░									░	░
Fruit/Pod				■	■	■	■	■	■	■	■	

Seasonal changes Deciduous. These trees only grow along rivers. Therefore it should be possible to identify them, as long as the pods are present.

239

RIVER THORN ACACIA

Acacia robusta   Brack Thorn Acacia

**MIMOSACEAE
ACACIA FAMILY**   **SA Tree Number 183.1**

AFRIKAANS Brakdoring   **N. SOTHO** Moku   **TSONGA** Munga, Mungamazi   **TSWANA** Moga
ZULU umNgamanzi

The species name **robusta** refers to the robust growth form of the tree.

Where you'll find this tree easily

The River Thorn Acacia grows singly, usually
along rivers.

- It is easiest to find in Riverine
  areas (H).

- It can also be found in the granite Ecozones A,
  B, C and D, as well as Olifants Rugged Veld (J)
  and Alluvial Plains (M).

Ecozones where this tree occurs

A	E	I	M
B	F	J	N
C	G	K	O
D	H	L	P

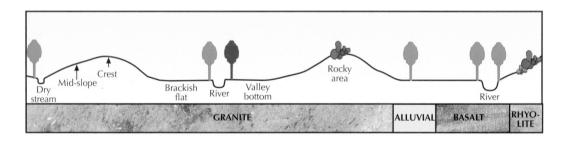

Striking features

- This is a large, upright Acacia, with dense,
  dark green, feathery foliage, forming a
  spreading canopy.
- The branches stay thick, even towards their
  ends.
- **The leaves are relatively long and droopy for
  an Acacia.**
- **There are prickly, dark "cushions" at the base
  of the new thorns and leaves.**
- The flower-balls are creamy-white and can be
  seen very early in spring.
- The pods are thick and hang from the tree in
  prominent bunches.

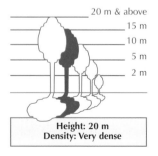

20 m & above
15 m
10 m
5 m
2 m

**Height: 20 m
Density: Very dense**

**Largest tree currently
registered**

Diameter: 1,45 m

Girth: 4,55 m

Height: 16 m

Nwanedi Resort
Venda

RIVER THORN ACACIA

Acacia robusta

Links with animals The leaves are browsed by kudu. Flowers attract bees and butterflies.

Human uses The underbark is used to make twine. Edible wood borer beetles are found in the wood. The bark is used for tanning.

Gardening This tree can be very attractive in a well-watered, warm garden. It will grow very fast from seed.

Wood The wood is pale with a dark heart. It is very tough, but not good for timber.

Look-alike trees This tree can be confused with other Acacias. See page 60 - 61 for comparisons.

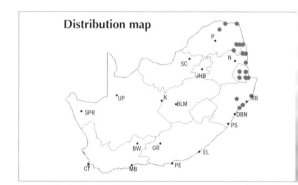

Distribution map

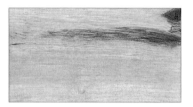

Later in summer the foliage colour deepens, from this bright, pale green of spring.

GROWTH DETAILS

This is a single-stemmed tree that divides into numerous large, upward-spreading branches, forming a dense, spreading canopy. Branches are thickened even towards their extremities, with the thick branches clearly visible in the canopy, giving the tree a robust appearance.

Pods   The slender, slightly sickle-shaped pods are rounded at the tip. Pods grow in bunches, are dark brown and burst open on the tree when ripe (October to February). (130 x 20 mm)

Leaves   Twice compound; tend to be grouped near thorns where they are clumped on cushions, but often not the same cushion as the thorns. Leaflets come off the leaf-stem at an acute angle and tend to look half-closed. Leaves consist of 2 - 6 feathers, each with 10 - 25 pairs of leaflets. (Leaf: 130 mm x 70 mm; leaflet: 12 x 3 mm)

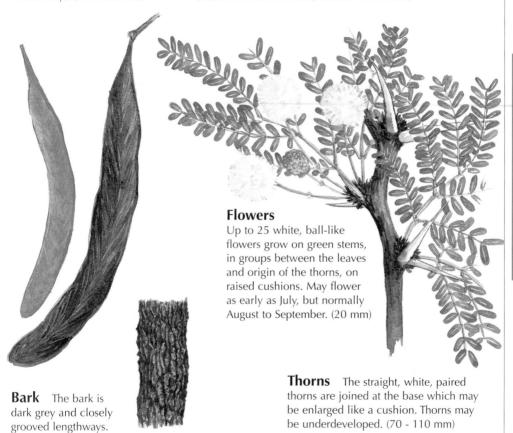

Flowers
Up to 25 white, ball-like flowers grow on green stems, in groups between the leaves and origin of the thorns, on raised cushions. May flower as early as July, but normally August to September. (20 mm)

Bark   The bark is dark grey and closely grooved lengthways.

Thorns   The straight, white, paired thorns are joined at the base which may be enlarged like a cushion. Thorns may be underdeveloped. (70 - 110 mm)

	Oct	Nov	Dec	Jan	Feb	Mar	Apr	May	Jun	Jul	Aug	Sep
Leaf	■	■	■	■	■							
Flower												
Fruit/Pod	■	■	■	■	■							

Seasonal changes   Deciduous. The dark cushions remain on the branches even after the leaves have dropped and make identification, on close inspection, possible even in winter.

243

SAUSAGE-TREE

Kigelia africana

BIGNONIACEAE
JACARANDA FAMILY

SA Tree Number 678

AFRIKAANS Worsboom   **N. SOTHO** Pidiso   **SISWATI** umVongotsi, umVongoti   **TSONGA** Mpfungurhu
TSWANA Moporota   **ZULU** umBongothi, uVunguti, umBele-le-wendlovu

The species name **africana** means of Africa.

Where you'll find this tree easily

The Sausage-tree grows singly along perennial
rivers, and may also be found further from rivers
in the higher rainfall areas.

- It is easiest to find this tree in Riverine
  areas (H).

- You will also find this tree along rivers and large
  drainage lines of the Mixed Bushwillow
  Woodlands (A), in Pretoriuskop Sourveld (B),
  Sabie/Crocodile Thorn Thickets (D), Knob
  Thorn/Marula Savannah (F) and Alluvial Plains (M).

Ecozones where this tree occurs

A	E	I	M
B	F	J	N
C	G	K	O
D	H	L	P

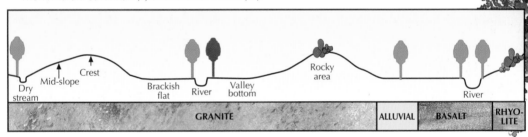

Dry stream | Mid-slope | Crest | Brackish flat | River | Valley bottom | Rocky area | River

GRANITE | ALLUVIAL | BASALT | RHYO-LITE

Striking features

- This is a large, riverine tree with a huge,
  low-branching trunk.
- The leaves are compound, large, leathery,
  and rigid.
- **The unique sausage-like fruit is visible most
  of the year, although not all trees carry
  fruit.**
- **The very prominent red-maroon flowers,
  that appear between July and October,
  make this tree easy to identify.**

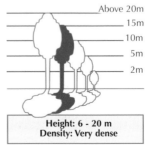

Above 20m
15m
10m
5m
2m

Height: 6 - 20 m
Density: Very dense

SAUSAGE-TREE

Kigelia africana

Links with animals Ripe fruit is eaten by baboon, monkey, porcupine and bushpig. The leaves are sometimes eaten by elephant and kudu. The flowers are very palatable and many buck species, such as nyala, impala and kudu, feed on fallen flowers. The nectar is drunk by baboon, monkey, sunbirds and insects. The caterpillars of the Charaxes butterflies feed on the trees.

Human uses The fruit is poisonous and inedible when green, but is used to brew beer when ripe. The seeds are fried and eaten. The wood is used for making canoes.

Gardening This is a lovely, ornamental shade tree for the larger garden. It is very susceptible to frost, especially when young, and is not drought-resistant. It is fast-growing and can be grown from seed.

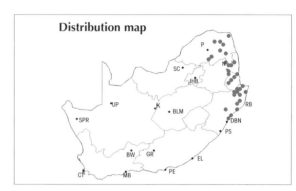

Distribution map

Wood The wood is whitish to yellowish or pale brown. There is no distinction between sapwood and heartwood.
It is moderately heavy (air-dry 720 kg/m³).

Look-alike trees Riverine trees with compound leaves can be confused with one another. See the comparisons of various once compound leaves on the Distinctive Striking Features, pages 57 - 58.

An unusually prolific crop of Sausage-tree pods

It has a single, gnarled, grooved, low-branching trunk. Main branches are prominent and split close to their origin from the trunk. Branches spread horizontally to form a round, very dense, slightly drooping canopy. Branchlets end in thick twigs.

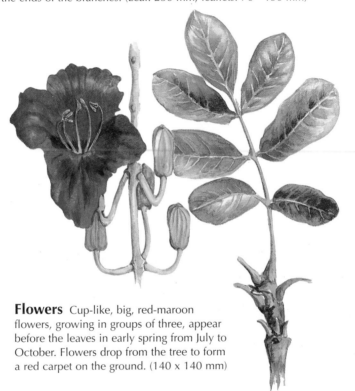

Leaves   Compound, with a single, rigid leaflet at the tip. The leaves are characteristically thick, leathery and rigid, with 2 - 5 pairs of leaflets. They are opposite and elliptic with a rounded tip and a smooth, wavy margin. Most end leaflets have serrated tips. The leaves are crowded near the ends of the branches. (Leaf: 250 mm; leaflets: 70 - 150 mm)

Flowers   Cup-like, big, red-maroon flowers, growing in groups of three, appear before the leaves in early spring from July to October. Flowers drop from the tree to form a red carpet on the ground. (140 x 140 mm)

Pods   Unique, huge, solid sausage-like fruit gives the tree its common English name. Ripe fruits fall from May through to April the following year. (500 x 100 mm)

Bark   The bark is smooth and peels in irregular blocks.

	Oct	Nov	Dec	Jan	Feb	Mar	Apr	May	Jun	Jul	Aug	Sep
Leaf	■	■	■	■	■	■	■	■	■		■	■
Flower	■									■	■	■
Fruit/Pod	■	■	■	■	■	■	■	■	■	■	■	■

Seasonal changes   Semi-deciduous. The leaves drop late in winter. In spring the fresh green foliage is very conspicuous. The short period without leaves, and the presence of the characteristic fruit, makes identification easy for most of the year.

WATER NUXIA

Nuxia oppositifolia   **Water elder**

LOGANIACEAE
WILD ELDER FAMILY   **SA Tree Number 635**

AFRIKAANS Watervlier   **ZULU** iNkhweza

The species name **oppositifolia** means opposite leaves.

Where you'll find this tree easily

The Water Nuxia grows in groups along the
perennial rivers.

- This tree can most easily be found growing
  in Riverine areas (H).
- It can also be found along rivers and large
  streams of the Sabie/Crocodile Thorn Thickets
  (D) and Alluvial Plains (M).

Ecozones where this tree occurs

A	E	I	M
B	F	J	N
C	G	K	O
D	H	L	P

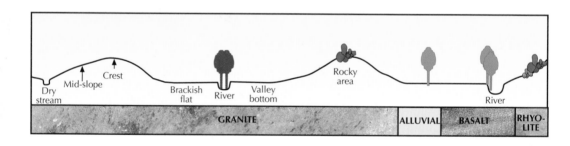

Striking features

- **This is a dense, pale-green, extremely finely
  leaved tree, only growing right on the edges
  of rivers and in river beds.**
- Leaves are thin, elliptic and long, and tend
  to stand upright.
- The branches form downward curves.
- The bark is light to dark brown with many
  distinct, lengthways fissures.

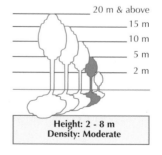

20 m & above
15 m
10 m
5 m
2 m

Height: 2 - 8 m
Density: Moderate

248

249

WATER NUXIA

Nuxia oppositifolia

Links with animals Leaves are eaten by kudu, bushbuck and elephant. Black Rhino eat the bark and leaves.

Human uses The wood is attractive and occasionally used for furniture.

Gardening Very little is known about growing this tree from seed but it is probably a slow grower. It needs to be grown very near to permanent water.

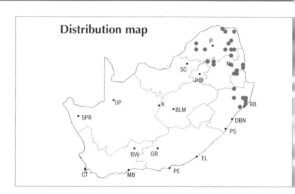

Distribution map

Water Nuxia are fine-leaved and beautiful along river banks.

Wood The wood is pale brown and fine-grained. It is hard and moderately heavy.

Look-alike trees The preferred habitat of this tree overlaps with that of the River Bushwillow (*Combretum erythrophyllum*), page 236, which has much broader leaves and four-winged pods.

GROWTH DETAILS

This is a multi-stemmed low-branching tree. The stems are fairly upright and slender. The branches are long and thin and older trees tend to have a V-shaped canopy.

Leaves   Simple, opposite, thin, long and narrowly elliptic. They are narrow at the base and rounded at the tip. They are slightly closed, light green and glossy above and dull below. Young leaves are covered by minute hairs and are slightly sticky. The veins are prominent and stand out underneath. The top third of the margin is toothed and wavy. (80 x 100 mm)

Flowers   Inconspicuous, white, trumpet-like flowers grow in sprays at the end of the branches. (October to February).

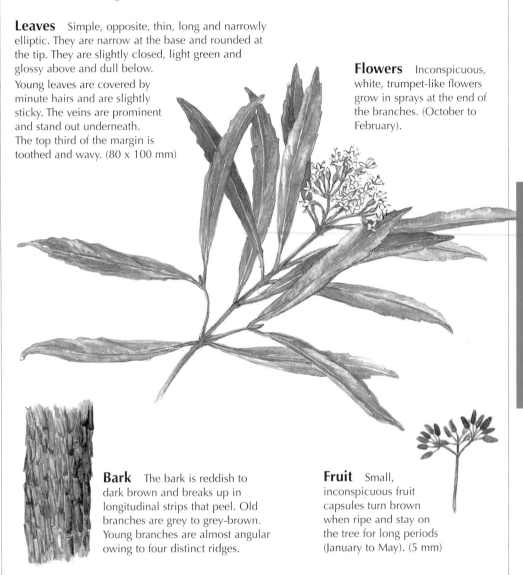

Bark   The bark is reddish to dark brown and breaks up in longitudinal strips that peel. Old branches are grey to grey-brown. Young branches are almost angular owing to four distinct ridges.

Fruit   Small, inconspicuous fruit capsules turn brown when ripe and stay on the tree for long periods (January to May). (5 mm)

	Oct	Nov	Dec	Jan	Feb	Mar	Apr	May	Jun	Jul	Aug	Sep
Leaf	■	■	■	■	■	■	■	■	■	■	■	■
Flower	■	■	■	■	■							
Fruit/Pod				■	■	■	■	■				

Seasonal changes   Evergreen. This tree can be identified throughout the year.

251

WEEPING BOER-BEAN

Schotia brachypetala

CAESALPINIACEAE **FLAMBOYANT FAMILY**	**SA Tree Number 202**

AFRIKAANS Huilboerboon   **ENGLISH** Tree fuchsia   **N. SOTHO** Molope   **SISWATI** uVovovo
TSONGA N'wavulombe   **ZULU** uVovovo; umGxamu

The term **brachypetala** means with short petals.

Where you'll find this tree easily

The Weeping Boer-bean grows singly along larger rivers and in higher rainfall areas, often on termite mounds.

- This tree can most easily be found in Riverine areas (H).

- It can also be found on termite mounds in Ecozones A, B, C, D, J.

Ecozones where this tree occurs

A	E	I	M
B	F	J	N
C	G	K	O
D	**H**	L	P

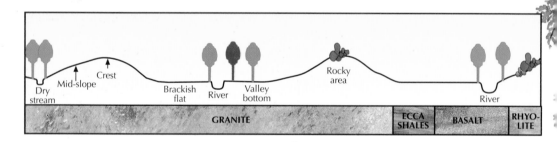

Dry stream   Mid-slope   Crest   Brackish flat   River   Valley bottom   Rocky area   River

GRANITE   ECCA SHALES   BASALT   RHYO-LITE

Striking features

- It has a single, straight trunk that branches low down, to form a round, very dense, dark green canopy.
- On the canopy edge, branchlets and twigs tend to curve downwards, and in game reserves are often bare from browsing.
- The compound leaves have no terminal leaflet, which can help to differentiate this tree from other common, riverine species.
- **Conspicuous, dark crimson flowers make identification easy from mid-August to October.**
- Broad, brown, bean-like pods burst open on the tree from March to September.

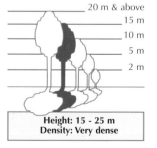

20 m & above
15 m
10 m
5 m
2 m

Height: 15 - 25 m
Density: Very dense

253

WEEPING BOER-BEAN

Schotia brachypetala

Links with animals Mature leaves are eaten by baboon, while young leaves are eaten by kudu, giraffe, impala and Black Rhino. The bark is also eaten by Black Rhino. Baboon, monkey, birds and insects drink the very sweet nectar.

Human uses The roasted seeds are edible. Extracts of the bark are used for treating heartburn and hangovers.

Gardening This decorative tree will grow in most gardens. It is sensitive to severe frost, but drought-resistant once established. It can be grown from seed and is fast-growing when planted in fertile soils and watered well.

Distribution map

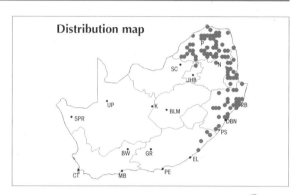

Wood The wood contains tannin and the sawdust causes eye irritation. It is rare and durable; very resistant; varnishes and polishes well. The sapwood is yellow-white, the heartwood is yellow-brown.

Look-alike trees The compound leaf of the Weeping Boer-bean is similar to other riverine trees, like the Sausage-tree, page 244, and Nyala-tree, page 214; however it is the only commonly found, large tree along rivers, with a compound leaf with a pair of leaflets at the tip. See the comparisons of various once compound leaves on the Distinctive Striking Features, pages 57 - 58.

Weeping Boer-bean flowers in spring, hanging over N'wanetsi Dam, Kruger.

GROWTH DETAILS

It has a single, straight trunk that branches low down. Twigs tend to hang downwards to form a rounded, very dense, leafy, dull, dark green canopy.

Leaves Compound, with 4 - 7 pairs of leaflets and a pair of leaflets at the tip, and leaflets opposite or sub-opposite. Broadly elliptic with a smooth margin. The central vein of each leaflet tends to be off-centre at the base. The leaves fall just before spring and are quickly replaced by new young leaves. (Leaf: 180 mm; leaflet: 65 x 40 mm)

Flowers Conspicuous sprays of attractive, red flowers with prominent stamens grow at the end of the older branches (mid-August to October). (Spray: 60 - 130 mm)

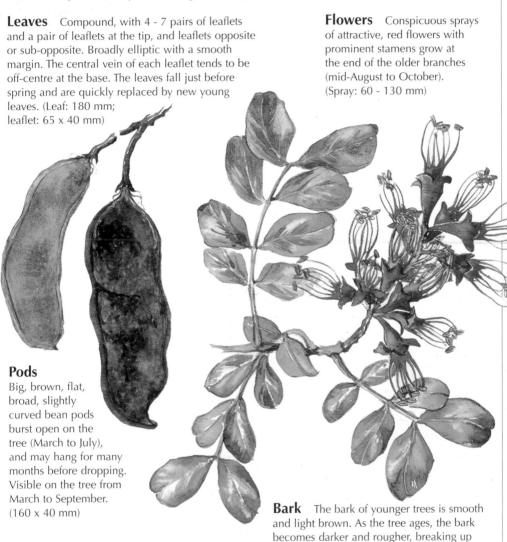

Pods
Big, brown, flat, broad, slightly curved bean pods burst open on the tree (March to July), and may hang for many months before dropping. Visible on the tree from March to September. (160 x 40 mm)

Bark The bark of younger trees is smooth and light brown. As the tree ages, the bark becomes darker and rougher, breaking up into small, nondescript blocks.

	Oct	Nov	Dec	Jan	Feb	Mar	Apr	May	Jun	Jul	Aug	Sep
Leaf	▉	▉	▉	▉	▉	▉	▉	▉	▉	▉	▉	
Flower	▉										▉	▉
Fruit/Pod						▉	▉	▉	▉	▉	▉	▉

Seasonal changes Deciduous to semi-deciduous. This tree loses its leaves very late, and often over a very short period, just before the flowers appear. It is therefore easy to identify, except for a short leafless period in early spring.

255

Find more Difficult Trees

BRACK LOVERS

Brack Areas in the Lowveld tend to be close to the inner bends of rivers. They are generally flat, and because of highly palatable grasses, often have patches of bare soil. Once you can identify Magic Guarri, page 278, you will recognise many more Brack Areas, as these small trees are indicators of the presence of sodic soils.

An open area with short grass surrounded by Magic Guarri is typical of Brack soils.

BUFFALO-THORN

Ziziphus mucronata

RHAMNACEAE
DOGWOOD FAMILY

SA Tree Number 447

AFRIKAANS Blinkblaar-wag-n-bietjie   **N. SOTHO** Moonaana   **SWAZI** umLalhabantu   **TSONGA** Mphasamhala   **TSWANA** Mokgalo   **VENDA** Mukhalu mutshetshete   **XHOSA** umPhafa   **ZULU** umPhafa, umLahlankosi, isiLahla, Umkhobonga

The species name **mucronata** refers to the pointed leaves on the tree.

Where you'll find this tree easily

The Buffalo-thorn is very widespread and grows singly in most Habitats. It is more common on brackish flats and koppies.

- It is easy to find this tree in Sabie/Crocodile Thorn Thickets (D).
- It can also be found in most other granite Ecozones, as well as the basalts F and K.

Ecozones where this tree occurs

A	E	I	M
B	F	J	N
C	G	K	O
D	H	L	P

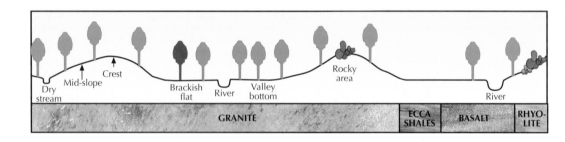

Striking features

- This is a small, single-trunked tree with an irregular spiky canopy.
- The canopy is formed by densely branched, angular, zigzag twigs and branchlets.
- The leaves are conspicuously shiny and light green with three veins from the base.
- **Round, berry-like fruit on the angular, zigzag branchlets and twigs make identification in winter possible.**

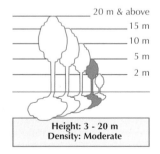

20 m & above
15 m
10 m
5 m
2 m

Height: 3 - 20 m
Density: Moderate

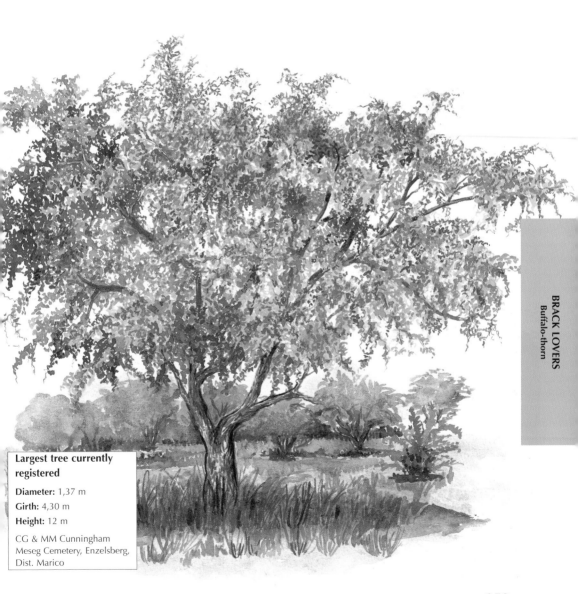

Largest tree currently registered

Diameter: 1,37 m

Girth: 4,30 m

Height: 12 m

CG & MM Cunningham
Meseg Cemetery, Enzelsberg,
Dist. Marico

259

BUFFALO-THORN

Ziziphus mucronata

Links with animals The fruit is eaten by many animals including Black Rhino, impala, warthog, baboon, monkey and nyala. The leaves are eaten by Black Rhino, impala, nyala, kudu and giraffe. Butterflies breed in the trees.

Human uses It is an important medicinal plant, used for stomach ailments, ulcers and chest problems. The fruit can be eaten, and is used for porridge and flour. The seeds are roasted as a coffee substitute. The wood is used for fencing posts.

In Zulu folklore the tree is supposed to deflect lightning and protect people sheltering under it in a thunderstorm. It is known as the burial tree of the Zulu, and branches of the Buffalo-thorn are laid on the graves of chiefs and royalty.

Gardening This is a very pretty tree, but because of its thorns, it is not a good tree for a garden with small children. The tree grows fast from seed and is fairly drought- and frost-resistant.

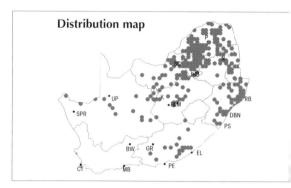

Distribution map

Wood The sapwood is yellow-white, the heartwood is yellow-brown, sometimes with reddish-brown, dark streaks. It is hard and suitable for turning, but warps easily.

The zig-zag branches and berry-like fruit make the Buffalo-thorn unmistakable.

GROWTH DETAILS

This is a single-trunked tree with a short, often crooked trunk that branches fairly low down to form a moderate spreading canopy. The trees often have mistletoe growing inside the canopy. Branchlets and twigs are zigzag-shaped and red-brown.

Leaves   Simple, alternate, grow on the angles of the twigs and are slightly folded. The leaves are bright, light green and shiny with serrated edges and they typically have three veins from the base. (40 x 30 mm)

Flowers   Inconspicuous star-like, small, yellow-green flowers grow in clusters at the base of the leaves (October to November). (5 mm)

Fruit   Round, berry-like fruit is hard and dark brown, and is often still visible on trees in winter when they have lost their leaves. It ripens from January onwards. (10 mm)

Thorns   Pairs of brown thorns, one straight and one curved, grow on the angles of the zigzag of twigs and branchlets. (Straight: 20 mm; curled: 7 mm)

Bark   The bark is grey and smooth when young, becoming grooved with age.

	Oct	Nov	Dec	Jan	Feb	Mar	Apr	May	Jun	Jul	Aug	Sep
Leaf												
Flower												
Fruit/Pod												

Seasonal changes   Deciduous. This tree is without leaves for long periods as it loses them early in autumn. The zigzag shape of the branchlets and twigs and the presence of fruit make identification possible in winter.

BUSHVELD GARDENIA

Gardenia volkensii   *Transvaal gardenia*

RUBIACEAE
GARDENIA FAMILY   **SA Tree Number 691**

AFRIKAANS Bosveldkatjiepiering   **SWANA** umValasangweni   **TSONGA** Ntsalala   **TSWANA** Morala
ZULU umGongwane umValasangweni

The species name **volkensii** is in honour of G. Volkens who collected on Mount Kilimanjaro from 1892 to 1894.

Where you'll find this tree easily

The Bushveld Gardenia grows singly in brack areas.

- It is easiest to find this tree growing in Sabie/Crocodile Thorn Thickets (D).
- This tree can also be found in Olifants Rugged Veld (J) and on Alluvial Plains (M).

Ecozones where this tree occurs

A	E	I	M
B	F	J	N
C	G	K	O
D	H	L	P

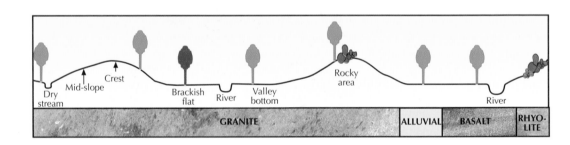

Striking features

- The bark of the trunk is pale grey and smooth and flakes off, showing patches of yellow underbark.
- The tree has an irregular canopy with pale grey, densely branched, upright branches.
- The pale grey branchlets are clearly visible in the sparse foliage of shiny, green leaves.
- The branchlets are short and thick and often at right angles to the branches, giving the tree a spiky appearance.
- **The large fruits and attractive white flowers are characteristic.**

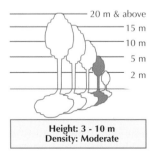

Height: 3 - 10 m
Density: Moderate

263

BUSHVELD GARDENIA

Gardenia volkensii

Links with animals The leaves are occasionally browsed by elephant, giraffe and kudu. Ripe fruit is eaten by baboon.

Human uses The tree was believed to have magical powers and was planted at the entrance to homesteads to keep evil sprits away. Infusion of the fruits and roots was used to induce vomiting. The wood is used for fences, sticks, spoons and firewood.

Gardening This tree is very decorative during the flowering season. It can be grown from seed and cuttings. It is slow-growing, fairly drought-resistant but not resistant to severe frost.

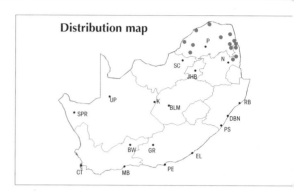

Distribution map

The presence of unique-shaped fruit helps recognition of Bushveld Gardenia.

Wood The wood is white, fine-grained, hard and heavy (air-dry 880 kg/m^3).

Look-alike trees The three pale-barked, brack-loving species can be confused with one another. The young leaves of the Jacket-plum *(Pappea capensis)*, page 274, are tooth-edged, and the short, stiff branchlets do not appear spiny. The simple leaves are leathery and rough and paler underneath when mature. The Bushveld Saffron *(Elaeodendron transvaalense)*, page 266, has simple, narrow-toothed leaves on short twigs; the branches are not as stiff as in the other species, but tend to be arching and often drooping.

This is a shrub or small tree with a short, sturdy stem that branches profusely low down to form a much-branched, irregular canopy. It may be single- or multi-stemmed. The foliage is sparse and the pale grey branches are clearly visible. The branchlets are short and thick, and often at right angles to the branches.

Fruit   The fruit is rounded and about the size of a hen's egg. It is covered with blunt longitudinal ribs and is rough. The skin is very thick and fibrous. Green fruit ripens to a grey-green (December to April). Fruit often remains on the tree until August. (60 x 30 - 50 mm)

Leaves   Simple leaves are clustered at the ends of branches in whorls of three. They are spoon-shaped with a broad, rounded tip and a sharp point with a narrow pointed base. Glossy green, and when mature, they are smooth and soft. The margin is smooth and slightly wavy. Leaves turn yellow in autumn. (30 - 50 x 25 - 40 mm)

Flowers   Sweet-scented, trumpet-like, white flowers grow singly at the end of the branches. They often appear before the leaves, from August to December, and go creamy to yellow with age. (80 x 100 mm)

Bark   The bark is pale grey with a yellow tinge. It is smooth and may be flaky.

	Oct	Nov	Dec	Jan	Feb	Mar	Apr	May	Jun	Jul	Aug	Sep
Leaf	███	███	███	███	███	███	███					
Flower												
Fruit/Pod			███	███	███	███	███	███	███	███	███	

Seasonal changes   Deciduous. The leaves turn yellow in autumn. Owing to the presence of the fruit and the particular growth form, this tree is recognisable for most of the year.

BUSHVELD SAFFRON

Elaeodendron transvaalense

Transvaal Saffron

**CELASTRACEAE
SPIKE-THORN FAMILY**

SA Tree Number 416

AFRIKAANS Bosveldsaffraan   **TSONGA** Shimapana   **ZULU** Ngwavuma

The species name **transvaalense** refers to the Transvaal.

Where you'll find this tree easily

The Bushveld Saffron tree grows singly, preferring brackish areas .

- It is easiest to find this tree in Sabie/Crocodile Thorn Thickets (D).
- This tree can also be found growing in Mixed Bushwillow Woodlands (A), Pretoriuskop Sourveld (B) and in Thorn Veld (E).

Ecozones where this tree occurs

A	E	I	M
B	F	J	N
C	G	K	O
D	H	L	P

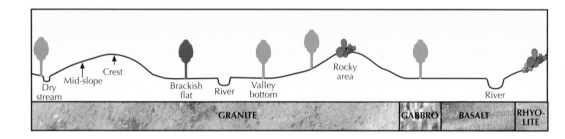

Striking features

- **This tree has a densely branched, untidy, roundish canopy.**
- It has long, thin, arching and drooping, pale grey branchlets showing clearly between the leaves.
- The bark of younger trees and branches is pale and fairly smooth, with darker, rougher patches on the older branches and stems, and on older trees.
- **The leaves are pale green and are arranged in groups on very short twigs coming off the branchlets at right angles.**

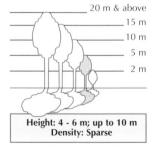

Height: 4 - 6 m; up to 10 m
Density: Sparse

267

BUSHVELD SAFFRON

Elaeodendron transvaalense

Links with animals The fruit is eaten by birds like the Purple-crested Turaco. The leaves and young shoots are eaten by elephant, giraffe, kudu and impala.

Human uses The wood is used for household utensils, spoons, pipes and cattle troughs. The bark is used for tanning and to make tea. It is reputedly an excellent treatment for stomach ailments.

Gardening This is a decorative tree and will grow in most gardens. It is difficult to grow from seed. It is slow-growing and probably susceptible to frost.

Wood The wood is pink when freshly cut and red-brown when dry. It is hard, finely textured and heavy (air-dry 960 kg/m³). It is insect-resistant and produces a smooth finish.

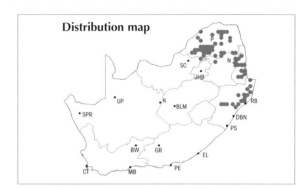

Distribution map

Look-alike trees The three pale-barked, brack-loving species can be confused with one another. The young leaves of the Jacket-plum *(Pappea capensis)*, page 274, are tooth-edged, and the short, stiff branchlets do not appear spiny. The simple leaves are leathery and rough and paler underneath when mature. The Bushveld Gardenia *(Gardenia volkensii)*, page 262, has spine-like branchlets which support clusters of spoon-shaped leaves, and the characteristic fruit is often present.

Pale, angular branchlets and very short twigs are distinctive of the Bushveld Saffron.

GROWTH DETAILS

This is a single-stemmed tree with a thick stem that branches low down to form a roundish canopy. The branches are arching and often drooping. Very short twigs, which carry the leaves, are pale and come off at right angles to the branchlets.

Leaves   Simple, narrow, elliptic, may be alternate but typically clustered in groups on very short twigs coming off the branchlets at right angles. The leaves are glossy, deep blue-green and leathery. The margin is smooth or slightly toothed. (20 - 70 x 10 - 30 mm)

Fruit   The berry-like fruit grows in bunches on the ends of the side branches or on long whip-like twigs. It is smooth and yellow when ripe and turns brown later (July to September). (20 x 16 mm)

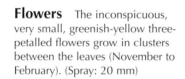

Flowers   The inconspicuous, very small, greenish-yellow three-petalled flowers grow in clusters between the leaves (November to February). (Spray: 20 mm)

Bark   The bark is pale grey and smooth in young branches and trees, and becomes darker and breaks into blocks in very old trees and branches. Branchlets are very fine and pale grey.

	Oct	Nov	Dec	Jan	Feb	Mar	Apr	May	Jun	Jul	Aug	Sep
Leaf	▓	▓	▓	▓	▓	▓	▓	▓	▓	▓		
Flower		░	░	░	░							
Fruit/Pod								▓	▓	▓	░	

Seasonal changes   Deciduous or semi-deciduous. As this tree is without leaves only for a short period, it can be identified for most of the year.

HORNED THORN ACACIA & SCENTED-POD THORN ACACIA

Acacia grandicornuta & Acacia nilotica

MIMOSACEAE ACACIA	SA Tree Number 168.1/179

HORNED THORN: AFRIKAANS Horingdoring **ZULU** umDongola, umNgampondo

SCENTED-POD THORN: AFRIKAANS Lekkerruikpeul **N. SOTHO** Moôka **SWAZI** isiThwethwe, umNcawe
TSONGA Nxangwa **TSWANA** Motabakgasi **ZULU** umNqawe, uBobe, uBombo, umQuwe

The species name **grandicornuta** means great-horned, and **nilotica** refers to the distribution of the tree along the Nile River.

Where you'll find this tree easily

The Horned-thorn Acacia and Scented-pod Thorn Acacia prefer brackish and clay soils. They often grow in groups.

- Both trees are easiest to find in groups, growing in brack areas in the Sabie/Crocodile Thorn Thickets (D).
- The Horned Thorn is common in Tree Mopane Savannah (O).
- The Scented-pod Thorn Acacia is common in Mixed Bushwillow Woodlands (A), Pretoriuskop Sourveld (B), Malelane Mountain Bushveld (C), Marula Savannah (F) and in Olifants Rugged Veld (J).

Ecozones where this tree occurs

HORNED THORN ACACIA

A	E	I	M
B	F	J	N
C	G	K	O
D	H	L	P

SCENTED-POD THORN ACACIA

A	E	I	M
B	F	J	N
C	G	K	O
D	H	L	P

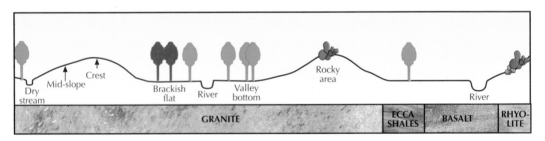

Crest · Mid-slope · Dry stream · Brackish flat · River · Valley bottom · Rocky area · River

GRANITE · ECCA SHALES · BASALT · RHYO-LITE

Striking features

- They are normally small Acacia trees or shrubs, with wide, V-shaped, irregular canopies.
- The huge, white, spiny thorns are conspicuous.
- **The Horned Thorn Acacia has white flower-balls, while the Scented-pod Thorn Acacia has yellow flower-balls.**
- **The pods of the Horned Thorn Acacia are sickle-shaped and flat, while those of the Scented-pod Thorn Acacia are swollen and enlarged over the seeds, giving them the appearance of a string of beads.**

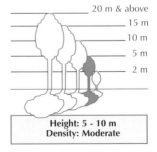

20 m & above
15 m
10 m
5 m
2 m

Height: 5 - 10 m
Density: Moderate

Horned Thorn Acacia

Scented-pod Thorn Acacia

HORNED THORN ACACIA
& SCENTED-POD THORN ACACIA

Acacia grandicornuta & Acacia nilotica

HORNED THORN ACACIA

Links with animals The leaves and pods are browsed by giraffe and impala. The seeds are eaten by baboon and monkey.

Human uses The wood is used for cooking fires.

Gardening This tree can be used to form a hedge. It will grow fast from seed in fertile soils and when it is well watered. It is fairly drought-resistant but not frost-resistant.

Wood The heartwood is reddish, has a very fine texture and is hard, durable and termite- and wood-borer resistant.

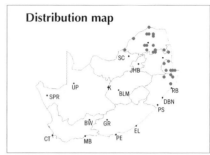

Distribution map

GROWTH DETAILS

These small, single-stemmed trees branch low-down to form V-shaped, irregular canopies.

Leaves Twice compound leaves grow in bunches of 3 - 5 at the origin of the thorns. Leaves consist of 3 - 10 feather pairs, each with 8 - 16 pairs of leaflets. Leaflets elliptic with a smooth margin. (Leaf: 70 mm; leaflet: 3 x 9 mm)

Flowers White, sweet-scented flower-balls grow in tufts of 4 - 12 at the leaf origin on new branchlets (October to March). (10 mm)

Pods Sickle-shaped, flat, brown, pods grow in bunches on the end of the twigs. Pods split open on the tree when ripe (April to July). (70 x 130 mm)

Thorns The long, spiny thorns are arranged spirally around the branchlets. Thorns are often thickened and are fused across the base. (90 mm)

	Oct	Nov	Dec	Jan	Feb	Mar	Apr	May	Jun	Jul	Aug	Sep
Leaf	■	■	■	■	■	■	■					
Flower												
Fruit/Pod							■	■	■	■		

Seasonal changes Deciduous. These trees are very difficult to differentiate from one another when the flowers and the pods are absent, but the leaf characteristics will help in summer.

272

SCENTED-POD THORN ACACIA

Links with animals The pods are readily eaten by all antelope.

Human uses The Voortrekkers used the pods to make ink. The wood is used for fuel, mining props and fence posts. Extracts of the pods are used for tanning. The gum is edible. An extract of the bark is used to treat coughs and as a sedative. Extracts of the root are used for the treatment of TB and colds.

Gardening These small trees will grow in most gardens. They can be grown from seed or root cuttings but grow slowly. They are fairly frost- and drought-resistant.

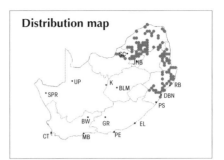
Distribution map

GROWTH DETAILS

These small, single-stemmed trees branch low-down to form V-shaped, irregular canopies.

Leaves Twice compound leaves grow in bunches of 3 - 4 at the origin of the thorns. Leaves consist of 3 - 9 feather pairs, each with 8 - 20 pairs of leaflets. Leaflets elliptic with a smooth margin. (Leaf: 40 mm; leaflet: 1 x 4 mm)

Flowers Yellow, scented balls on hairy stalks grow in groups of four on the new branchlets. The tree may flower over a long period although it is never covered in flowers (October to February). (12 mm)

Pods The characteristic pods are swollen over the seeds to give them a beaded appearance. Young, green pods are covered with fine, reddish hairs but they turn black when mature. They do not split open. Mature pods have a strong, sweet scent (March to August). (15 x 120 mm)

Bark The bark is reddish-brown and smooth in young branches, but dark grey to black and rough with grooves in older branches and trees.

Thorns Paired, white thorns vary in size; curve slightly backwards; grow from a single base. (50 - 90 mm)

	Oct	Nov	Dec	Jan	Feb	Mar	Apr	May	Jun	Jul	Aug	Sep
Leaf	▓	▓	▓	▓	▓	▓	▓	▓				
Flower	▓	▓	▓	▓	▓							
Fruit/Pod						▓	▓	▓	▓	▓	▓	

Seasonal changes Deciduous. These trees are very difficult to differentiate from one another when the flowers and the pods are absent, but the leaf characteristics will help in summer.

JACKET-PLUM

Pappea capensis

SAPINDACEAE **LITCHI FAMILY**	**SA Tree Number 433**

AFRIKAANS Doppruim   **N. SOTHO** Morôba-diêpê   **TSONGA** Gulaswimbi   **XHOSA** iliTye, umGqalutye
ZULU umKhokhwane, umQhoqho, umVuma, iNdaba

The species name **capensis** means from the Cape.

Where you'll find this tree easily
The Jacket-plum grows singly in brack areas.

🌿 This tree can most easily be found in
   Sabie/Crocodile Thorn Thickets (D).

🌿 It can also be found in Ecozones A, B, C,
   E, I, J, L. It often grows on old termite
   mounds.

Ecozones where this tree occurs

A	E	I	M
B	F	J	N
C	G	K	O
D	H	L	P

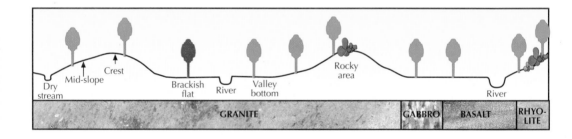

Striking features
- The rounded canopy is formed by an intense
  tangle of short, grey branchlets and twigs.
- The tree has an overall dull-green
  appearance with very visible short, tangled,
  pale grey branches.
- The leaves appear to form rosettes at the
  ends of the drooping branchlets.
- Leaves are hard and leathery with a
  prominent, sunken, pale central vein.
- **The velvety-green, berry-like fruit that
  bursts open to show a bright red jelly-like
  flesh is characteristic (December to July).**

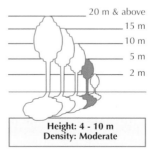

Height: 4 - 10 m
Density: Moderate

Young leaf   Older leaf

275

JACKET-PLUM

Pappea capensis

Links with animals The fruit is eaten by a wide variety of animals and birds. The leaves are not palatable and are seldom eaten.

Human uses The wood is white and easy to work with, heavy and tough and may be used for poles, yokes, furniture and spoons. The fruit is edible and tasty. Vinegar and jelly are made from the fruit. The seeds contain oil that is used for various purposes. The tree is still important in traditional medicine today.

Gardening This is an attractive tree that will flourish in most gardens. It grows well from seed but extremely slowly; is fairly drought-resistant.

Look-alike trees The three pale-barked, brack-loving species can be confused with one another. Young leaves of the Jacket-plum are tooth-edged; short, stiff branchlets do not appear spiny. The simple leaves are leathery and rough and paler underneath when mature. The Bushveld Gardenia (*Gardenia volkensii*), page 262, has spine-like branchlets which support clusters of spoon-shaped leaves; characteristic fruit is often present. The Bushveld Saffron (*Elaeodendron transvaalense*), page 266, has simple, narrow-toothed leaves on short twigs; the branches are not stiff as in the other species but tend to be arching and often drooping.

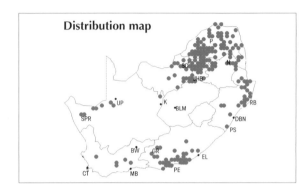

Distribution map

Wood The wood is white and easy to work. It is heavy and tough.

The pale grey bark and rigid, leathery leaves with yellowish central veins make this tree easy to find.

GROWTH DETAILS

Even within the Lowveld the growth form and the leaf size of this tree are highly variable. Under well-watered conditions it is a tall tree with a dense rounded canopy and larger leaves. In relatively drier areas it is a tree with a short trunk that branches low down to form an intricately branched, roundish canopy, and smaller leaves.

Leaves   Simple, alternate in the older growth and crowded towards the end of the twigs; elliptic with a rounded base and tip but very variable in size, dependent on the rainfall. The margins are smooth when mature, but sharply toothed in young leaves. The leaves are rigid, leathery, rough, dark olive-green above and pale underneath, with a conspicuous yellow central vein that is visible from both sides. (5 - 10 x 80 - 160 mm)

Fruit   The velvety-green, berry-like fruit grows in bunches. When ripe it bursts open to expose a shiny, bright red jelly covering the black seeds (December to July). The dark shells of the fruit may be seen long after the fruit has dropped. (20 mm)

Bark   The bark of young branches is smooth and pale grey and may be broken into small blocks. The bark of older trees and branches is darker and rough with irregular patches of light and dark bark. It is often covered in lichen. Branchlets are pale grey.

Flowers   Small, pale creamy-green, scented flowers grow in spikes between the leaves. Male and female flowers grow on separate trees (September to March). (Spike: 25 - 160 mm)

	Oct	Nov	Dec	Jan	Feb	Mar	Apr	May	Jun	Jul	Aug	Sep
Leaf	▓	▓	▓	▓	▓	▓	▓	▓	▓	▓		▓
Flower												
Fruit/Pod			▓	▓	▓	▓	▓	▓	▓	▓		

Seasonal changes   Deciduous to evergreen. As this tree has leaves for most of the year, it is normally easy to recognise.

MAGIC GUARRI

Euclea divinorum

EBENACEAE EBONY FAMILY	SA Tree Number 595

AFRIKAANS Towerghwarrie **N. SOTHO** Mohlakola **TSONGA** Nhlangula **TSWANA** Mothakola
VENDA Mutangule **ZULU** umHlangula

The species name **divinorum** refers to the use of tree parts by diviners.

Where you'll find this tree easily

The Magic Guarri grows in groups in brack areas.

- This tree is easily found in Mixed Bushwillow Woodlands (A).
- It is also easy to find this tree in most other Ecozones.

Ecozones where this tree occurs

A	E	I	M
B	F	J	N
C	G	K	O
D	H	L	P

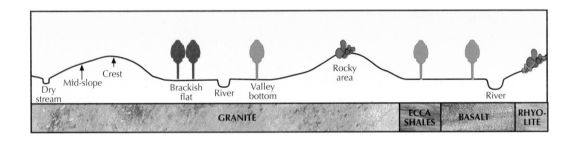

Dry stream · Mid-slope · Crest · Brackish flat · River · Valley bottom · Rocky area · River

GRANITE · ECCA SHALES · BASALT · RHYO-LITE

Striking features

- Its preference for brackish flats and growing in groups is characteristic.
- Bare, grey stems and branches grow upwards, carrying an evergreen, dense, rounded canopy.
- **The leaves have a shiny, grey-green upper-surface and a lighter under-surface.**
- **The margins of the leaves are usually very wavy.**
- The pale grey stems are covered by smooth bark in younger trees, and with coarse, blocky bark in older trees.

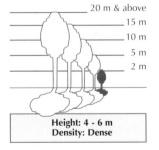

20 m & above
15 m
10 m
5 m
2 m

Height: 4 - 6 m
Density: Dense

279

MAGIC GUARRI

Euclea divinorum

Links with animals The fruit is eaten by birds such as hornbills. Black Rhino eat the bark. When other food is scarce, the leaves are browsed by Grey Duiker, rhino, giraffe, kudu and impala.

Human uses The fruit is used as a purgative. Leafy branches are broken off and used to beat out veld fires. The frayed ends of the twigs are used as tooth-brushes.

Gardening Although this tree does not seem very attractive in the veld, it can be used very effectively in gardens or as wind-breaks in the drier areas, as it is fairly drought- and frost-resistant. A slow-growing tree that prefers brackish soil, it can be easily grown from seed. The seeds should be sown in the locality where the trees are needed as they do not transplant well.

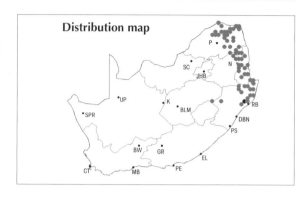

Distribution map

Wood The wood is pale red to red-brown and finely grained. It is hard, tough and moderately heavy (air-dry 820 kg/m³).

Look-alike trees The simple undulating leaf and round berries are similar to the Jackal-berry (*Diospyros mespiliformis*) page 210, but growth form of both species precludes confusion. The similarities are not surprising – both trees belonging to the Ebony family.

Heavily laden fruit on a branch of a Magic Guarri

GROWTH DETAILS

Usually multi-stemmed, but sometimes single, this tree branches low down, from the base, or has side branches from the main trunk. There is a rounded, dense canopy. The trunk is pale grey.

Leaves   Simple, opposite, elliptic with a smooth, very wavy margin. The leaf is leathery. The upper-surface is a shiny, grey-green while the under-surface is lighter. The leaf form distinguishes this tree from other Eucleas. (105 x 25 mm)

Fruit   Small, round bunches of berries turn purple when ripe (October to March). (6 mm)

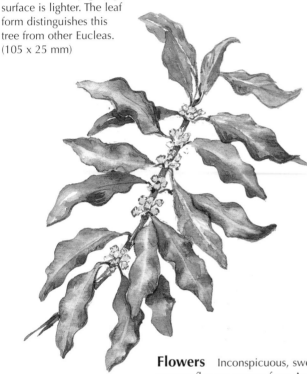

Flowers   Inconspicuous, sweet-scented, creamy flowers appear from August to September. Male and female flowers grow on separate plants. (3 - 5 mm)

Bark   The stem is covered by smooth, light grey bark in younger trees, and by dark grey, coarse, blocky bark in older trees.

	Oct	Nov	Dec	Jan	Feb	Mar	Apr	May	Jun	Jul	Aug	Sep
Leaf												
Flower												
Fruit/Pod												

Seasonal changes   Evergreen. This is often the only green tree in the brackish flats in winter. It is therefore easily identified at this time.

281

Find more Difficult Trees

SMALLER TREES IN GROUPS

These eight trees would be difficult to identify on their own. However, they all tend to grow in groups of many similar-sized small trees, fairly close together, making identification very easy.

Elephant rolling a long branch of a Round-leaved Bloodwood *(Pterocarpus rotundifolius)* through his mouth to debark it (see page 296).

FLAKY THORN ACACIA

Acacia exuvialis   **Flaky Thorn**

| MIMOSACEAE ACACIA FAMILY | SA Tree Number 164.1 |

AFRIKAANS Skilferdoring   **TSONGA** Risavana   **ZULU** umSabane

The species name **exuvialis** refers to the bark stripping off the tree.

Where you'll find this tree easily

The Flaky Thorn Acacia grows in fairly dense groups, in the granite Ecozones (A,B,C, and P).

- It is easiest to find on the edges of roads in Sabie/Crocodile Thorn Thickets (D).
- It also grows in sandy soils in mixed Bushwillow Woodlands (A), Lebombo Mountain Bushveld (I), Olifants Rugged Veld (J), Mopane Shrubveld (L) and Mopane/Bushwillow Woodlands (P).

Ecozones where this tree occurs

A	E	I	M
B	F	J	N
C	G	K	O
D	H	L	P

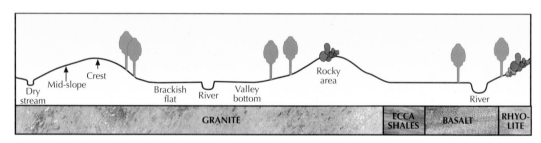

Striking features

- **The bark is smooth and peels in large, orange-brown flakes leaving a smooth, yellow-brown under-surface.**
- It is a small thorn tree, often multi-stemmed and has fine, feathery foliage.
- The thorns are very long and white.
- **It has a few yellow flower-balls for most of the summer.**

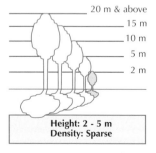

Height: 2 - 5 m
Density: Sparse

284

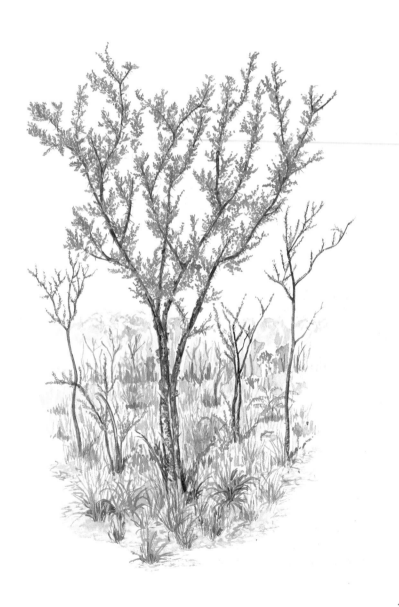

285

FLAKY THORN ACACIA

Acacia exuvialis

Links with animals Leaves and pods are eaten by impala and duiker.

Human uses Roots are cooked like vegetables in the same way as Sweet Potatoes.

Gardening This tree is small and untidy and seldom used in the garden.

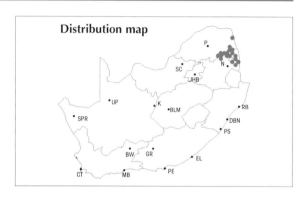

Distribution map

Look-alike trees This tree can be confused with other Acacias. See page 60 - 61 for comparisons.

Fresh spring leaves, white thorns and flaky, orange bark of the Flaky Thorn Acacia

This is a multi-stemmed or low-branching tree or shrub with a sparse, V-shaped canopy.

Leaves Twice compound, with 1 - 6 pairs of feathers, each with 3 - 6 pairs of opposite leaflets. Leaflets elliptic with a rounded end, a sharp tip and a smooth margin. (Leaflet: 3 - 10 x 1,5 - 4,5 mm)

Flowers The yellow, ball-like flowers on long, slender stalks may be seen sporadically from September to February. They are never abundant but the tree may flower for long periods. (10 mm)

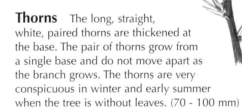

Pods Sickle-shaped, segmented, brown to reddish-brown, flat pods are covered by glands that secrete a sticky fluid (February to May). (10 x 65 mm)

Thorns The long, straight, white, paired thorns are thickened at the base. The pair of thorns grow from a single base and do not move apart as the branch grows. The thorns are very conspicuous in winter and early summer when the tree is without leaves. (70 - 100 mm)

Bark Smooth, grey to dark grey, and peels in large, orange-brown skins leaving a smooth, yellow-brown under-surface. The under-surface tends to have an oily / shiny appearance owing to the presence of resin.

	Oct	Nov	Dec	Jan	Feb	Mar	Apr	May	Jun	Jul	Aug	Sep
Leaf	■	■	■	■	■	■	■	■				
Flower	░	░	░	░	░							░
Fruit/Pod					■	■	■	■				

Seasonal changes Deciduous. The presence of the flaky bark and obvious white thorns makes identification possible throughout the year.

LARGE-FRUIT BUSHWILLOW

Combretum zeyheri

Large-fruited Bushwillow

COMBRETACEAE
BUSHWILLOW FAMILY

SA Tree Number 546

AFRIKAANS Raasblaar   **N. SOTHO** Moduba-tshipi   **TSONGA** Mafambaborile   **TSWANA** Modubana
VENDA Mufhatela-thundu   **ZULU** umBondwe-wasembudwini

The species name **Zeyheri** is named in honour of the German Plant collector C.L.P. Zeyher.

Where you'll find this tree easily

The Large-fruit Bushwillow grows singly on granite crests in higher rainfall areas.

- It is easiest to find this tree in Pretoriuskop Sourveld (B).

- It can also be found in Mixed Bushwillow Woodlands (A), in Malelane Mountain Bushveld (C), in the Lebombo Mountain Bushveld (I) as well as in Sandveld (N).

Ecozones where this tree occurs

A	E	I	M
B	F	J	N
C	G	K	O
D	H	L	P

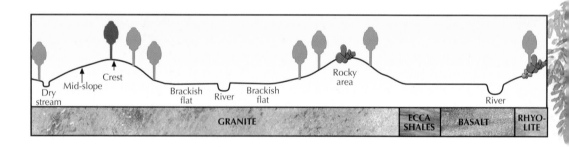

Striking features

- **This tree has huge, brown, four-winged pods for most of the year.**

- It is a single, or multi-stemmed tree with large, drooping leaves.

- The leaves are darkish-green, leathery and dull.

- The branches curve downwards and may hang to the ground.

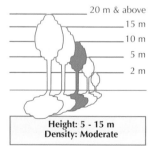

20 m & above
15 m
10 m
5 m
2 m

Height: 5 - 15 m
Density: Moderate

Largest tree currently registered

Diameter: 0,97 m

Girth: 3,04 m

Height: 13 m

E.A. Galpin
'Mosdene', Zyferkraal 528
Dist. Potgietersrus

LARGE-FRUIT BUSHWILLOW

Combretum zeyheri

Links with animals This tree is not very palatable. The leaves are eaten by giraffe and elephant. Ripe seeds are eaten by baboon.

Human uses The wood makes good timber and is also used for yokes. Part of the roots are used to make baskets and fishing traps. Leaf extracts are used to treat backache and eye ailments. The bark is used to treat gallstones, and root extracts are taken for bloody diarrhoea. Powdered bark is used to arrest menstrual flow and as eye lotions.

Gardening This tree can be a very decorative addition to the garden. It can be grown from seed, grows slowly and is not very resistant to cold.

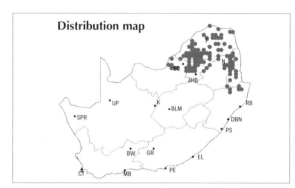

Distribution map

Wood Fresh wood is yellow, becoming whitish-yellow as it dries out. The wood is easy to work, but is not durable unless thoroughly seasoned.

Look-alike trees
This tree can be confused with other Bushwillows. See page 62 - 63 in the Distinctive Striking Features section, for comparisons.

Striking flowers of the Large-fruit Bushwillow

GROWTH DETAILS

This is a single-stemmed or multi-stemmed tree that branches low down to form a moderately dense, irregular, roundish canopy, with branches that tend to hang down.

Leaves The large leaves are simple and opposite, with a long, hairy leaf stem (15 mm). Leaves have wavy margins, and prominent veins especially on the under-surface. They are covered with soft hair when young, but are hairless and leathery when mature. Leaves are elliptic to broadly elliptic with a rounded tip which may be pointed or notched and a rounded to broadly tapering base. They are yellow-green to dark green above and paler below, and leaves turn brilliant yellow in autumn. (25 - 140 x 30 - 85 mm)

Flowers The small yellow-green to yellow flowers grow in dense spikes, singly, in the angle formed by the leaf. The flowers appear just before or with the new leaves and may be pleasantly or unpleasantly scented (August to November). (Flower spike: up to 75 x 25 mm)

Pods The conspicuous pods are the largest of the characteristic, four-winged pods of the Bushwillow family. The pods are found in bunches and are produced in such abundance that they weigh down the branches and branchlets. They are green, turning light brown when ripe and may stay on the tree until October (February - October). (Individual pod: 50 - 100 mm diameter).

Bark The bark is smooth and light. In older trees the bark becomes greyish-brown with patches of rougher bark that may peel off in small blocks, to show a red or orangey tinge below.

	Oct	Nov	Dec	Jan	Feb	Mar	Apr	May	Jun	Jul	Aug	Sep
Leaf												
Flower												
Fruit/Pod												

Seasonal changes Deciduous. It can be identified for most of the year while the pods are present.

RED BUSHWILLOW

Combretum apiculatum

COMBRETACEAE
BUSHWILLOW FAMILY

SA Tree Number 532

AFRIKAANS Rooiboswilg **N. SOTHO** Mohwelere-Tshipi **TSONGA** Xikukutsu **TSWANA** Mogodiri
ZULU umBondwe, umBondwe-omnyama

The species name **apiculatum** refers to the sharp tip of the leaf.

Where you'll find this tree easily

The Red Bushwillow is most common in large groups on granite crests.

- It is easiest to find this tree in Mixed Bushwillow Woodlands (A).
- This tree can also be found in all other granite, gabbro and rhyolite Ecozones, and the Sandveld Ecozone N.

Ecozones where this tree occurs

A	E	I	M
B	F	J	N
C	G	K	O
D	H	L	P

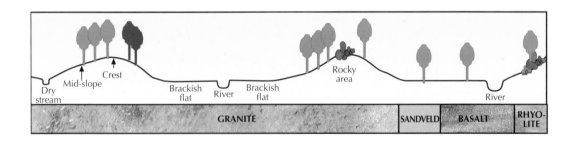

Striking features

- **The medium-sized, russet, four-winged pods are visible most of the year.**
- This tree has a short, often curved stem and is often multi-stemmed.
- It has a spreading, mostly formless, canopy.
- The leaves are shiny green but yellow leaves are seen amongst them most of the year.

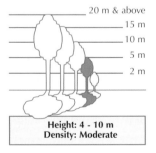

20 m & above
15 m
10 m
5 m
2 m

Height: 4 - 10 m
Density: Moderate

RED BUSHWILLOW

Combretum apiculatum

Links with animals Only young and fallen leaves are eaten regularly, but kudu, bushbuck, eland, giraffe and elephant also eat the mature green leaves. The fruit is eaten by Brown-headed Parrots.

Human uses The very heavy wood is used to make furniture.

Gardening This tree will grow in most gardens, preferring sandy soil or rocky areas with clay soil. It is not very attractive, but may grow into a lovely shade tree. It is fairly drought-resistant but cannot take severe frost. This tree is slow-growing and can be grown easily from seed.

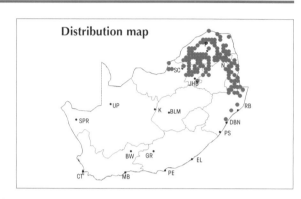

Distribution map

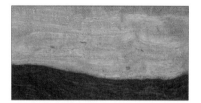

Wood The wood is exceptionally hard and durable, with black heartwood and yellow sapwood. It is suitable for turning.

Look-alike trees This tree can be confused with other Bushwillows. See page 62 - 63 in the Distinctive Striking Features section, for comparisons.

Relatively formless, inconsistently-shaped trees, Red Bushwillow are distinctive in groups.

GROWTH DETAILS

The tree is often multi-stemmed. Smaller, younger branchlets are green to light brown, while older branchlets are grey-brown.

Leaves   Simple, opposite, broad elliptic with a smooth margin. The leaves are a shiny green but yellow leaves may be seen amongst them for most of the year. The tip of the leaf is characteristically twisted and points downwards. (65 x 35 mm)

Flowers   The sweet-smelling, cylindrical spikes are not very conspicuous and arise from red buds with the new leaves in spring (September to November). One can smell the flowers when driving through areas where Red Bushwillows are common. (Spike: 70 x 20 mm)

Pods   The characteristic four-winged pods, with a single seed in the centre, hang in bunches which ripen in late summer and autumn. (25 x 20 mm)

Bark   The bark is grey to red-brown and breaks off in flat, uneven pieces.

	Oct	Nov	Dec	Jan	Feb	Mar	Apr	May	Jun	Jul	Aug	Sep
Leaf												
Flower												
Fruit/Pod												

Seasonal changes   Deciduous. The beautiful autumn colours range from reddish-yellow to yellow-green and dark brown. Some fruit is present most of the year.

295

ROUND-LEAVED BLOODWOOD

Pterocarpus rotundifolius   **Round-leaved Teak**

FABACEAE **PEA FAMILY**	**SA Tree Number 237**

AFRIKAANS Dopperkiaat   **SWAZI** inDlebezindlovu   **TSONGA** Muyataha, Ncelele
VENDA Mushusha-phombwe   **ZULU** iNdlandlovu

The species name **rotundifolius** refers to the round leaflets.

Where you'll find this tree easily

The Round-leaved Bloodwood grows in groups.

- This tree is most easily found in Mixed Bushwillow Woodlands (A).

- It can also be found in Sabie/Crocodile Thorn Thickets (D), in Thorn Veld (E), in Marula Savannah (F) as well as in the Lebombo Mountain Bushveld (I).

Ecozones where this tree occurs

A	E	I	M
B	F	J	N
C	G	K	O
D	H	L	P

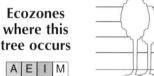

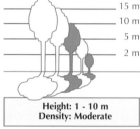

20 m & above
15 m
10 m
5 m
2 m

Height: 1 - 10 m
Density: Moderate

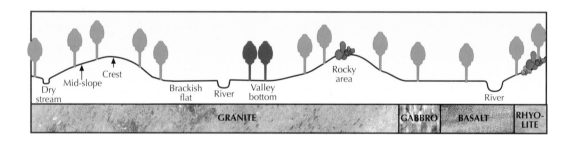

Striking features

- This is usually a multi-stemmed shrub with an irregular or round canopy and many dead branches sticking out after veld fires.
- It can be a tall tree with bare trunk and rounded canopy.
- **Leaves are characteristic and are large, very glossy, compound, with firm, large, round leaflets on a long leaf-stalk.**
- **The yellow flowers are conspicuous and characteristic.**
- **The pods are characteristic but relatively inconspicuous.**

297

ROUND-LEAVED BLOODWOOD

Pterocarpus rotundifolius

Links with animals Elephant find the leaves and young twigs very palatable and they often break the trees and branches when eating. The leaves are also browsed by kudu and impala.

Human uses The wood is durable and insect-proof and is used for wagon wheels, furniture and household articles.

Gardening This can be a very attractive tree for the small garden. It is quick-growing from seed but not frost-resistant.

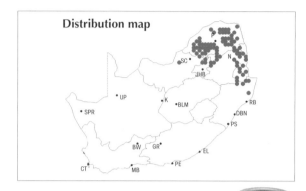

Distribution map

Wood
The wood is yellow with brown markings and moderately heavy (air-dry 848 kg/m³).

As a tree-spotter or game-watcher it adds to your interest to know elephant enjoy eating the shiny leaves of Round-leaved Bloodwood!

This tree is very susceptible to veld fires, and because of regular burning, large trees are seldom seen.It is normally a multi-stemmed shrub and branches low down to form a moderately dense, rounded canopy. In tree form it has a tall, bare trunk with a roundish canopy.

Leaves   Compound, large and shiny with 1 or 2 pairs of alternate leaflets with a larger terminal leaflet. Leaflets almost round, and the herringbone pattern of the veins is conspicuous. The leaflet margin is smooth. Leaflets are dark green above and much paler below. Leaves turn yellow and brown in autumn. (Leaf: 100 - 300 mm; leaflet: 35 - 110 mm and almost as broad)

Pod   The pod consists of a central hard core surrounded by a thin, hard, very wavy membrane. The pod is yellow-green to dark brown and ripens in autumn. It may remain on the tree through winter (November to July). (60 x 35 mm)

Flowers   The conspicuous, deep yellow, pea-shaped flowers grow in sprays on the ends of mature stems. The flowers last for 2 - 3 weeks, and are sweet-scented and have crinkled petals. This tree normally flowers only after good rains, but may flower more than once in a season (September to February). (Spray: 150 - 300 mm)

Bark   Bark is grey to light brown, smooth when young. In older trees it is rough and breaks up into irregular blocks that peel off.

	Oct	Nov	Dec	Jan	Feb	Mar	Apr	May	Jun	Jul	Aug	Sep
Leaf												
Flower												
Fruit/Pod												

Seasonal changes   Deciduous. This tree may be without leaves from June to October, but will be recognisable as long as the fruit is present.

RUSSET BUSHWILLOW

Combretum hereroense

COMBRETACEAE	
BUSHWILLOW FAMILY	**SA Tree Number 538**

AFRIKAANS Kierieklapper **N. SOTHO** Mokabi **TSONGA** Mpotsa **TSWANA** Mokabi **VENDA** Mugavhi **ZULU** umHlalavane

The species name **hereroense** refers to the Herero people of Namibia.

Where you'll find this tree easily

The Russet Bushwillow grows in loose groups often around pans, on rocky areas and sometimes along smaller drainage lines.

- It is easiest to find in Mixed Bushwillow Woodlands (A).

- This tree can also be found in Sabie/Crocodile Thorn Thickets (D).

Ecozones where this tree occurs

A	E	I	M
B	F	J	N
C	G	K	O
D	H	L	P

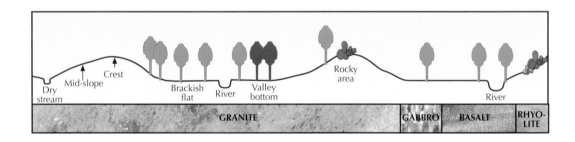

Striking features

- **The pods are characteristically the four-winged *Combretum* shape, but are smaller than those of similar-sized *Combretum* trees.**
- This is a small, multi-stemmed tree with one or more thick, crooked, often curved stems.
- **It has an overall coppery appearance from March to July, owing to the presence of large numbers of red-brown pods that grow conspicuously on the canopy.**
- It is densely branched, with new young branches forming very straight, upward shoots.

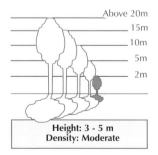

Height: 3 - 5 m
Density: Moderate

301

RUSSET BUSHWILLOW

Combretum hereroense

Links with animals The leaves are eaten by kudu, impala, steenbok, elephant and giraffe.

Human uses The wood is used as supports in mines, and to make pick and hoe handles. Straight branches are used to make kieries (walking sticks), hence the Afrikaans name 'Kierieklapper'. Root extracts are used for stomach complaints, and as enemas for venereal diseases and pains in the body. Bark is used for heart disease and heartburn. Dried young shoots are used for tonsillitis and coughs.

Gardening Not a very attractive garden plant, except in autumn when it is covered by coppery pods. It should grow well in most gardens as it is drought-resistant and can take fairly sharp frost. It can be grown from seed and will grow quite fast in well-watered gardens. The seeds are thought to be poisonous.

Look-alike This tree can be confused with other Bushwillows. See page 62-63 in the Distinctive Striking Features section for comparisons.

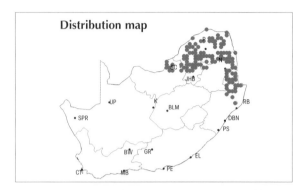
Distribution map

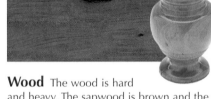

Wood The wood is hard and heavy. The sapwood is brown and the heartwood reddish-brown with dark markings. It is termite- and borer-proof.

This is a particularly large, distinctive Russet Bushwillow, laden with pods in late May.

GROWTH DETAILS

It is multi-stemmed with branchlets growing vertically upwards from bigger, horizontal branches.

Leaves   The simple leaves are opposite and have a smooth margin. They are small for the Bushwillow family, and they vary in shape, but usually broadly elliptic to heart-shaped. They have a rounded tip, that often ends in a small sharp point, and rounded or broadly tapering base. The leaves are dark green above and pale yellow-green below. The undersurface is often covered in rusty-brown hairs. (20 - 70 x 10 - 45 mm)

Bark   The yong bark is covered in hairs, peels in strips, and changes colour from green to red-brown, to grey. Older bark is rough and fissured lengthways, and is light grey to dark grey-brown.

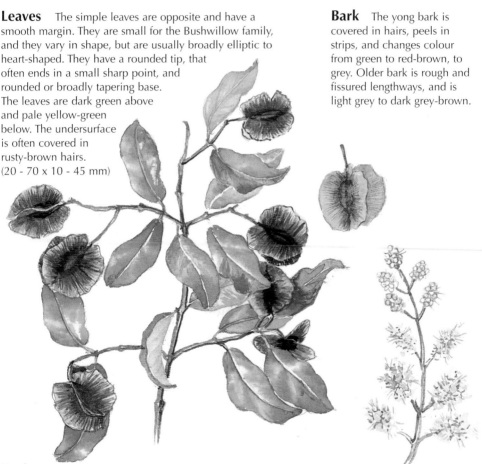

Pods   The four-winged pods grow abundantly in prominent bunches, and are characteristic of the Bushwillow family. They are brilliant russet-red in summer, changing to light, coppery-brown later in the season. Pods appear in mid- to late-summer and remain on the tree for long periods, often until July. (Approximately 23 x 20 mm).

Flowers   The sweet-smelling flowers are white to cream-coloured, to yellow, and are found in dense spikes that grow in the angle made by the leaves, or on the tips of twigs. The flowers appear before or with the new leaves (August to November). (Flower spike: up to 60 x 15 mm)

	Oct	Nov	Dec	Jan	Feb	Mar	Apr	May	Jun	Jul	Aug	Sep
Leaf												
Flower												
Fruit/Pod												

Seasonal changes   Deciduous. Leaves and fruit fall in late autumn, after which identification is difficult.

SICKLE-BUSH

Dichrostachys cinerea   Small-leaved Sickle-bush

**MIMOSACEAE
ACACIA FAMILY**   **SA Tree Number 190**

AFRIKAANS Sekelbos **PEDI** Moretshe, Mongana, Moselesele **SISWATI** umSilazembe **TSONGA** Ndzenga
TSWANA Mosêlêsêlê **VENDA** Murenzhe **ZULU** uGagane, umZilazembe, umThezane, uMnukelambiba

The species name **cinerea** refers to the ashy colour of the bark.

Where you'll find this tree easily

The Sickle-bush grows in dense groups and
prefers clay soils.

- This tree can easily be found growing in
  Sabie/Crocodile Thorn Thickets (D).
- This tree can also be found in most other
  Ecozones.

Ecozones where this tree occurs

A	E	I	M
B	F	J	N
C	G	K	O
D	H	L	P

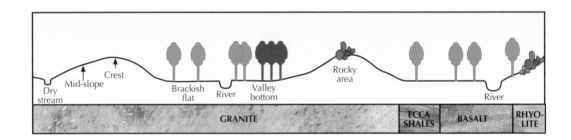

Striking features

- This smallish, multi-stemmed shrub (or
  occasionally tree), has a heavily intertwined
  or matted canopy with fine feathery foliage.
- The branches and twigs have long, straight
  spines.
- **The flowers resemble Chinese lanterns.**
- **Tightly coiled pods are very distinctive.**

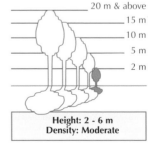

Height: 2 - 6 m
Density: Moderate

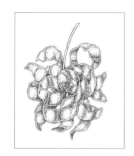

Largest tree currently registered

Diameter: 0,67 m
Girth: 2,10 m
Height: 6 m

JJH Engelbrecht
Maroelasfontein,
Dist. Waterberg

SICKLE-BUSH

Dichrostachys cinerea

Links with animals The pods are very nutritious and are eaten by a wide variety of animals including rhino, monkey, giraffe, bushpig and buffalo.

Human uses Roots, bark, pods and leaves are used for medicinal purposes including the treatment of toothache, snakebite and skin diseases. The leaves are said to have local anaesthetic properties. The wood is used for fence poles. Fresh bark is used to make fibre.

Gardening With its very attractive flowers, sharp spines and tendency to encroach, the Sickle-bush can make an attractive, impenetrable hedge for the indigenous garden. This bush is fairly drought-and frost-resistant. It grows slowly but can be grown from seed easily.

Look-alike trees This tree can be confused with the Acacias and Albizias. See page 59-61 for comparisons.

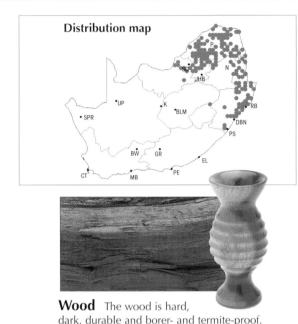

Distribution map

Wood The wood is hard, dark, durable and borer- and termite-proof. It is suitable for turning and produces good quality charcoal.

Search the Sickle-bush shapes in mist, and find the Pearl-spotted Owl!

GROWTH DETAILS

This is a small, multi-stemmed, low-branching tree. The stems and branches divide profusely to form a densely intertwined, matted canopy of branchlets and twigs with fine feathery foliage.

Leaves The long, twice compound, olive-green leaves are alternate. The very small delicate leaflets are elliptic with a smooth margin. There are 8 - 12 pairs of feathers and 15 - 30 pairs of leaflets. (Leaf: 30 - 200 mm; leaflet: 3 x 0,5 mm)

Spines The long, straight, light grey spines are modified side branchlets, and are so tough that they can puncture tractor tyres. Sometimes they have leaves growing on them. (20 - 40 mm)

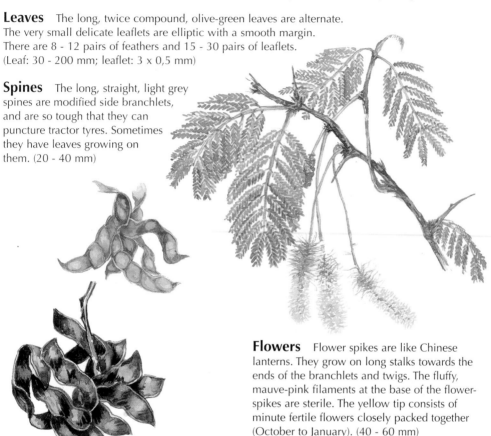

Flowers Flower spikes are like Chinese lanterns. They grow on long stalks towards the ends of the branchlets and twigs. The fluffy, mauve-pink filaments at the base of the flower-spikes are sterile. The yellow tip consists of minute fertile flowers closely packed together (October to January). (40 - 60 mm)

Pods The closely packed, fertilised flowers mature to form many tightly coiled pods growing bunched together from each flower-spike. The clusters of pods ripen to dark brown and do not split open on the tree. Pods may remain on the tree even after the leaves have dropped (May to September). (Cluster: 70 -100 mm diameter)

Bark The bark is light brown to ash-grey as the scientific name indicates, with shallow lengthways grooves.

	Oct	Nov	Dec	Jan	Feb	Mar	Apr	May	Jun	Jul	Aug	Sep
Leaf												
Flower												
Fruit/Pod												

Seasonal changes Deciduous. This tree can be identified in winter by its growth form, spines and pods.

WHITE-LEAVED RAISIN & SANDPAPER RAISIN

Grewia bicolor & Grewia flavescens

White Raisin & Sandpaper Raisin

| TILIACEAE LINDEN FAMILY | SA Tree Number 458/459.2 |

WHITE-LEAVED RAISIN: AFRIKAANS Witrosyntjie   **SANDPAPER RAISIN: AFRIKAANS** Skurwerosyntjie

The species name **bicolor** means of two colours, and **flavescens** means becoming yellow or yellowish.

This is a large group of trees and shrubs that is very widely spread in South Africa. They are all similar in appearance, and often grow in groups. The following two species are typical, common Raisins.

Where you'll find these trees easily

White-leaved Raisin

The White-leaved Raisin grows in groups, often to be found in large stands growing along the side of the road.

- You can easily find this tree in the Sabie/Crocodile Thorn Thickets (D).
- You will also find this tree growing in most other Ecozones.

Ecozones where this tree occurs

WHITE-LEAVED RAISIN

A	E	I	M
B	F	J	N
C	G	K	O
D	H	L	P

SANDPAPER RAISIN

A	E	I	M
B	F	J	N
C	G	K	O
D	H	L	P

Sandpaper Raisin

The Sandpaper Raisin grows in groups, often to be found in large stands growing along the side of the road.

- You can find this tree easily in the Sabie/Crocodile Thorn Thickets (D).
- This tree can also be found in the Lebombo Mountain Bushveld (I), Olifants Rugged Veld (J) and in Mopane/Bushwillow Woodlands (P).

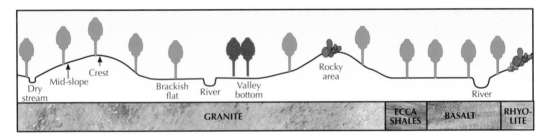

Striking features

- These trees or shrubs often grow in large, uniform groups.
- They are multi-stemmed and densely branched, forming a very irregular, leafy canopy.
- The leaves are broad and hairy.
- The leaf tips may be rounded or pointed, and this will help with specific identification.
- Some species have square branches, which will also help with identification.
- **They have yellow, star-like flowers.**
- **The fruit is berry-like and hard, but the size and number of lobes differ between species.**

WHITE-LEAVED RAISIN

- 20 m & above
- 15 m
- 10 m
- 5 m
- 2 m

Height: 2 - 5 m
Density: Moderate

SANDPAPER RAISIN

- 20 m & above
- 15 m
- 10 m
- 5 m
- 2 m

Height: 1 - 5 m
Density: Moderate

WHITE-LEAVED RAISIN

SANDPAPER RAISIN

309

WHITE-LEAVED RAISIN
& SANDPAPER RAISIN

Grewia bicolor & Grewia flavescens

Links with animals Klipspringer and impala eat Sandpaper Raisin leaves. The fruit of all bushes are eaten by birds, especially hornbills, and also by baboon and monkey.

Human uses The fruit is edible. The wood is used for sticks and knobkieries. The young branchlets are used to weave baskets.

Gardening These small shrubs are not really attractive or neat enough to use except in very large indigenous gardens.

GROWTH DETAILS: WHITE-LEAVED RAISIN

This is a multi-stemmed shrub and often has twisted branches. The bark is dark grey and rough and peeling. Young stems are smooth grey. Branchlets are velvety-grey or brown.

Leaves Simple and alternate. The form is variable but the under-surface is always distinctly paler and covered with velvety-grey hairs. The edges are smooth or slightly toothed. Leaf tips are round. Leaves are held horizontally or drooping. (10 - 32 x 15 - 70 mm)

Fruit The berry-like fruit is hard and is normally one to two-lobed. It is reddish-brown when mature. (December to April). (Each lobe 6 mm)

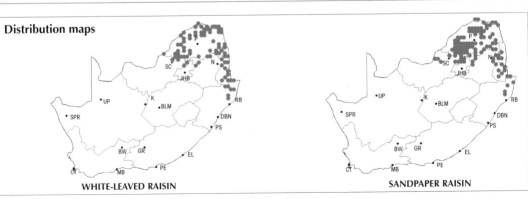

Distribution maps

WHITE-LEAVED RAISIN

SANDPAPER RAISIN

GROWTH DETAILS: SANDPAPER RAISIN

This is a multi-stemmed scrambling shrub. The stems are square and fluted, especially the mature branches, which have four distinct angles. The branchlets are covered with coarse hairs.

Leaves   Simple, alternate, and hairy and light green on both sides. Edges are irregularly toothed; stalk is short and velvety; leaf tips are pointed. (30 x 70 mm)

Fruit   The berry-like fruit is hard and is normally two-lobed (may be one to four-lobed), slightly grooved and covered by whitish hair. It ripens to a yellow-brown (March to July). (Each lobe 8 - 14 mm)

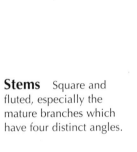

Stems   Square and fluted, especially the mature branches which have four distinct angles.

Flowers of both species
Yellow, star-like flowers grow in the base of the leaves. (20 mm)
(**White-leaved Raisin:** October to December)
(**Sandpaper Raisin:** December to March)

	Oct	Nov	Dec	Jan	Feb	Mar	Apr	May	Jun	Jul	Aug	Sep
Leaf	▓	▓	▓	▓	▓	▓	▓	▓	▓	▓		
Flower	░	░	░									
Fruit/Pod			▓	▓	▓	▓	▓					

Seasonal changes: White-leaved Raisin   Deciduous.

	Oct	Nov	Dec	Jan	Feb	Mar	Apr	May	Jun	Jul	Aug	Sep
Leaf	▓	▓	▓	▓	▓	▓	▓	▓	▓	▓		
Flower			░	░	░	░						
Fruit/Pod						▓	▓	▓	▓	▓		

Seasonal changes: Sandpaper Raisin   Deciduous. This is easy to identify in
winter because of the berries and square stems.

Kruger Trails

TREE TRAILING IN 2002

These Trails have been designed for beginner tree
spotters who want the excitement of finding their own,
unmarked trees, using the principles of Sappi Tree
Spotting. Each Trail covers trees that are common to
that area, and easy to find once you have a Search Image
in mind.

There are 11 Trails on the following pages. There is
one for each Main Camp – with the exception of
Punda Maria where the density of trees, as well as the
vast variety, make a Beginners' Trail impossible.

Weeping Boer-bean, page 252, and Knob Thorn Acacia,
page 132, often flower together in early Spring –
with spectacular results!

How to make the most of a Trail

If you have a GPS, you can simply use it to find the trees. However you should still read from 2 to 6 below.

1 Note that the start and reset points at intersections – when both road surfaces are either tar or sand – are taken with your vehicle already in the new road, with the back of the vehicle lining up with the previous crossroad. When the intended road changes from tar to sand, or vice versa, reset your kilometre reading with your front tyres on the new surface, and your back tyres on the old surface.

2 Look up the next tree in this book before you arrive at the new spot. You should have a very clear Search Image of the tree you want to identify. Take a note of the Striking Features, like flowers, fruit and autumn leaf colour, and be aware that in certain winter months deciduous trees are likely to be leafless and hard to identify.

3 The readings, GPS or kilometre, are approximates, and are only intended to get you within 20 - 25 metres of the tree. Approach the indicated spot very slowly, using the rest of the "clue" to help you look in the right place. Remember that individual vehicles will have their own variance in reading distance. You should be able to notice if your car under- or over-reads relative to our recordings. Unless otherwise stated, most readings are taken with your vehicle directly in line with the trunk of the tree. In a few cases you are specifically told to stop before the tree to improve your view – however this is usually a good idea anyway, especially with very large trees that are close to the road.

4 Virtually all the trees are within a few metres of the reading, reasonably close to the road. They have been chosen because they are good examples of the Search Image described in this book, and are usually standing alone to avoid confusion.

5 If you are unable to find a tree, add a few metres to your kilometre reading (if you have reversed and forwarded while searching), then add the kilometres to the next tree, and set off again, optimistically with a new Search Image!

6 On most of the Trails once a tree has been identified, it does not feature on that Trail again. When this "rule" is broken it is usually because of attractive/ideal/unusual growth forms. Once you have found, and identified a specific tree, we hope you will remember its Striking Features, and as you drive the rest of the Trail you will recognise others of the same species. It is quite possible that if you drive the 4 - 8 km (that is the average of most Trails) with enthusiasm, commitment and joy in tree spotting, even a novice should be able to recognise an average of 10 trees in that area – forever!

7 Remember that trees are vulnerable to death from old age, fire and elephant damage. As the years go by and your book is "older", even if it is a new book for you, the tree could have died, or even, in a few instances, be hidden by another tree that grew faster and larger.

Scented-pod Thorn Acacia, page 270

314

BERG-EN-DAL

START: Intersection S110 to Berg-en-Dal
Camp Gate and S110 Matjulu Loop
25 25.72 S
31 26.63 E
ROUTE: Matjulu Loop to Matjulu Pan
END: Matjulu Pan
25 24.17 S
31 26.20 E

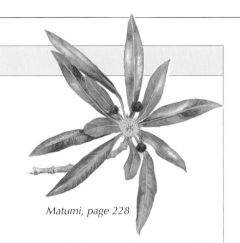

Matumi, page 228

Trail tree no.	Distance to next tree	Tree name	Directions and clues	GPS
1	0.2 km	Knob Thorn Acacia	North-east (right); large, old specimen	25 25.71 S 31 26.59 E
2	0.1 km	Large-fruit Bushwillow	Just past the 40 km sign on both sides of the road	25 25.70 S 31 26.55 E
3	0.48 km	Marula	West (left); just off the road	25 25.73 S 31 26.33 E
4	0.15 km	Apple-leaf	Middle of Metjula River; west (left); north bank of river; 35 m away	25 25.67 S 31 26.27 E
5		Matumi	East (right); north bank of river	
6	0.13 km	Pride-of-De Kaap Bauhinia	West (left); and others slightly ahead on east (right)	25 25.65 S 31 26.19 E
7	0.6 km	Jackal-berry	North (right); on termite mound; and another one ahead	25 25.46 S 31 26.45 E
8	0.39 km	Weeping Boer-bean	North-west (left); close to the road	25 25.31 S 31 26.55 E
9	0.65 km	Sycamore Fig	Stop on bridge; east (right); north bank of river; 45 m away	25 24.97 S 31 26.48 E
Take the road to Matjula Pan; reset				
10	0.45 km	African-wattle	West (left); close to the road; notice the landslide on the hill west (left)	25 24.56 S 31 26.40 E
Include short loop to river on west (left) side; finish the loop and continue on Matjula Pan road without resetting				
11		Leadwood Bushwillow	At the Matjula Pan circle; facing the pan, south, ahead; 50 m away; used as a rubbing post	25 24.17 S 31 26.20 E

CROCODILE BRIDGE

START: Junction of H4-2 and S25
      25 20.85 S
      31 53.03 E
ROUTE: H 4-2 out of Crocodile Bridge Camp; turn west along
      S25; then south towards the Hippo Pools on the S27
END: Hippo Pools at end of S27
      25 21.97 S
      31 51.12 E

Apple-leaf,
page 128

Trail tree no.	Distance to next tree	Tree name	Directions and clues	GPS
1	0.65 km	Knob Thorn Acacia	Both sides of the road	25 20.94 S 31 52.68 E
2	1.01 km	Jackal-berry	West (left); close to the road	25 20.85 S 31 52.12 E
3	0.24 km	Many-stemmed Albizia	North-east (right) 10 m off the road, a few trees; also on the south-west (left) side ahead	25 20.78 S 31 51.98 E
4	0.55 km	Delagoa Thorn Acacia	North-east (right); just before the road curves and the old railway line crosses the road	25 20.60 S 31 51.73 E
5	0.2 km	Knob Thorn Acacia	South- and north- east corners each have large specimens	25 20.58 S 31 51.60 E
Turn right down the S27				
6 7	0.15 km	Buffalo-thorn Delagoa Thorn Acacia	East (left); very close to the road All along the road for a number of metres on the east (left); then on the west (right) as well	25 20.66 S 31 51.59 E
8	0.55 km	Apple-leaf	North-east (left); 10 m off the road; smaller ones near the road	25 20.94 S 31 51.68 E
9	0.1 km	False Marula	South-west (right); 5 m off the road	25 21.99 S 31 51.72 E
10	0.5 km	Marula	West (right); 15 m off the road	25 21.24 S 31 51.82 E
11	0.7 km	Tamboti	As you cross a small drainage line on the North-east river bank (left); 8 m off the road	25 21.60 S 31 51.89 E
12	0.25 km	African-wattle	West (right)	25 21.72 S 31 51.99 E
13	0.28 km	Sickle-bush	At first on the west (right); then a few rolls further on, on the east (left) the road	25 21.85 S 31 52.07 E
14 15 16	0.1 km	Sausage-tree Jackal-berry Sycamore Fig	Just before end of road, on river side, south (left); side of the inlet Growing round a Sausage-tree	25 21.91 S 31 52.07 E
17	0.15 km	Large-leaved Rock Fig	On the east (left); on the west side of the rocky outcrop, near the top; this small tree which has white roots, clings to the rock	25 21.97 S 31 51.12 E

LOWER SABIE

Jackal-berry, page 210

START: At the junction of Lower Sabie camp road and H4-2
25 07.20 S
31 04.83 E
ROUTE: H4-2 then South on S28 until the hide at Nthandanyathi
END: Hide at Nthandanyathi

Trail tree no.	Distance to next tree	Tree name	Directions and clues	GPS
1		Umbrella Thorn Acacia	At the T junction; west, ahead	25 07.27 S 31 54.84 E
2	1.35 km	Knob Thorn Acacia	Just east of H-10 junction; north-east (left); 5 m off road; another one a few metres ahead	25 07.43 S 31 55.48 E
3	0.41 km	Leadwood Bushwillow	North-east (left); close to the road	25 07.43 S 31 55.72 E
4	0.43 km	Sickle-bush	Both sides of the road	25 07.49 S 31 55.96 E
5	0.82 km	Jackal-berry River Thorn Acacia	North (left); on both sides of the Jackal-berry	25 07.66 S 31 56.44 E
6	0.7 km	Apple-leaf	River side of road; east (left); 3 quite small trees	25 07.98 S 31 56 .62 E
7	0.11 km	Lala-palm	East (left)	25 08.06 S 31 56.62 E
8	0.6 km	Sausage-tree	East (left)	25 08.38 S 31 56.54 E
After 2.3 km turn left on the S28				
9	0.82 km	Fever Tree Acacia	North (left); in the drainage line, on the far east (left) side of the drainage line; young, but typical of the species	25 09.86 S 31 56.21 E
10	0.59 km	Tree Wisteria	West (right); 5 m off the road	25 10.12 S 31 56.38 E
11	1.2 km	Small Knob Thorn Acacia	East (left)	25 10.74 S 31 56.63 E
12		Leadwood Bushwillow	West (right)	
13	0.2 km	Marula	West (right); 40 m off the road a number of trees in the large pan area	25 10.84 S 31 56.68 E
After 3.4 km turn east (left) to Nthandanyathi Viewing; enter the Hide and sit in the middle seats				
14	Across river	Sycamore Fig	Over the river from the hide; on the eastern bank	
15	Right of hide	River Thorn Acacia	5 trees in a row along the river bank; the same side as the hide; from 50 m away; south to north	
16	Right of hide	Jackal-berry		
17	Right of hide	Weeping Boer-bean	This is the canopy over the hide	
18	Left of hide	Wild Date-palm		
19	Left of hide	Sycamore Fig		

PRETORIUSKOP

START: H1-1/H2-1 junction
      25 09.48 S
      31 15.70 E
ROUTE: Route H1-1 west; S1 north as far as
      turnoff to Mestel Dam
End: At turnoff to Mestel Dam
      25 07.82 S
      31 12.58 E

*Silver Cluster-leaf,
page 148*

Trail tree no.	Distance to next tree	Tree name	Directions and clues	GPS
1	0.1 km	Red Thorn Acacia	East (right); slim, smallish Acacia	25 09.43 S 31 15.66 E
2	0.78 km	Silver Cluster-leaf	South (left); a row of 4 smallish, then 1 large tree; reset at the large tree	25 09.25 S 31 15.27 E
3	0.58 km	Kiaat Bloodwood	North (right); 30 m – well off the road	25 09.20 S 31 14.94 E
4		Silver Cluster-leaf	North and further east (right); close to the road	
5	0.3 km	Marula	Junction Circle Road and H1-1; south-east corner (left) of the Junction; a magnificent specimen	25 09.26 S 31 14.79 E
6	0.83 km	Sycamore Fig	South (left); ± 10 m; small Natal-mahogany growing under it, on its east (left)	25 09.48 S 31 14.37 E
7	4.18 km	Black Monkey-orange	Just before the H1-1 and S1 junction south (left); 5 m	25 09.37 S 31 12.05 E
Route: Turn north S-1 dirt road				
8	At junction	Jackal-berry	North-west corner of junction (left); on an old termite mound a couple of trunks or separate trees	25 09.35 S 31 12.03 E
9	0.2 km	Black Monkey-orange	East (right); very old tree	25 09.23 S 31 12.11 E
10	0.7 km	Sickle-bush	East (right); close to road; a series of small bushes along road side	25 08.87 S 31 12.27 E
11	0.5 km	Jackal-berry	North-west (right); 10 m off the road; very tall tree	25 08.59 S 31 12.29 E
12		Natal-mahogany	A little further on; north-west (right)	
13	2.05 km	African-wattle	South-east (right); 15 m off the road;	25 07.82 S 31 12.58 E
After 13 it is worth doing a round trip to Mestel Dam – although we have not included any trees				

SKUKUZA

START: H1-2 at the far end of the low level bridge across
Sabie River, still on the bridge 24 59.35 S; 31 36.10 E
ROUTE: H1-2 and Maroela Loop
END: Before the Maroela Loop joins the H1-2
24 56.98 S
31 39.43 E

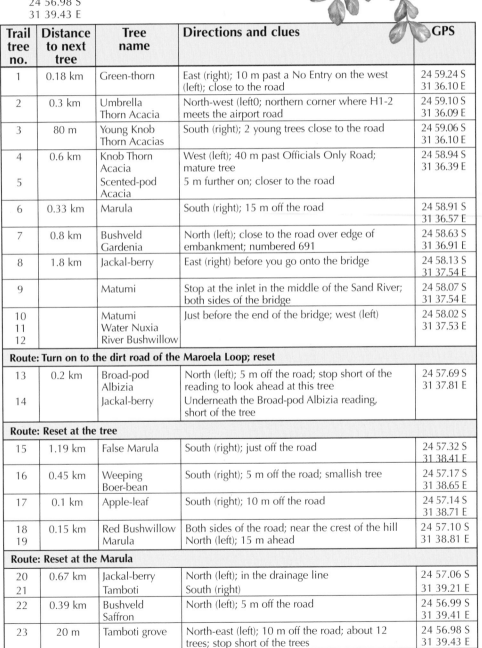

*Weeping
Boer-bean,
page 252*

Trail tree no.	Distance to next tree	Tree name	Directions and clues	GPS
1	0.18 km	Green-thorn	East (right); 10 m past a No Entry on the west (left); close to the road	24 59.24 S 31 36.10 E
2	0.3 km	Umbrella Thorn Acacia	North-west (left0; northern corner where H1-2 meets the airport road	24 59.10 S 31 36.09 E
3	80 m	Young Knob Thorn Acacias	South (right); 2 young trees close to the road	24 59.06 S 31 36.10 E
4	0.6 km	Knob Thorn Acacia	West (left); 40 m past Officials Only Road; mature tree	24 58.94 S 31 36.39 E
5		Scented-pod Acacia	5 m further on; closer to the road	
6	0.33 km	Marula	South (right); 15 m off the road	24 58.91 S 31 36.57 E
7	0.8 km	Bushveld Gardenia	North (left); close to the road over edge of embankment; numbered 691	24 58.63 S 31 36.91 E
8	1.8 km	Jackal-berry	East (right) before you go onto the bridge	24 58.13 S 31 37.54 E
9		Matumi	Stop at the inlet in the middle of the Sand River; both sides of the bridge	24 58.07 S 31 37.54 E
10 11 12		Matumi Water Nuxia River Bushwillow	Just before the end of the bridge; west (left)	24 58.02 S 31 37.53 E
Route: Turn on to the dirt road of the Maroela Loop; reset				
13	0.2 km	Broad-pod Albizia	North (left); 5 m off the road; stop short of the reading to look ahead at this tree	24 57.69 S 31 37.81 E
14		Jackal-berry	Underneath the Broad-pod Albizia reading, short of the tree	
Route: Reset at the tree				
15	1.19 km	False Marula	South (right); just off the road	24 57.32 S 31 38.41 E
16	0.45 km	Weeping Boer-bean	South (right); 5 m off the road; smallish tree	24 57.17 S 31 38.65 E
17	0.1 km	Apple-leaf	South (right); 10 m off the road	24 57.14 S 31 38.71 E
18 19	0.15 km	Red Bushwillow Marula	Both sides of the road; near the crest of the hill North (left); 15 m ahead	24 57.10 S 31 38.81 E
Route: Reset at the Marula				
20 21	0.67 km	Jackal-berry Tamboti	North (left); in the drainage line South (right)	24 57.06 S 31 39.21 E
22	0.39 km	Bushveld Saffron	North (left); 5 m off the road	24 56.99 S 31 39.41 E
23	20 m	Tamboti grove	North-east (left); 10 m off the road; about 12 trees; stop short of the trees	24 56.98 S 31 39.43 E

SATARA

START: At junction of H1-3 and S110
24 24.37 S
31 47.15 E
ROUTE: Along S110 for approximately 4 km
END: 24 23.92 S
31 49.51 E

Magic Guarri,
page 278

Trail tree no.	Distance to next tree	Tree name	Directions and clues	GPS
1	0.2 km	Marula	Check south (right); set back off road	24 24.38 S
2		Sickle-bush	A scraggly Sickle-bush in front	31 47.32 E
3	1.2 km	Leadwood Bushwillow	North (left); close to the road	24 24.57 S 31 47.99 E
4		Knob thorn Acacia	South (right); typical shape	
5	0.5 km	Magic Guarri	Both sides of road; this indicates brack area	24 24.70 S 31 48.26 E
6	0.1 km	Delagoa Thorn Acacia	South (right); this tree is normally in Ecozone G which is about 6 km from here. This indicates it is probably growing here in a small area of Ecca shale soil	24 24.73 S 31 48.32 E
7	0.5 km	Apple-leaf	South/river side of road; 3 tall trees roughly in a line	24 24.42 S 31 48.57 E
8		Magic Guarri	In front of Apple-leaf	
9	0.7 km	Feverberry Croton	South (right); close to the road	24 24.06 S 31 48.61 E
10		Leadwood Bushwillow	Ahead on on south (right)	
11	0.2 km	Lala-palm	West (left); spread over an open area	24 23.95 S 31 48.58 E
Route: At 0.7 km take small inlet towards the river				
12	0.75 km	Sycamore Fig	Across the river, straight ahead; 2 old specimens	24 23.80 S 31 48.86 E
13		Natal-mahogany		
14	0.3 km	Buffalo-thorn	South side (right); at start of small bridge	24 23.78 S 31 49.05 E
15	0.85 km	Jackal-berry	South (right); on the road	24 23.92 S 31 49.51 E

ORPEN

START: Junction H7 and S106, about 10 km from Orpen Camp
      24 28.02 S
      31 27.84 E
ROUTE: East along S106 until junction H7;
      head west for a few kilometres only
END: Rabelais Dam
      24 27.57 S
      31 29.96 E

Long-tail Cassia,
page 102

Trail tree no.	Distance to next tree	Tree name	Directions and clues	GPS
1	0.9 km	Knob Thorn Acacia	South (right); big tree as you go into the first drainage line you cross	24 27.99 S 31 27.84 E
2	10 m	Row of Wild Date-palms	South (right); in the drainage line ahead	24 27.98 S 31 27.86 E
3	0.3 km	Leadwood Bushwillow	North (left); next to the road	24 27.95 S 31 28.01 E
4	2.5 km	Marula	South (right); this tall tree is halfway up a crest; a on the road	24 27.91 S 31 28.14 E
5	0.85 km	Apple-leaf	North (left); close to the road	24 27.82 S 31 28.61 E
6	0.4 km	Bushveld Gardenia	North (left); close to the road; 2-3 m off the road	24 27.78 S 31 28.85 E
7	10 m	African-wattle	North (left); on the side of the road	24 27.77 S 31 28.89 E
8	0.25 km	Magic Guarri	All around the brackish flats – best example south (right); fairly close to the road	24 27.75 S 31 29.03 E
9	0.25 km	Silver Cluster-leaf	You will notice many of these trees halfway up the crest; leaf the north (left)	24 27.72 S 31 29.12 E
10	0.2 km	Green-thorn	South (right); just off the road south (right); ahead	24 27.71 S 31 29.30 E
11		Large-fruit Bushwillows	South (right); ahead	
12		Red Bushwillows	North (left); around Green-thorn and just ahead	
13	0.5 km	Russet Bushwillow	North (left); close to the road	24 27.69 S 31 29.58 E
Take the left turn at the split of the road towards Rabelais Dam				
14	0.2 km	Flaky Thorn Acacia	20 m after turnoff; south (right); close to the road	24 27.65 S 31 29.71 E
15		Long-tail Cassia	South-west (right); behind the Flaky Thorn	
16	0.7 km	Jackal-berry	At the second parking at Rabelais Dam; on a termite mound	24 27.57 S 31 29.96 E

OLIFANTS

START: Junction H8 and S93
  23 59.83 S
  31 43.94 E
ROUTE: Turn north up S93; south-west down S44
END: Just before S44 junction with S93
  23 58.98 S
  31 46.31 E

Sandpaper Raisin, page 308

Trail tree no.	Distance to next tree	Tree name	Directions and clues	GPS
1	10 m	Mopane	As you roll off the tar there are thickets on both sides of the road	23 59.83 S 31 43.94 E
Route: At 0.29 km turn east (right) on a small loop to the dam				
2	30 m	Purple-pod Cluster-leaf	West (right); 10 m off the road	23 59.32 S 31 43.82 E
Route: Position your car to face the dam				
3		Russet Bushwillow	Still on loop; at dam; west of dam; between the car and the dam	23 59.63 S 31 43.85 E
Route: Take the middle of the 3 roads and return to S93; reset				
4	0.27 km	Tall Mopane	West (left); 6 m off road; 2 trees close together	23 59.55 S 31 43.76 E
5	0.9 km	Knob Thorn Acacia	East (right); on a small bridge over a drainage line	23 59.06 S 31 43.89 E
6	0.25 km	Leadwood Bushwillow	East (right); wtih Mopane in front; close to the road	23 58.91 S 31 43.92 E
7	0.72 km	White-leaved Raisin		
8		Knob Thorn Acacia	A small Knob Thorn is south of the White-leaved Raisin	23 58.54 S 31 43.97 E
Route: Turn on to the S44; reset; at 1.3 km take the loop road to the river; reset				
9	20 m	Knob Thorn Acacia	South-east (right); 2 smallish trees are close to the road browsed into the triangular shape typical of Econzone L	23 56.81 S 31 44.11 E
10	At river	Leadwood Bushwillow	In front of you	
11		Knob Thorn Acacia	In front of you	
Route: Reset; turn right and continue the loop back to S44; drive to Olifants Lookout				
12	At lookout	Red Bushwillow	Facing the river; west (right) 2 trees	23 58.92 S
13		Shepherds-tree	Facing the river; west (right; very, very small – but good to see leaves and bark!	31 46.48 E
Route: Turn around; reset				
14	0.55 km	Leadwood Bushwillow	East (left) of road; 7 m	23 58.98 S
15		Knob Thorn Acacia	East (left) of road; 12 m	31 46.31 E

LETABA

START: H1-6 and S95 junction
  23 49.79 S
  31 35.19 E
ROUTE: North-east on S95
END: Before the end of the S95
  23 48.99 S
  31 35.16 E

*Natal-mahogany,
page 232*

Trail tree no.	Distance to next tree	Tree name	Directions and clues	GPS
1		Mopane	At the start of the trail, Mopane are on both sides and all around in Ecozone L	23 49.79 S 31 35.19 E
2	0.5 km	Mopane	On S95; on both sides of the road are tall Mopane	23 49.78 S 31 35.23 E
3		Umbrella Thorn Acacia	Move a few metres only; north (left)	
Reset				
4	0.2 km	Apple-leaf	South (right); on the river side of the road; 3 trees	23 49.71 S 31 35.34 E
5	0.6 km	Jackal-berry	At 0.6 km take loop down owards the river; on the river side a group of trunks look like one large specimen, but are in fact separate trees of the same species	23 49.45 S 31 35.52 E
6		Feverberry Croton	River side	
Route: Return to the S95				
7		Feverberry Croton	Just before you rejoin the S95; east (right); there are 2 good examples	
Reset				
8	1.8 km	Leadwood Bushwillow	Take the small loop to river; on the river side of the road; used as a rubbing post	23 49.34 S 31 35.58 E
9		Natal-mahogany	There are a few trunks with easy-to-recognise leaves – but poor tree shape	
10	1.88 km	Shepherds-tree	South (left); multi-stemmed	23 48.78 S 31 35.29 E
11	0.49 km	Sickle-bush	South (right)	23 48.99 S 31 35.16 E

MOPANI

START: S142 at junction with H1–6 south of Mopani Camp
   23 31.99 S
   31 25.14 E
ROUTE: NW along S142; include Mopani Viewing and
   Bird Hide; return to S142 heading north-west
END: 1 km after Bird Hide at Mopani Viewing
   23 31.58 S
   31 23.89 E

*Mopane,
page 144*

Trail tree no.	Distance to next tree	Tree name	Directions and clues	GPS
1	10 m	Mopane	In this Ecozone there are plenty of these trees, after which the camp, the Ecozone are named	23 31.99 S 31 25.15 E
2	0.7 km	Knob Thorn Acacia	Stop in the first drainage line you get to; on the hillside; west (left)	23 31.87 S 31 24.74 E
3	0.1 km	A group of Bushveld Candelabra Euphorbias	Stop in the Tsendze River; south (left)	23 31.87 S 31 24.65 E
4	Tsendze River Bridge	Marula	Move to the end of the bridge; west (left) of Tsendze River	
5		Bushveld Candelabra Euphorbias	West (left); on rocky outcrop are trees 5,6,7,8 and 9	23 31.81 S 31 24.56 E
6		Marulas	Amongst the Candelabra Euphorbias	
7		White Kirkias	Halfway up the rocky area	
8		Knob Thorn Acacia	Close to the road	
9		Small Baobabs	Close together; towards the top of the rocky area	
Route: Drive to Mopani Viewing; lock your car and get out to enjoy the hide				
10	Mopani Viewing	Silver Cluster-leaf	On the left of the gate; good to get a close look at the leaves, but the tree is very young	23 31.60 S 31 23.86 E
11		Tamboti	Outside the actual hide door, just before you enter the hide, overhanging the walkway	
Route: Reset before leaving the Hide; take the left hand road towards the river				
12	5 m	Sickle-bush	As you start on the river road; south (right)	23 31.59 S 31 23.87 E
13	8 m	Scented-pod Thorn Acacia	North-west (left)	23 31.58 S 31 23.89 E
This road will take you back to the S142				

SHINGWEDZI

START: At the junction main Shingwedzi Camp road and S134
   23 06.25 S
   31 25.70 E
ROUTE: Complete the S134 circle; continue along the S50
   towards Kanniedood Dam
END: About 5 km along the S134 on a river loop,
   before Kanniedood Dam
   23 06.64 S
   31 26.98 E

*Nyala-tree,
page 214*

Trail tree no.	Distance to next tree	Tree name	Directions and clues	GPS
1	20 m	Mopane	On both sides of the road; these tall Mopanes are common in amongst the shrub Mopane that dominate Ecozone L, nearby	23 06.27 S 31 25.68 E
2	0.2 km	Narrow-leaved Mustard-tree	Just after the No Entry sign; both sides of the road; these bushy shrubs are interesting because they are specific to Ecozone M; the southern (right) shrub has a large, old, leaning trunk	23 06.36 S 31 25.60 E
3	75 m	Umbrella Thorn Acacia	Both sides of the road; almost make a canopy across the road	23 06.41 S 31 25.59 E
Route: Reset the intersection of Mashagadzi Pan road and S134				
4	0.68 km	Shrub Mopane	Notice the change from Ecozone M to Ecozone L; dominant shrub Mopane ahead	23 06.76 S 31 25.43 E
5	0.37 km	Purple-pod Cluster-leaf	A hedge of small bushes along the west (right); the biggest tree is about 3 m off the road behind the smaller bushes	23 06.96 S 31 25.48 E
6	4.05 km	–	Unusually dramatic and visible end of Ecozone L; enter Ecozone M; note that there are now fewer Mopanes	23 07.76 S 31 25.43 E
7	0.2 km	Lala-palm	Just after the No Entry sign; on South (right); just off the road	25 06.59 S 31 26.55 E
Route: Turn on to the first loop on the east (left), river side; do not reset				
8	0.49 km	Large-leaved Rock Fig	A number of trees on both sides of the road; the largest is on the north-west (left)	23 06.61 S 31 26.80 E
9	0.85 km	Apple-leaf	Ahead; tall tree; north-west (left); on the road; used as a rubbing post	
Route: continue towards the river along this loop				
10	50 m	Leadwood Bushwillow	North (left); look ahead about 10 m, before moving to tree itself; interesting bark; very old tree	23 06.12 S 31 26.63 E
11	50 m	Jackal-berry	South-west (right); about 10 m ahead; 3 m off the road; roll alongside the tree itself to reset	23 06.60 S 31 26.89 E
12		Fever Tree Acacia	Across the river; north (left)	
Route: Continue along this loop				
13	0.15 km	Nyala-tree	South-west (right)	23 06.64 S 31 26.98 E
14		Jackal-berry	North-east (left)	
15		Wild Date-palm	Ahead on north-east (left)	
16		Sycamore Fig	Close to the river; north-east (left)	

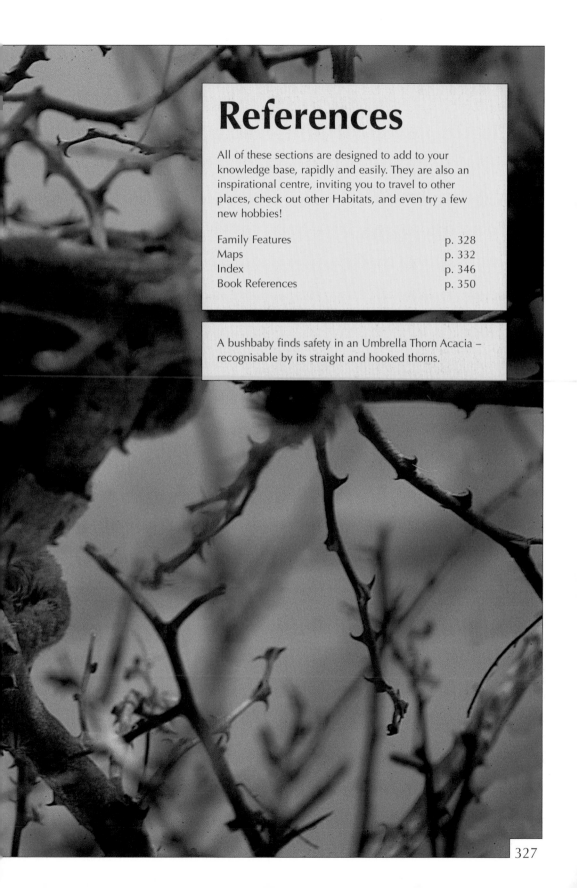

References

All of these sections are designed to add to your knowledge base, rapidly and easily. They are also an inspirational centre, inviting you to travel to other places, check out other Habitats, and even try a few new hobbies!

A bushbaby finds safety in an Umbrella Thorn Acacia – recognisable by its straight and hooked thorns.

Family Features

All living things have relatives that share certain distinctive features. In plants this can be similar growth form, seed dispersal mechanism, or leaf, flower, fruit or pod structure. Scientists classify plants by their flower features which can be minute details, hardly visible to the naked eye.

As a pleasure-seeking tree spotter you will find that knowing some visible similarities between family members will help you build up methods of recognising new trees wherever you go in Africa or further afield.

The scientific classifications tend to change quite regularly, so these statistics of world and South African distribution are simply there to give you an idea of the family size and distribution.

The information includes the Ecozones where you are most likely to find each family member. This is shown by the letter A to P in brackets. With this information you can look for related trees in one area. Remember to check their Habitat distribution on the Ecozone Tree Lists, pages 41 - 46.

ACACIA Mimosaceae
Worldwide - 58 genera, 3 100 species, mainly tropical regions; South Africa - 8 genera, 100 tree species (3rd largest woody family).
Family Features
- Leaves - twice compound, the leaves of certain species fold up at night
- Flowers - balls or spikes, protruding stamens
- Seeds - protected by palatable bean-like pods

Trees in this book
Black Monkey Thorn Acacia (A,G,H,I) p 32; Delagoa Thorn Acacia (G) p 158; Fever Tree Acacia (F,M) p 72; Flaky Thorn Acacia (A,D,I,J,L) p 284; Horned Thorn Acacia (D,O) p 270; Knob Thorn Acacia (A,B,C,D,E,F,H,J,K,L,O,P) p 132; Red Thorn Acacia (A,B,C,G,H,I) p 182; River Thorn Acacia (A,B,C,D,F,H,J, M) p 240; Scented-pod Thorn Acacia (A,B,F,C,D) p 270; Umbrella Thorn Acacia (A,C,D,E,F,G,J,K,L,M,O,P) p 80 Broad-pod Albizia (D,F,H) p 94; Bushveld Albizia (C,E,F,I,L,M,P); Many-stemmed Albizia (G) p 174; Sickle-bush (A,B,C,D,F,G,I,J,K,L,M,O,P) p 304

Flaky Thorn Acacia, page 284

BUSHWILLOW Combretaceae
Worldwide – 60 genera, 400 species; South Africa – well represented with 5 genera, 41 tree species.
Family Features
- Leaves - simple
- Flowers - spiked
- Seeds - four-winged

Trees in this book
Flame Climbing Bushwillow (D,H,J,M) p 98; Large-fruited Bushwillow (A,B,C,I) p 288; Leadwood Bushwillow (A,C,F,H,J,M,O) p 136; Red Bushwillow (A,B,C,D,E,I,J,N,P) p 292; River Bushwillow (D,H) p 236; Russet Bushwillow (A,B,C,D,E,F,J,L,M,O,P) p 300; Weeping Bushwillow (A,B,C,J,N) Purple-pod Cluster-leaf (C,D,L,J,P) p 110; Silver Cluster-leaf (A,B,C,N,P) p 148

CAPER Capparaceae
Worldwide - 46 genera and about 700 species; South Africa - 40 species.
Family Features
- Leaves - variable
- Flowers - 4 free petals, numerous long stamens

Trees in this book
Bushveld Bead-bean (F,G,J,K,L,O) p 39; Shepherds-tree (I,J,M,O,P) p 34

DOGWOOD / BLINKBLAAR Rhamnaceae
Worldwide - 52 genera, 600 species; South Africa - 7 genera, 20 tree species.
Family Features
- Leaves - shiny, simple, alternate
- Flowers - small, inconspicuous, nectar-rich

Tree in this book
Buffalo-thorn (A,B,C,D,F,K) p 258

EBONY Ebenaceae
Worldwide - 2 genera, 485 species, mostly
tropical regions; South Africa - 2 genera, 35 tree
species; wood traded by ancient merchants.
Family Features
• Very variable
• Leaves - simple, smooth margin
Trees in this book
Jackal-berry (A,B,C,D,F,H,J,M,P) p 210;
Magic Guarri (A,B,C,D,F,G,M,O,P) p 278

EUPHORBIA Euphorbiaceae
Worldwide - 2 000 species; South Africa -
100 species; 2nd largest woody family.
Family Features
• Latex - milky or watery, often poisonous
• Leaves - simple, usually alternate,
  toothed margin
• Fruit - small, 3-lobed capsule
Trees in this book
Bushveld Candelabra Euphorbia (D,I) p 192;
Lebombo Euphorbia (I) p 33; Naboom Euphorbia
(A,B,C,D,I) p 194; Rubber-hedge Euphorbia
(D,E); Feverberry Croton (F,H,L,P)
p 37, Lebombo-ironwood (I,N) p 170;
Tamboti (A,B,C,D,G,H,M,O,P) p 222

FLAMBOYANT Ceasalpiniaceae
Worldwide - 162 genera, 2 000 species,
mainly tropics; South Africa - 50 species;
one of the largest woody families.
Family Features
• Leaves - compound, alternate, paired leaflets
  at tip, swelling at base of leaf-stalk
• Flowers - large, showy, 5 symmetrical petals
• Seeds - usually more pod-encased, usually
  more than one seed
Trees in this book
African-wattle (A,B,C,D,E,F,I,J,K,L,P) p 90;
Long-tail Cassia (I,F,D,P) p 102; Mopane
(I,M,O,H,L,P) p 144; Pod-mahogany (A,I,N) p 200;
Pride-of-De Kaap Bauhinia (B,N,H) p 106;
Small False Mopane (N,P) p 40; Weeping
Boer-bean (A,B,J,C,D,H) p 252

GARDENIA Rubiaceae
Worldwide - 400 genera, 5 000 - 6 000
species, warmer parts of the world;
South Africa - 47 genera.
Family Features
• Leaves - hairy pits in axils of veins
  (under-surface), untoothed margin,
  opposite or whorled
Trees in this book
Bushveld Gardenia (A,D,J,M) p 262;
Matumi (D,H,J,M) p 228

GREEN-THORN Balanitaceae
Family Features
• Leaves - compound, 2 leaflets
Tree in this book
Green-thorn (D,E) p 162

JACARANDA Bignoniaceae
South Africa - 11 native species
Family Features
• Leaves - pinnately compound, opposite
  or whorled and without stipules
• Flowers - large, bell- or funnel-shaped
  and very showy
• Fruit - dehiscent and resembles a long,
  narrow pod, usually with winged seeds
Tree in this book
Sausage-tree (D,F,H,M) p 244

KAPOK Bombacaceae
Worldwide - about 21 genera, 150 species;
only tree of this family in Africa.
Family Features
• Trunks - swollen, bottle-shaped or
  barrel-shaped
• Leaves - alternate, often palmately compound
• Flowers - large with 5 free petals and
  numerous stamens
• Fruit - capsule or nut
Tree in this book
Baobab (I,M,P) p 68

Sickle-bush,
page 304

LINDEN Tiliaceae
Worldwide - 44 genera, 500 species;
South Africa - 30 tree and shrub species.
Family Features
• Leaves - simple, alternate, 3-veined from base, toothed margin, star-shaped hairs
Trees in this book
Sandpaper Raisin (D,I,P) p 308; White-leaved Raisin (A,B,C,D,F,G,H,J,K,L,M, O,P) p 308

LITCHI Sapindaceae
Worldwide - 120 genera, about 1 000 species;
South Africa - about 30 species.
Family Features
• Leaves - variable
• Flowers - small and inconspicuous in local species
• Fruit - small, fleshy parts (arils) of many species are edible
Tree in this book
Jacket-plum (A,B,C,D,E,I,J,L) p 274

MAHOGANY Meliaceae
Worldwide - in Asia a well known Seringa;
South Africa - 6 genera, 20 tree and shrub species.
Family Features
• Leaves - alternate, compound, crowded towards end of branchlets
• Flowers - stamens fused into a tube, 5 free petals
Tree in this book
Natal-mahogany (D,F,H,J) p 232

MANGO Anacardiaceae
Worldwide - 60 genera; South Africa - 10 genera, 80 species
Family Features
• Trees have watery latex
• Leaves - three leaflets (Karee members only)
• Flowers - separate male and female flowers, on separate trees
• Fruit - edible in most species
• Bark - rich in resin
Trees in this book
Bushveld Resin –tree (F,P) p 31;
Drooping Resin-tree (F,I,L) p 31;
False Marula (A,B,D,E,F,H,I,L) p 29;
Marula (A,B,D,E,F,H,I,J) p 140

MULBERRY Moraceae
Worldwide - tropical and sub-tropical area,
1 000 species; South Africa - Ficus genus,
35 species.
Family Features
• Leaves - alternate, rounded leaf-buds
• Latex - milky
Trees in this book
Large-leaved Rock Fig (A,B,C,D,E,I,J,P) p 196;
Red-leaved Fig (A,B,C,D) p 24; Sycamore Fig (B,D,F,H,J) p 218

MUSTARD Salvadoraceae
Family Features
• Leaves - opposite, simple, elliptic to round, with smooth margins
Tree in this book
Narrow-leaved Mustard-tree (M) p 178

MYRRH Burseraceae
Worldwide - 200 species, mainly Africa and Arabia; South Africa - 26 species; linked to biblical times; produced frankincense and myrrh from resin.
Family Features
• Latex - milky
• Leaves - compound, aromatic
• Bark - thin, papery, flaky (in some species)
Trees in this book
Firethorn Corkwood (F,I,J,L,N) p 188;
Tall Firethorn Corkwood (A,F,I,J,L,M,N,P) p 186

MYRTLE Myrtaceae
Worldwide – large tropical and sub tropical family; 2 000 species; South Africa - 25 species.
Family Features
• Leaves - simple, simple, opposite, smooth margin
• Flowers – many stamens
• Fruit – tipped with remains of flower
Trees in this book
Umdoni/Waterberry (A,B,D,H) p 22

Many-stemmed
Albizia,
page 174

PALM Arecaceae

Worldwide - 140 genera, 100 species; South Africa - 7 shrub or tree species; strongly associated with humans.

Family Features
- Flowers - small spray enclosed in sheath
- Fruit - berry-like

Trees in this book

Northern Lala-palm (H,M) p 76;
Southern Lala-palm (F,H,M,P) p 76;
Wild Date-palm (F,H) p 84

PEA Fabaceae

Worldwide - 437 genera, 11 300 species; South Africa - 2 genera, 35 tree species.

Family Features
- Flowers - pea-like, broad, erect upper petal, 2 narrower wings on both sides, 2 lowest petals joined (boat-like keel)
- Seeds - encased in pods usually covering more than one seed

Trees in this book

Apple-leaf (A,C,D,F,G,H,J,L,M,P) p 128;
Kiaat Bloodwood (B,C) p 166;
Nyala-tree (D,H,J,M) p 214; Round-leaved Bloodwood (A,D,E,F,I) p 296;
Tree Wisteria (A,B,E,F,G) p 118;
Zebrawood (A,E,F,O,P) p 122

SPIKE-THORN Celastraceae

Worldwide - 60-70 genera, South Africa - 60 tree species, widely distributed.

Family Features
- Very variable

Trees in this book

Bushveld Saffron (D,E) p 266;
Common Spikethorn (A,F,H) p 25;
Red Spike-thorn (D,F,H,J,M) p 114

STAR-CHESTNUT Sterculiaceae

Worldwide - 50 genera. 1 000 species; South Africa - 3 genera. Cocoa tree family member.

Family Features
- Leaves - star-shaped clumps of hairs (visible only with magnifying glass)

Tree in this book

Wild-pear Dombeya (A,B,C,N) p 27

TREE-OF-HEAVEN Simaroubaceae

Worldwide - 30 genera and over 100 species; South Africa - about 4 indigenous tree species.

Family Features
- Leaves - alternate, compound leaves with a leaflet at the tip, and toothed margins
- Flowers - some have separate male and female flowers
- Fruit - may be dry and woody, or fleshy

Trees in this book

Mountain Kirkia (B,C) p 28; White Kirkia (I,J,L,N,P) P 204

WILD ELDER Loganiaceae

Worldwide - 5 genera, 21 species; South Africa - 20 species.

Family Features
- Very varied
- Leaves - simple, opposite or in threes
- Flowers - bisexual

Trees in this book

Black Monkey-orange (A,B,C,N,P) p 154;
Water Nuxia (D,H,M) p 248

Weeping Bushwillow, page 26

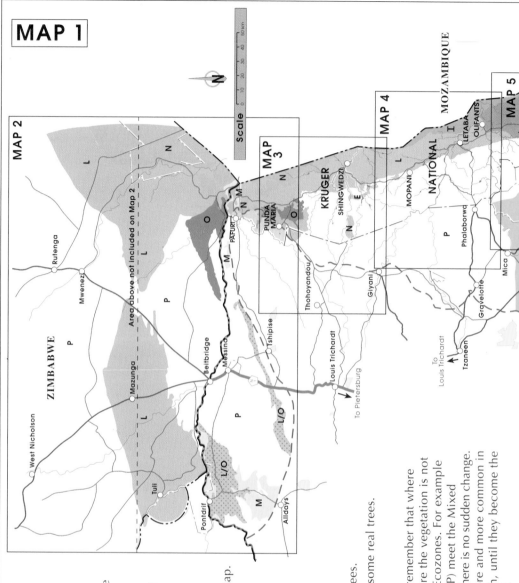

The Lowveld

Use the following Maps to make tree spotting easy.

For details of how the Lowveld was defined, and for a full description of Ecozones and Habitats, read pages 18 - 47.

Find trees by Ecozone

1. Work out where you are on the Map.

2. Which Ecozone are you in? What is its letter?

3. Look up the Ecozone Tree List, pages 41 - 46, and decide which trees you might be able to find in your Ecozone.

4. Look up these trees in the book.

5. Create a Search Image for these trees.

6. Check your Search Image against some real trees.

When using Ecozones to find trees, remember that where Ecozones meet, there is an area where the vegetation is not really characteristic of either of the Ecozones. For example where the Mopane Ecozones (L and P) meet the Mixed Bushwillow Woodlands (Ecozone A), there is no sudden change. Pockets of Mopane trees become more and more common in Ecozones A and J as one moves north, until they become the dominant trees, in Ecozones L and P.

Base information obtained from official maps produced by the Chief Directorate of Surveys and Land Information

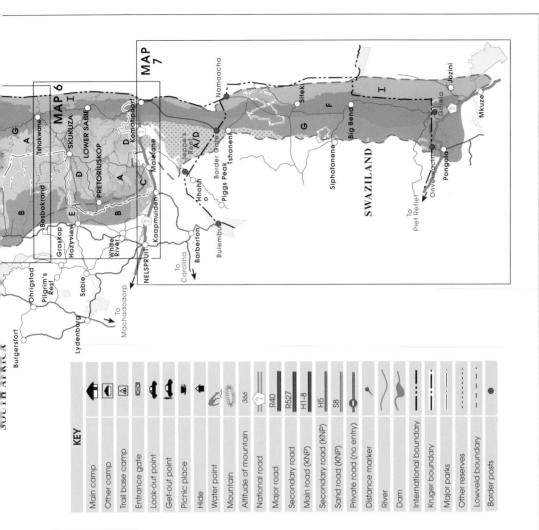

MAP 6

G · Tshokwane

A

I · SKUKUZA

LOWER SABIE

D · PRETORIUSKOP

E

B · Bosbokrand

Graskop

Hazyview

White River

Sabie

Ohrigstad

Pilgrim's Rest

Lydenburg

Burgersfort

To Machadodorp

NELSPRUIT

Kaapmuiden

To Carolina

Barberton

Bulembu

Piggs Peak

Tshaneni

Mhlume

Malelane

Komatipoort

Border Gate

Jeppe's Reef

A/D

C

MAP 7

Namaacha

Siteki

F

G · Big Bend

SWAZILAND

Siphofanene

To Piet Retief

Onverwacht

Pongola

Jozini

Golela

Mkuze

H

KEY

	Main camp
	Other camp
	Trail base camp
	Entrance gate
	Look-out point
	Get-out point
	Picnic place
	Hide
	Water point
	Mountain
366	Altitude of mountain
	National road
R40	Major road
R527	Secondary road
H1-8	Main road (KNP)
H5	Secondary road (KNP)
S8	Sand road (KNP)
	Private road (no entry)
	Distance marker
	River
	Dam
	International boundary
	Kruger boundary
	Major parks
	Other reserves
	Lowveld boundary
	Border posts

Ecozones

See the Ecozone Tree List pages 41 - 46.

A Mixed Bushwillow Woodlands (on granite)
B Pretoriuskop Sourveld (on granite)
C Malelane Mountain Bushveld (on granite)
D Sabie / Crocodile Thorn Thickets (on granite)
E Thorn Veld (on gabbro)
F Knob Thorn / Marula Savannah (on basalt)
G Delagoa Thorn Thickets (on Ecca shale)
H Riverine
I Lebombo Mountain Bushveld (on rhyolite)
J Olifants Rugged Veld (on rhyolite / basalt)
K Stunted Knob Thorn Savannah (on basalt)
L Mopane Shrubveld (on basalt)
M Alluvial Plains
N Sandveld
O Tree Mopane Savannah (on Ecca shale)
P Mopane / Bushwillow Woodlands (on granite)

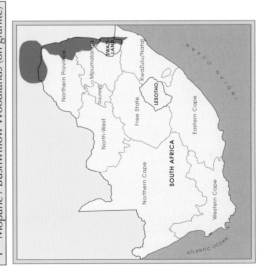

Northern Province

Mpumalanga

SWAZILAND

Gauteng

North-West

Free State

KwaZulu/Natal

LESOTHO

Northern Cape

SOUTH AFRICA

Eastern Cape

Western Cape

INDIAN OCEAN

ATLANTIC OCEAN

333

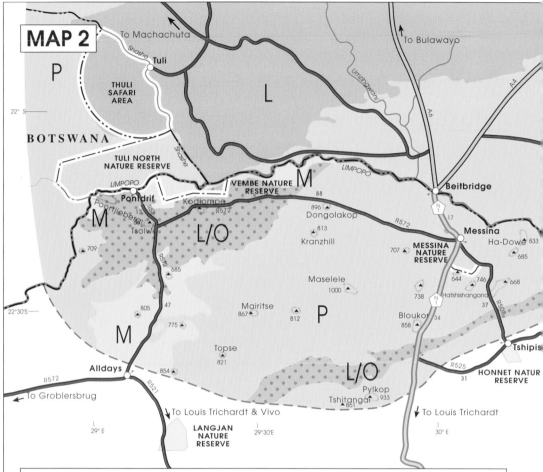

MAP 2

To Machachuta

To Bulawayo

P

Tuli

THULI
SAFARI
AREA

L

22° S

BOTSWANA

TULI NORTH
NATURE RESERVE

Shashe

LIMPOPO

LIMPOPO

VEMBE NATURE
RESERVE

M

88

Beitbridge

Pontdrif

Kodiompe

Dongolakop

896

R572

17

M

Poortjiebel

Tsolw

R52

L/O

813

Kranzhill

MESSINA

Messina

Ha-Dowe 833

709

685

707

MESSINA
NATURE
RESERVE

685

R572

Maselele
1000

644

746

668

22°30'S

805

47

Mairitse
867

738

Hatshishangana

M

775

812

P

Blouko

858

34

37

Topse
821

L/O

Tshipis

Alldays

854

R525

HONNET NATUR
RESERVE

R572

R521

31

To Groblersbrug

Pylkop
Tshitangaf 933
861

To Louis Trichardt

29° E

To Louis Trichardt & Vivo

LANGJAN
NATURE
RESERVE

29°30'E

30° E

Northern Province and Zimbabwe

The Zimbabwe part of this Map was created by integrating the "Vegetation of Zimbabwe" Map with practical experience and knowledge of the area.

This whole area is dominated by Mopane trees and shrubs. In the more sandy areas, the Silver Cluster-leaf and Pod-mahogany are more numerous in the Lowveld of Zimbabwe than in similar vegetation types in Kruger.

The green dotted line indicates the Lowveld as defined by the National Botanical Institute's Vegetation Map of South Africa, Lesotho and Swaziland (1996). The area to the west of this green dotted line (which is shown in colour on this Map, between Punda Maria and Pafuri), is in fact not part of the Lowveld. It is, however, included here in colour because it is part of the Kruger National Park.

Ecozones

See the Ecozone Tree List pages 41 - 46.

L	Mopane Shrubveld (on basalt)
M	Alluvial Plains
N	Sandveld
O	Tree Mopane Savannah (on Ecca shale)
P	Mopane / Bushwillow Woodlands (on granite)

To Thohoyandou

Base information obtained from official maps produced by the Chief Directorate of Surveys and Land Information

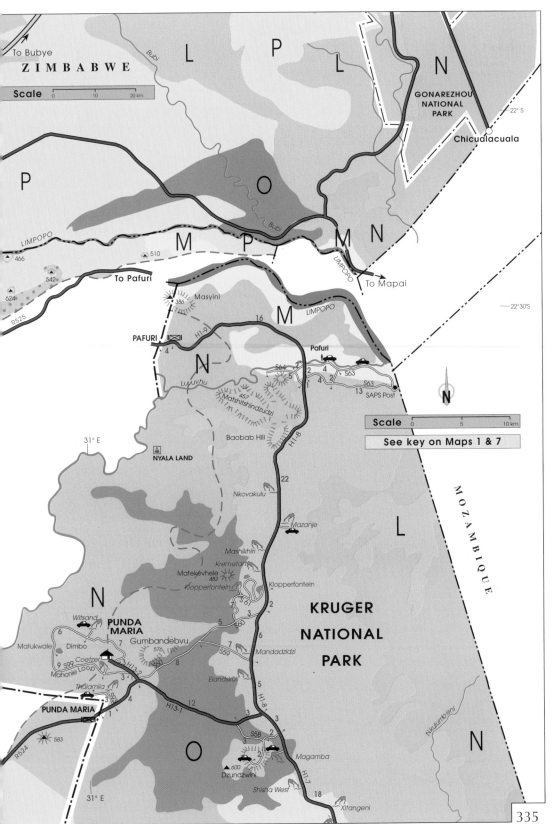

ZIMBABWE

To Bubye

L P L N

GONAREZHOU
NATIONAL
PARK

Chicualacuala

22° S

P

P

O

M P M N

LIMPOPO

To Mapai

466

510

542

624

R525

To Pafuri

M

LIMPOPO

22°30'S

386 Masyini

16

H1-9

N

PAFURI

4

Pafuri

S64 2

4 S63

Luvuvhu

5

4

13 SAPS Post

S63

457 Matshitshindzudzi

N

Scale 0 5 10 km

See key on Maps 1 & 7

Baobab Hill

H1-8

NYALA LAND

22

Nkovakulu

M
O
Z
A
M
B
I
Q
U
E

Mazanje

L

Mashikhiri

Kremetart

Matekevhele
482

Klopperfontein

Klopperfontein

S61

N

Witsand

2

KRUGER

PUNDA
MARIA

NATIONAL

6

Gumbandebvu

5

S60

6

PARK

Matukwale Dimbo

7

576

7

Coetzer

S59 Mandadzidzi

9 S99

8

Mahonie Loop

3 H13-2

Thulamila

3

Elandskui

5

PUNDA MARIA

4

H13-1

12

H1-8

3

R524

583

S58

O

Magamba

600
Dzundzwini

H1-7

31° E

Shisha West

18

Xitangeni

31° E

N

335

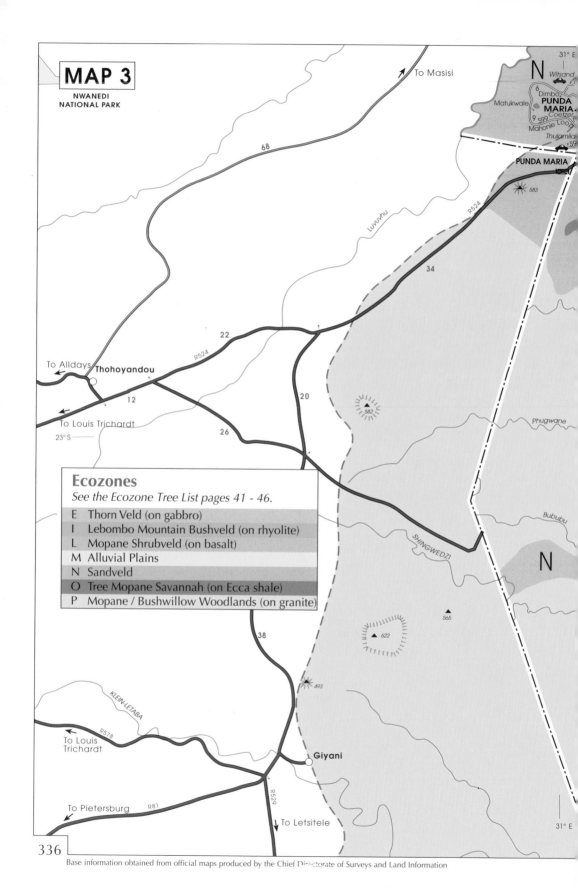

MAP 3

NWANEDI
NATIONAL PARK

To Masisi

31° E

N

Witsand

6 Dimbo
Matukwale PUNDA
MARIA
9 S99 Coetzer
Mahonie Loop
Thulamila
S9

PUNDA MARIA

583

R524

68

Luvuvhu

34

22

R524

20

Phugwane

To Alldays **Thohoyandou**

582

12

To Louis Trichardt

23° S

26

Bububu

SHINGWEDZI

N

Ecozones
See the Ecozone Tree List pages 41 - 46.

E	Thorn Veld (on gabbro)
I	Lebombo Mountain Bushveld (on rhyolite)
L	Mopane Shrubveld (on basalt)
M	Alluvial Plains
N	Sandveld
O	Tree Mopane Savannah (on Ecca shale)
P	Mopane / Bushwillow Woodlands (on granite)

565

622

38

493

KLEIN-LETABA

R578

To Louis
Trichardt

Giyani

To Pietersburg R81

R529

To Letsitele

31° E

Base information obtained from official maps produced by the Chief Directorate of Surveys and Land Information

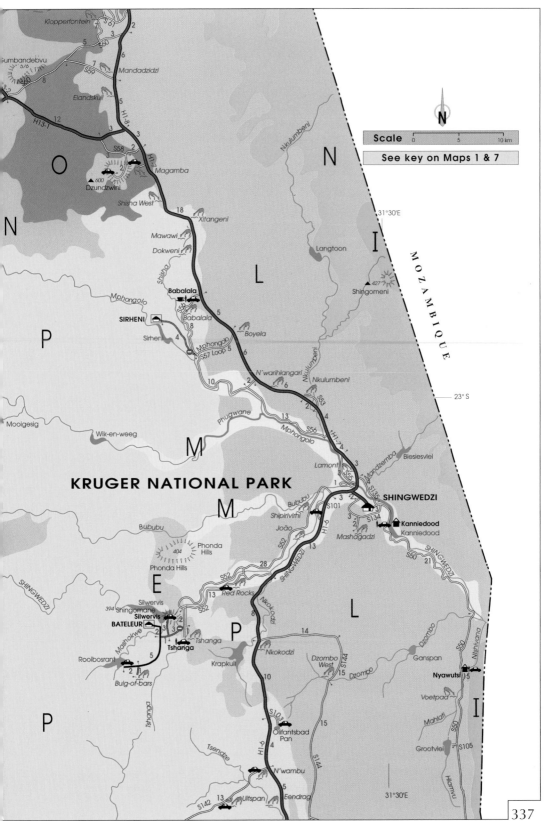

Scale 0 5 10 km

See key on Maps 1 & 7

KRUGER NATIONAL PARK

MOZAMBIQUE

Extracts of map reproduced under Government Printer Copyright Authority no. 10263 dated 25 October 1996

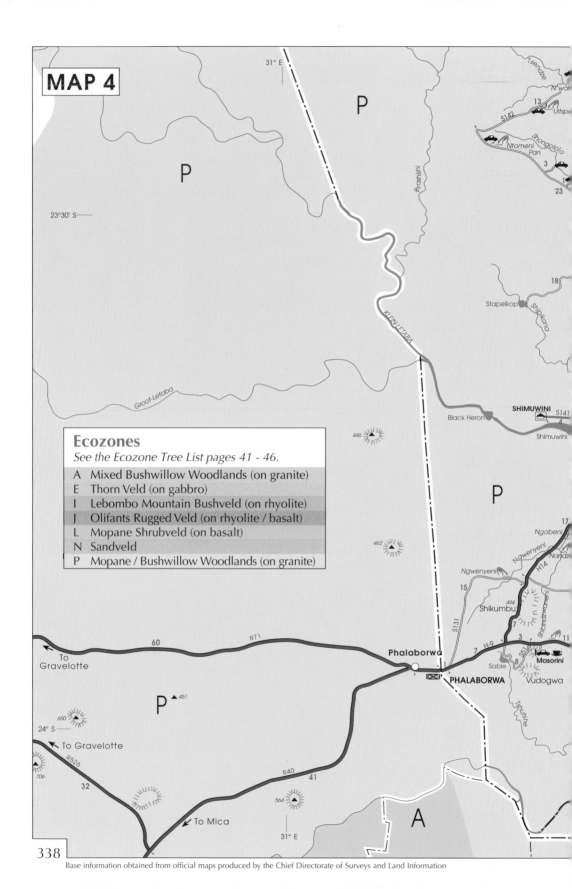

MAP 4

P

P

31° E

23°30' S

Tsenzse

N'wa

13   Uitspe

S142

Ntomeni
Pan   3

23

18

Byashishi

Stapelkop   Shilkorna

KLEIN-LETABA

Groot-Letaba

Black Heron   **SHIMUWINI**   S141
4
Shimuwini

446

Ecozones
See the Ecozone Tree List pages 41 - 46.

A   Mixed Bushwillow Woodlands (on granite)
E   Thorn Veld (on gabbro)
I   Lebombo Mountain Bushveld (on rhyolite)
J   Olifants Rugged Veld (on rhyolite / basalt)
L   Mopane Shrubveld (on basalt)
N   Sandveld
P   Mopane / Bushwillow Woodlands (on granite)

P

17
Ngobeni

462   Ngwenyeni   Nandze

H14

Ngwenyeni
15   494
Shikumbu

S131   Shitandzwaneni   11
7   3
H-9   7   Sable   8   **Masorini**
1

60   R71   **Phalaborwa**   **PHALABORWA**   Vudogwa

To
Gravelotte   Ighutshe

P ▲ 451

650   706

24° S

← To Gravelotte

R526

32   R40   41

564

To Mica

A

31° E

338

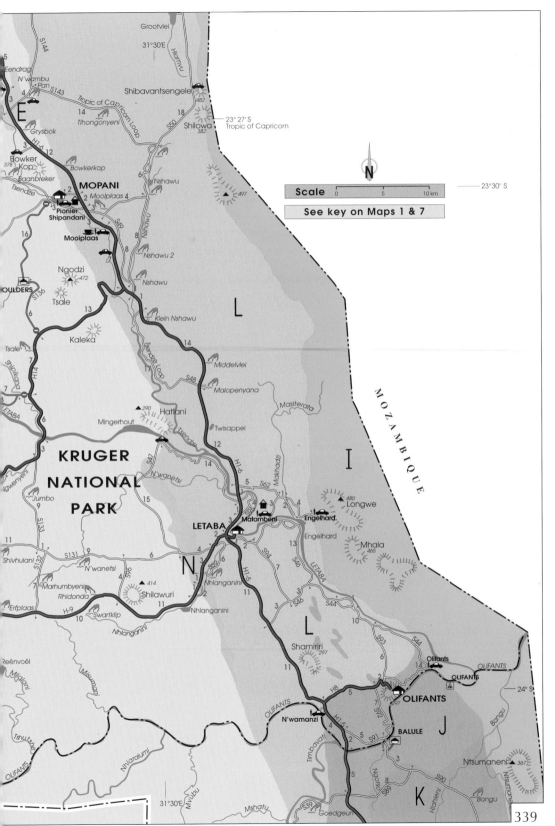

Grootvlei

31°30'E

Eendrag
N'wambu
Pan S143
S144

E
3
4

14
Tihongonyeni

Grysbok
H1-4
12

Bowker
378 Kop
Baanbreker
Tsendze

MOPANI
2
2 Mooiplaas 4
3
Pionier
Shipandani

16
Mooiplaas

Ngodzi
472
OULDERS S136
Tsale

6
Tsale
13
Kaleka

Shipikana
H14
7

Shibavantsengele
482

23° 27' S
Tropic of Capricorn
Shilowa
382

Tropic of Capricorn Loop
S50
18
S50

Nshawu

Nshawu
8
Nshawu 2
8
Nshawu

Nshawu
1

Klein Nshawu
14

Tsendze Loop
17
Middelvlei
S48
Malopenyana

Masiferata

Hatlani
290
Mingerhout
Tsendze
Twisappel
12
14
H1-6

L

I

MOZAMBIQUE

Scale
0   5   10 km
See key on Maps 1 & 7

23°30' S

N

KRUGER

NATIONAL

PARK

Ngwenyeni
Jumbo
9
S133

11
Shivhulani S131
6
N'wanetsi
4
7 Marhumbyeni
Rhidonda
Erfplaas
10 Swartklip
Nhlanganini

S7
N'wanetsi
15

414
Shilawuri
11
Nhlanganini
2
Nhlanganini

LETABA
2
3
Matambeni
3

5 S62
1
3
4

Engelhard
480 Longwe
Engelhard

13
S46
S44

Mhala
465

L
10

Shamiriri
297
6
S92
S44

Olifants
14 OLIFANTS
OLIFANTS

24° S

11
H8
OLIFANTS
N'wamanzi
H1-5
S92
297
OLIFANTS
BALULE
J

Timbavati
5 S91
3

Ntsumaneni 367

Reênvoël
Mitjalani

Tshutshe
Nhlaralumi
OLIFANTS
Mvubu
Mshatu
S39
Goedgeun
K
Hlatheni
S90
Bangu
Ntsumani

31°30'E

339

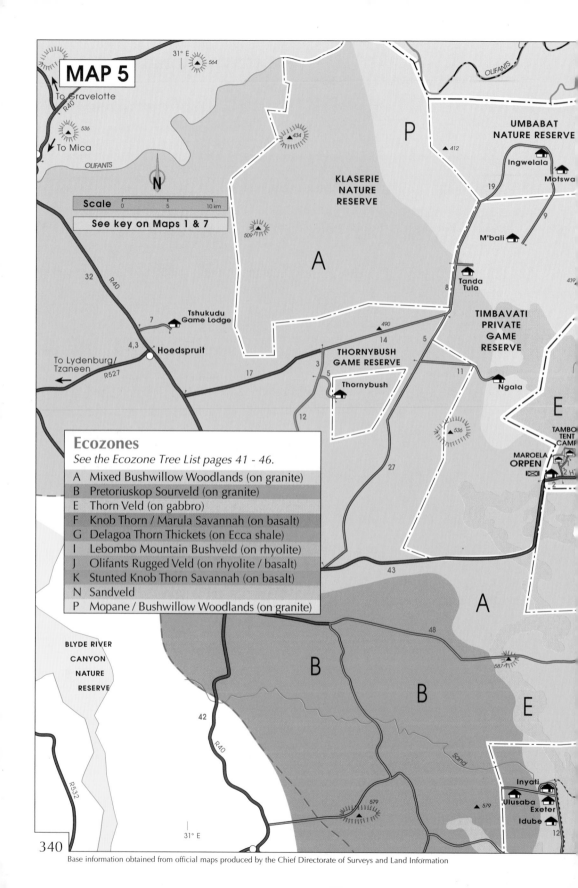

MAP 5

31° E ▲ 564

To Gravelotte

R40

▲ 536

To Mica

OLIFANTS

N

Scale 0 — 5 — 10 km

See key on Maps 1 & 7

OLIFANTS

P

UMBABAT
NATURE RESERVE

▲ 412

Ingwelala

Motswa

▲ 434

KLASERIE
NATURE
RESERVE

19

9

M'bali

509 ▲

A

Tanda
Tula

8

▲ 439

32

R40

7

Tshukudu
Game Lodge

4,3 ● Hoedspruit

To Lydenburg/
Tzaneen
R527

←

17

490 ▲

14

TIMBAVATI
PRIVATE
GAME
RESERVE

5

THORNYBUSH
GAME RESERVE

3

5

Thornybush

11

Ngala

E

12

536 ▲

TAMBO
TENT
CAMP

MAROELA
ORPEN

27

2

Ecozones

See the Ecozone Tree List pages 41 - 46.

A   Mixed Bushwillow Woodlands (on granite)
B   Pretoriuskop Sourveld (on granite)
E   Thorn Veld (on gabbro)
F   Knob Thorn / Marula Savannah (on basalt)
G   Delagoa Thorn Thickets (on Ecca shale)
I   Lebombo Mountain Bushveld (on rhyolite)
J   Olifants Rugged Veld (on rhyolite / basalt)
K   Stunted Knob Thorn Savannah (on basalt)
N   Sandveld
P   Mopane / Bushwillow Woodlands (on granite)

43

48

A

BLYDE RIVER
CANYON
NATURE
RESERVE

587 ▲

42

R40

B

B

Sand

E

R532

579 ▲

Inyati

Ulusaba

Exeter

▲ 579

Idube

12

31° E

Base information obtained from official maps produced by the Chief Directorate of Surveys and Land Information

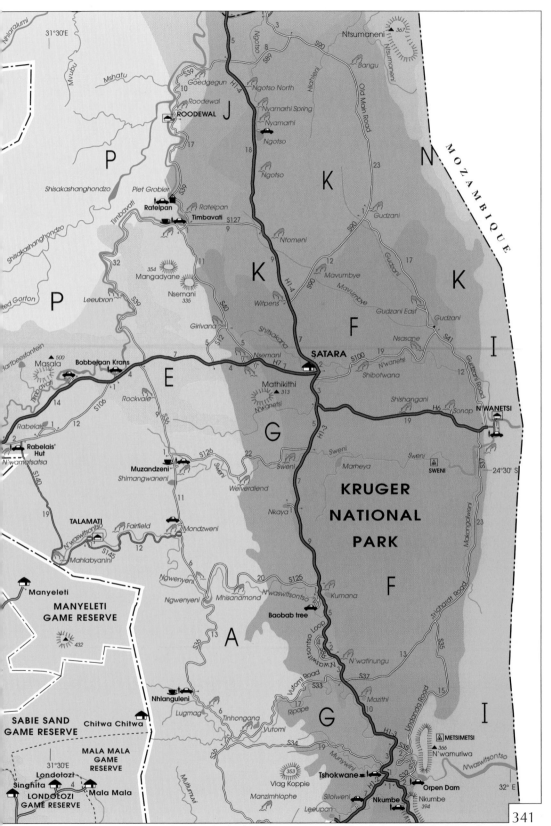

acana

341

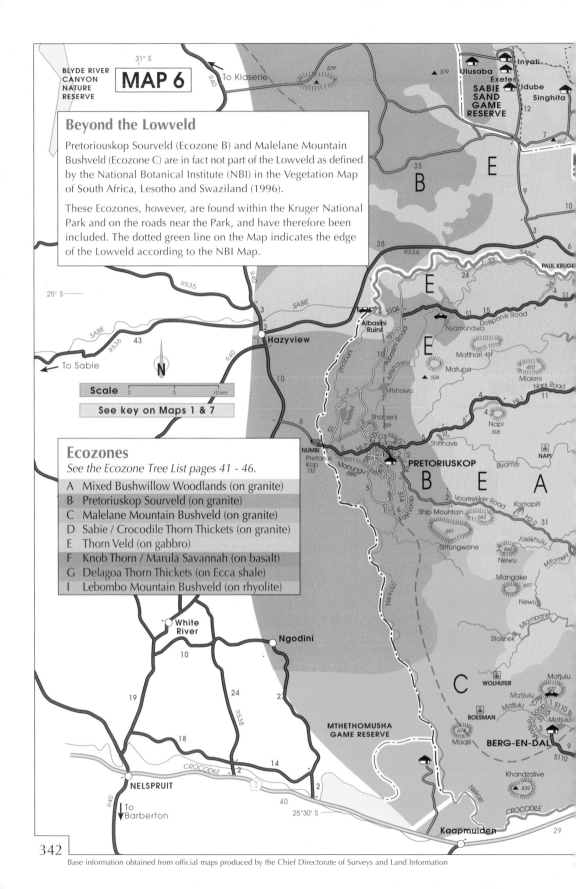

BLYDE RIVER CANYON NATURE RESERVE

31° E

MAP 6

To Klaserie

579

Ulusaba

Inyati

Exeter

Idube

SABIE SAND GAME RESERVE

Singhita

12

7

452

E

B

35

9

10

Beyond the Lowveld

Pretoriuskop Sourveld (Ecozone B) and Malelane Mountain Bushveld (Ecozone C) are in fact not part of the Lowveld as defined by the National Botanical Institute (NBI) in the Vegetation Map of South Africa, Lesotho and Swaziland (1996).

These Ecozones, however, are found within the Kruger National Park and on the roads near the Park, and have therefore been included. The dotted green line on the Map indicates the edge of the Lowveld according to the NBI Map.

38

R536

SABIE

PAUL KRUGE

E

24

4

S1

6

25° S

R535

3

SABIE

Dolspane Road

15

S1

Nyamundwa

Albasini Ruins

S104

SABIE

R536

43

To Sabie

N

Hazyview

R40

10

Albasini Road

Mtshawu

10

Matlhari 451

Matupa

504

492

Mlaleni

Napi Road

11

Scale
0   5   10 km

See key on Maps 1 & 7

Phabeni

7

Mestel

Mtshawu

Shabeni 359

8

5

Shithave

4

Napi

505

NUMBI

Pretorius Kop 732

Manungu 689

5

5

Biyamiti

NAPI

PRETORIUSKOP

B   E   A

Ecozones
See the Ecozone Tree List pages 41 - 46.

A Mixed Bushwillow Woodlands (on granite)
B Pretoriuskop Sourveld (on granite)
C Malelane Mountain Bushveld (on granite)
D Sabie / Crocodile Thorn Thickets (on granite)
E Thorn Veld (on gabbro)
F Knob Thorn / Marula Savannah (on basalt)
G Delagoa Thorn Thickets (on Ecca shale)
I Lebombo Mountain Bushveld (on rhyolite)

S1

6

Fayi Loop

S14

2

Voortrekker Road

Komapiti

Ship Mountain

662

H2-2

31

691

josékhulu

Sitfungwane

666

Newu

Mitomeni

Mangake

697

Newu

Mlambane

White River

Ngodini

10

Stolsnek

C

WOLHUTER

Matjulu

627

19

24

27

R538

Matjulu

Matjulu

S110 b

Loop

S112

Matjulu

3

BOESMAN

674

Maqili

BERG-EN-DAL

9

S110

18

MTHETHOMUSHA GAME RESERVE

Nsikazi

Khandzalive

839

14

NELSPRUIT

CROCODILE

2

N4

2

R40

To Barberton

40

25°30' S

CROCODILE

Kaapmuiden

29

Base information obtained from official maps produced by the Chief Directorate of Surveys and Land Information

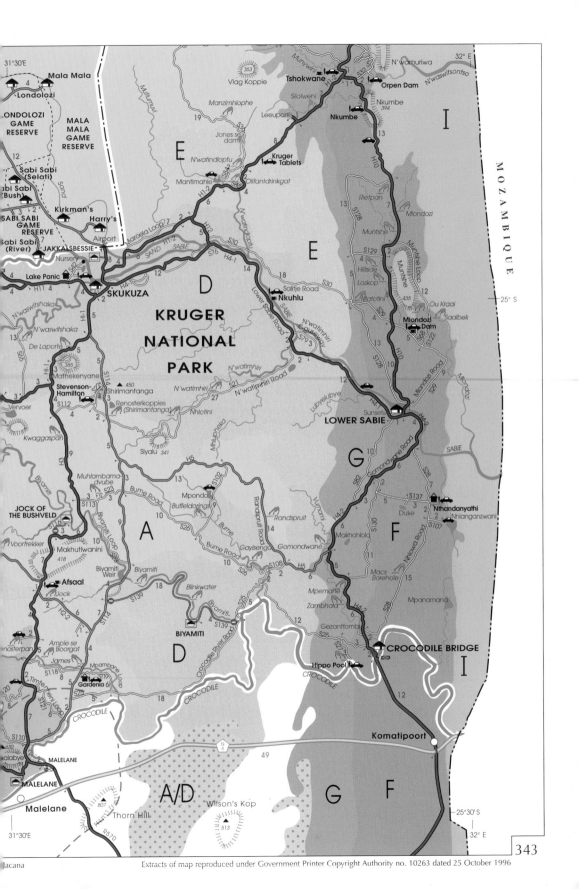

343

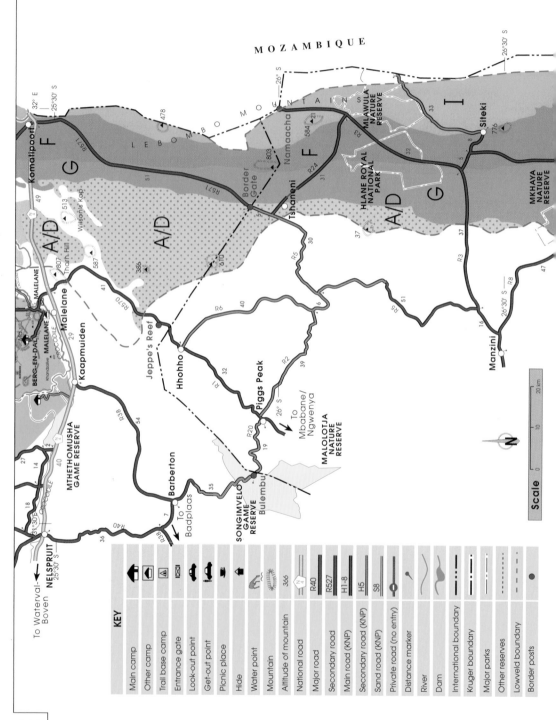

MAP 7

MOZAMBIQUE

26°30' S

32° E
25°30' S

Komatipoort

MALELANE

BERG-EN-DAL

Malelane

Kaapmuiden

MTHETHOMUSHA GAME RESERVE

To Waterval-Boven

NELSPRUIT
25°30' S

To Badplaas

Barberton

Jeppe's Reef

Hhohho

SONGIMVELO GAME RESERVE

Bulembu

Piggs Peak

26° S

To Mbabane/Ngwenya

MALOLOTJA NATURE RESERVE

LEBOMBO MOUNTAINS

478

513

Wilson's Kop

807

Tharh Hill

587

366

610

Border Gate

803

Tshaneni

Namaacha

584

MLAWULA NATURE RESERVE

HLANE ROYAL NATIONAL PARK

Siteki

776

MKHAYA NATURE RESERVE

Manzini

26°30' S

26°30' S

A/D

F

G

I

A/D

F

G

Scale

0   10   20 km

N

KEY

	Main camp
	Other camp
	Trail base camp
	Entrance gate
	Look-out point
	Get-out point
	Picnic place
	Hide
	Water point
	Mountain
366	Altitude of mountain
	National road
R40	Major road
R527	Secondary road
H1-8	Main road (KNP)
H5	Secondary road (KNP)
S8	Sand road (KNP)
	Private road (no entry)
	Distance marker
	River
	Dam
	International boundary
	Kruger boundary
	Major parks
	Other reserves
	Lowveld boundary
	Border posts

Base information obtained from official maps produced by the Chief Directorate of Surveys and Land Information

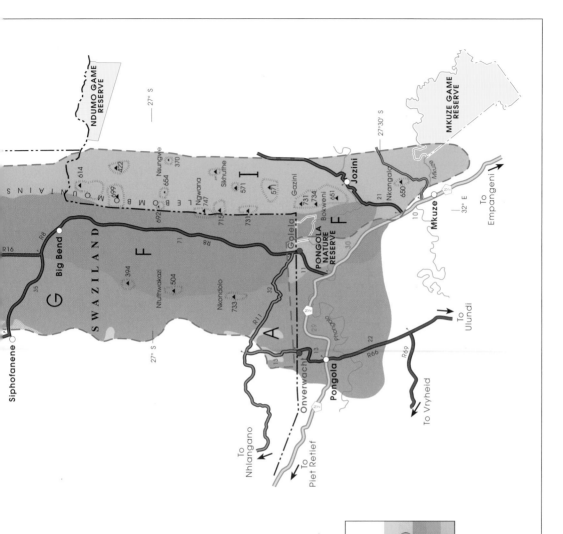

Southern Mpumalanga, Northern Natal & Swaziland

The Ecozone boundaries, as well as the trees listed on pages 41 - 46, are not as accurate for this area as they are for the Kruger National Park. However, it will give you a good idea of what types of trees to expect in the general area.

Ecozones

See the Ecozone Tree List pages 41 - 46.

A   Mixed Bushwillow Woodlands (on granite)
D   Sabie / Crocodile Thorn Thickets (on granite)
F   Knob thorn / Marula Savannah (on basalt)
G   Delagoa Thorn Thickets (on Ecca shale)
I   Lebombo Mountain Bushveld (on rhyolite)

Scale
0   10   20 km

Index

Pod-mahogany, page 200

Umdoni/Waterberry,
page 22

Tree Wisteria,
page 118

Book References

Acocks, JPH, 1988, *Veld Types of South Africa*, No. 57, *Botanical Research Institute, Pretoria.*

Carr, JD, 1976, *The South African Acacias*, Conservation Press Pty Ltd, Johannesburg.

Carr, JD, 1988, *Combretaceae in South Africa*, Tree Society of Southern Africa, Johannesburg.

Coates Palgrave, K, 1977, *Trees of Southern Africa*, 1st edition, C. Struik, Cape Town.

Gertenbach, W, 1983, *Landscapes of the Kruger National Park*, Koedoe 26:9-121.

Hutchings, A, Scott, AH, Lewis, G & Cunningham, A B, 1996, *Zulu Medicinal Plants - An Inventory*, University of Natal Press, Pietermaritzburg.

Palmer, E & Pitman, N, 1972 & 1973, *Trees of Southern Africa*, 3 Vols, AA Balkema, Cape Town.

Pooley, E, 1993, *The Complete Field Guide to Trees of Natal, Zululand & Transkei*, 1st edition, Natal Flora Publications Trust, Durban.

Steyn, Marthinus, 1996, *SA Ficus Identification Guide for Wild Figs in South Africa*, Promedia, Marks Street, Waltloo.

Van Wyk, 1973, *Bome van die Nasionale Krugerwildtuin*, Perskor-Uitgewery, Johannesburg.

Van Wyk, B & Van Wyk, P, 1997, *Field Guide to Trees of Southern Africa*, Struik Publishers (Pty) Ltd, Cape Town.

Van Wyk, BE, Van Oudtshoorn, B & Gericke, N, 1997, *Medicinal Plants of South Africa*, 1st edition, Briza Publications, Pretoria.

Van Wyk, P, *Trees of the Kruger National Park*, Vols 1 & 2.

Venter, F & JA, 1996, *Making the most of Indigenous Trees*, 1st edition, Briza Publications, Pretoria.

Venter, FJ, 1990, *A classification of land use for management planning in the Kruger National Park*, Ph.D, Pretoria, University of South Africa.

Von Breitenbach, F, 1995, *National List of Indigenous Trees*, 3rd edition, Dendrological Foundation, Pretoria.

Watt, JM & Breyer-Brandwijk, MG, 1962, *Medicinal and Poisonous Plants of Southern and Eastern Africa*, 2nd edition, E & S Livingstone Ltd, Edinburgh and London.

Sausage-tree, page 244